D1163665

PRAISE FOR ***THE DIAMOND PROCESS***

"*The Diamond Process* takes a number of pieces of leadership and management, some of which we "kind of know" and organizes them in a logical way to help leaders gain intentionality and focus in their work. Starting with a logical "left brain" approach, Mike and Chris have shared great real life stories from their experiences to give examples for us right-brained folks. It's a powerful book that will liberate many aspiring leaders and managers."

—**LEE ELLIS**, author of *Engage With Honor*

"There are lots of books on leadership, but few that combine outstanding pedigree, highly practical ideas, and a sensibility that can help anyone become a more effective leader. The power of simplicity has never been greater."

—**SYDNEY FINKELSTEIN**, professor and bestselling author of *Superbosses*

"Mike Diamond and Christopher Harding bring their professional and military experience to bear in this thoughtful and precise leadership guide. If you are looking for a thorough understanding of how to lead processes as well as people, *The Diamond Process* has much to offer."

—**MARSHALL GOLDSMITH**, executive coach, business educator, and *New York Times* bestselling author, ranked number one leadership thinker by Thinkers50

"Is leadership about people or process? Major General Mike Diamond answers that question once and for all. Few people understand how to focus on both the way he does. And *The Diamond Process* now makes it possible for all of us to learn how. A book for every leader!"

—**BARRY BANTHER**, bestselling author of *A Leaders Gift—How to Earn the Right to Be Followed*

The DIAMOND PROCESS

HOW TO FIX YOUR ORGANIZATION AND EFFECTIVELY LEAD PEOPLE

MG (RET.) MIKE J. DIAMOND
& CHRISTOPHER R. HARDING

This publication is designed to provide accurate and authoritative information in regard to the subject matter covered. It is sold with the understanding that the publisher and author are not engaged in rendering legal, accounting, or other professional services. If legal advice or other expert assistance is required, the services of a competent professional should be sought.

Published by Greenleaf Book Group Press
Austin, Texas
www.gbgpress.com

Distributed by Greenleaf Book Group

For ordering information or special discounts for bulk purchases, please contact Greenleaf Book Group at PO Box 91869, Austin, TX 78709, 512.891.6100.

Design and composition by Greenleaf Book Group
Cover design by Greenleaf Book Group

Cataloging-in-Publication data is available.

Print ISBN: 978-1-62634-392-4

eBook ISBN: 978-1-62634-393-1

Part of the Tree Neutral® program, which offsets the number of trees consumed in the production and printing of this book by taking proactive steps, such as planting trees in direct proportion to the number of trees used: www.treeneutral.com

Printed in the United States of America on acid-free paper

17 18 19 20 21 22 10 9 8 7 6 5 4 3 2 1

First Edition

This book is dedicated to all leaders—from the devoted housewife and mother to the corporate executive and military member—who strive to be the best, every day, that they can be. We trust this book will provide an invaluable road map for you along your path to successful leadership. Whether you are the hero of your family or your organization, we pray that you draw inspiration to achieve greatness in your leadership role and set an example for those who come behind you to proudly follow.

"Leadership, like courtship, is a journey that engages the person but is more about the PROCESS to reach your destination."

—Major General (Retired) Mike Diamond

CONTENTS

ACKNOWLEDGMENTS

I have enjoyed learning and *leading* in military, corporate, and nonprofit sectors. I have thrived under exceptionally stellar leaders and role models but, at the same time, had to endure some ghastly, incompetent leaders. However, through it all I realized that there are valuable lessons to be learned no matter how good, bad, or ugly the leadership. My sincerest appreciation goes to those leaders who were the best of the best and took time to mentor me. You know who you are!

To those who have worked with me or served with me through the years, thanks for being good teammates. I hope that you have learned as much from me as I have learned from you.

The team at Greenleaf Publishing has been most accommodating toward the success of the book. We could not have had a better editor than Chris Benguhe. Chris, you were successful in getting us to follow your tried-and-true process rather well. You have certainly raised the quality of the book compared to what it might have been. Scott James, thank you for helping us understand that the book is a step in the overall process of establishing our new brand.

I have been blessed to be mentored by two outstanding authors who have advised me along the writing process. Lee Ellis introduced me to Greenleaf and facilitated the whole book-writing process. Thanks, Lee, for guiding me along the way and being a great resource in authorship. Thanks a million to Barry Banther for getting me on the right track initially and redirecting my efforts toward a more effective and meaningful product.

I appreciate the contributions of my inner circle. They served as reviewers and have been a great sounding board throughout the entire process. Jim Gauldin, COL (Ret) Mike Ford, COL (Ret) Bob Burch, and Chuck Walsh have been very instrumental in shaping this content. I am deeply indebted to COL (Ret) Jeff Carra and MAJ (Ret) John Wilson who both provided extensive time and effort to help make the Diamond Process Model a successful paragon for organizations striving for excellence in their capability and performance. John, your expertise and timeless efforts in the visuals and graphics are unsurpassed, and I am most grateful for your contributions.

To my coauthor and son, Capt. Chris Harding, I could not have done this without your sacrifices, suggestions, research, and fluid writing style. Your unique ideas and right-brained approach helped balance my left-brained, analytical style in making this a much more balanced book. To my daughter-in-law, Katie Martin, thank you for your sacrifices, which enabled Chris to contribute.

Lastly, this endeavor would not have gotten out of the starting blocks without my most supportive wife, Bernadette. Without your support, this book would remain a dream and a missed opportunity. You have been there through the birth, rearing, and presentation, and I can't thank you enough. The IOUs keep piling up!

—Mike Diamond

INTRODUCTION

Throughout our careers, in both military and civilian sectors, we have noticed some axioms that seem to prevail: First, it is safe to assume most people come to work each day to be productive members of a winning team with the intentions of doing "right things right." Second, most workers have reasonable expectations from their leadership regarding appropriate leader behaviors, as well as a keen awareness when those expectations are not met. Subordinates may not be adept at dissecting particular leadership failures but they can usually recognize when something is not right. Finally, when workers recognize these shortcomings, they expect resolution from someone in the leadership chain.

To see evidence of the aforementioned axioms, leaders need only pay attention to the overwhelming volume of feedback that follows a change of personnel or process. Questions such as "What took you so long to make this change?" may indicate a leadership decision took longer than expected; or "Why didn't someone ask us about what was going on?" may reveal subordinate dissatisfaction with the lack of group decision making. Comments such as "It's about time someone saw what we did" may indicate workers feel a lack of recognition; or "I don't know how they didn't realize this, because everyone knows what's been going on" can signify subordinates feel leadership is out of touch with the organization. Each comment represents a worker who feels leadership did not meet his or her expectation. The mere existence of a comment, and frustration for that matter, represents that subordinates care about the work they are performing and that they have hope that someone will change things for the better.

Unfortunately for these hopeful workers, we live in an age where bad leadership seems to be the rule rather than the exception. Poor leadership is so common we've been reduced to making comedy movies to cope. One popular example is the cult classic *Office Space,* where the main boss, Bill Lumbergh, continually harasses employees over not filling out TPS reports. This represents the common frustration of supervisors ignoring the things they should be concerned about and focusing instead on mindless paperwork. In the popular movie *Horrible Bosses*, three workers hate their bosses so much that they devise a plan where each friend will kill another friend's boss so the police won't be able to find a motive. The success of these movies indicates we all have similar shared experiences. For those who may have not seen these films, we've compiled a couple of character types that represent typical bosses we've had the pleasure of encountering in our careers, many of which you may find familiar.

The first type of bad leader is the one Chris refers to as "the Incompetent Mole." To understand the mole is to understand that there is no understanding the mole. He is not an intelligent creature and is likely in his current position not because he is qualified, but because either he knew someone important or his last supervisor promoted him out of the office so he wouldn't have to look at his ugly mug. Similar to a mole who will simply burrow and hide in the presence of a threat, this boss never makes a decision, but rather passes things right on through to the next person. He also has poor eyesight like a mole, so he will have no idea what you do for him as a subordinate. Since the mole has no awareness of whether or not you are doing a

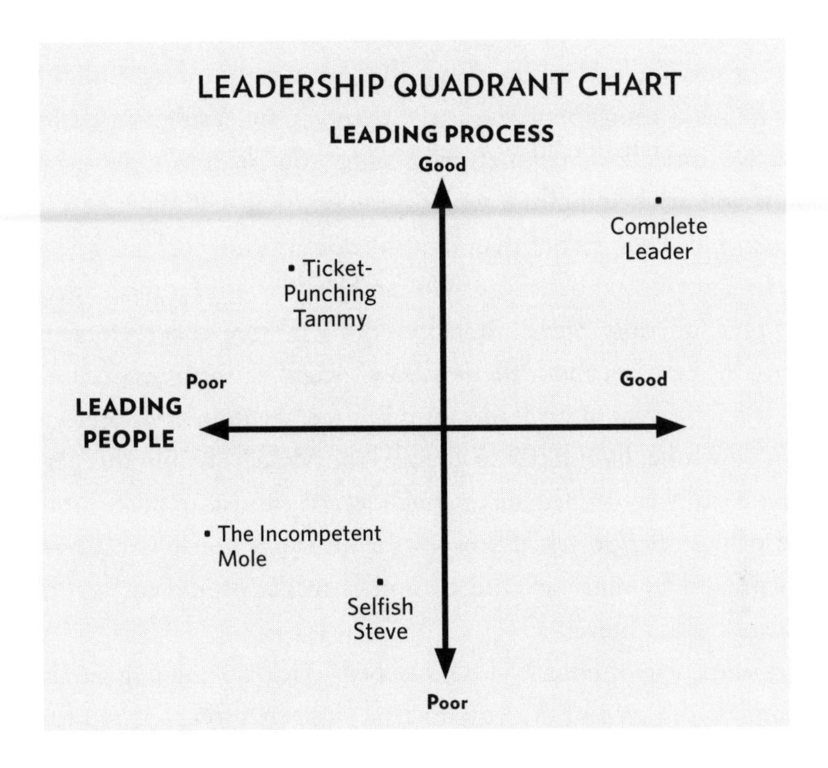

good job, he will probably not recognize your hard work and superior performance. As if this isn't bad enough, when it comes to performance awards, the mole will likely reward the guy sitting next to you who does nothing but waste oxygen all day because that is the decision that makes no sense and is the most illogical. The mole does not have the mental capacity to focus on what is important, so if a subordinate seeks his counsel with a problem, he or she likely leaves the mole's presence with more problems, no solutions, and at least three erroneous tasks that will not lead to a solution. Hence, in order to survive, one must avoid the mole at all costs.

The next type of bad leader we've experienced is called "Selfish Steve." As the name implies, this leader cares only about himself and his success. Steve is usually a shrewd individual and usually holds a leadership position that is much higher than yours. This is because

Steve is very focused on the things that get him promoted, and therefore he looks much better on paper than you do. You may be a more effective leader, but Steve gets paid more. You are Steve's favorite person if you are helping him with a problem that will make him look better to his boss. Other than that, he doesn't know or care who you are; he cares only about those who can help him appear more successful to his superiors. Steve cares about himself more than the organization. Oh, he cares about the *perceived* success of the organization, as this is a reflection of his leadership. But faced with a decision to promote someone, he is likely to choose "the Mole," because this person is more easily controlled and is much less of a threat to his accumulation of personal power. If you've ever known a horrible leader who gets praised by outsiders and continues to get promoted, you have known "Selfish Steve."

A third type of poor leader is dubbed "Ticket-Punching Tammy." Tammy is the type of leader who typically gets promoted in organizations where "time in grade," "time in service," or a quota system is the promotion requirement. We find Tammy in governmental or unionized organizations where she is comfortable stepping on and over others to get herself promoted. Tammy has neither character nor ability, but thrives in a system where she can wait out others who have less seniority. She slides into power vacuums created when others like her retire or move on to other positions.

Simply stated, these examples represent the ignorant, the selfish, and the power-hungry positional leader. We like to feel that most leaders, like most workers, do not represent these characters and really want to do a good job. However, we also feel many of you are somewhat misguided in your approach to leadership. Much literature has been written about the expectations leaders have for their subordinates, but often overlooked are the expectations that workers have for managers and those aspiring to be leaders. The chasm and void created by leaders in all sectors—corporate, military, government, nonprofit, etc.—who do not meet or exceed worker expectations is what inspired us to write this book.

We created this book as a guide to help those in leadership positions, and others who aspire to be leaders, to not only live up to the basic expectations that subordinate workers have, but also to help them progress toward a more lofty standard we refer to as the "complete leader." This book will enable managers and leaders to learn how to be the most effective leader that their subordinates *want* them to be and that their organizations *need* them to be.

We will illustrate what Mike has seen time and time again both as a Major General in the US Army and as a consultant: Many leaders are incomplete in their approach to leadership because they focus on leading people and neglect to lead processes. This makes their leadership approach incomplete, as both must come under a leader's direction. Without leading both, managers leave too much to chance. Furthermore, many leaders are not fulfilling their positional obligations in numerous situations because they lead according to what appeals to their strengths and interests—rather than what their organization needs.

Although we may be able to learn some important lessons from bad leaders, some of us have never had good examples. Mike has also experienced many individuals in leadership positions who want to do *right things right*, but simply do not understand what *right* looks like within their organization. For this, we offer a solution called the *Diamond Process Model (DPM)*. The DPM is a holistic model that can be tailored to any organization, large or small. It is a recipe for success for any size organization and is a great tool for any leader who desires to maintain organizational control in order to meet expectations and increase efficiency and effectiveness.

Anyone from a mother at home leading the family unit to a corporate leader in a Fortune 1000 company can benefit from this book; it will help you understand the fundamentals of leading people and processes and will provide a common sense perspective that will change the way you view leadership and enable you to identify the missing piece(s) of your leadership approach. We feel that DPM is a fundamental way of thinking that should be adopted by corporate managers, leaders from government and nonprofit organizations, military leaders, and students, because it is universal in that it can be used at any level within any organization.

Corporate leaders will benefit by gaining insights into the intricacies of their organizations. This holistic understanding of the interdependencies between people and processes will enable leaders to leverage organizational resources so as to focus on long-term goals, maintain capability to handle short-term challenges, and increase profits by gaining unparalleled knowledge about their organizations. By increasing process awareness, these leaders will be better equipped to react to internal opportunities or external threats, all the while maintaining cost control. Additionally, by understanding organizational balance and the Diamond Process Model, corporate leaders can propel themselves into performing as a *complete leader*.

Leaders of government and nonprofit organizations will benefit from DPM as it will enable them to streamline processes in order to navigate many of the inherent constraints consistent with this type of organizational structure. Process leadership is extremely critical when it comes to the *color of money*—that is, allocating funds in accordance with federal, state, and municipal restrictions. Additionally, these types of organizations are known for red tape and have much to benefit from streamlining processes as many internal practices are process-centric. Furthermore, by utilizing DPM, leaders in these organizations can save costs, reduce waste, and improve regulatory compliance in a fiscally constrained environment. Finally, supervisors will learn how to lead, since most are not afforded the opportunity to be trained on management and leadership—especially many first-line supervisors and middle-management professionals.

Military leaders stand to gain a great deal from this book as well. Most military leaders have a defining moment in their careers, and DPM will better prepare them for handling that defining moment. As military leaders ourselves, we understand that much of the professional development offered by DoD service organizations is geared toward leading people only. Some training in process improvement is available, but as you will see, process improvement is at the micro level, whereas DPM resides at the macro level. Military organizations boast at having some of the best training programs available, but this book is an ideal augmentation to the current training they receive, as it provides the missing piece: process leadership. Military leaders are often thrust into situations where they are required to accept people and processes as they are and *win*. DPM will provide these leaders an overall understanding of all the variables and will enable them to quickly adapt to their environments by understanding which elements should have priority for resources.

We also suggest this book to students studying academic leadership or any type of management curriculum. By understanding DPM, students will be able to develop a fundamental cognitive map that will provide a base upon which further learning can take place. This awareness will make it easier to categorize new information encountered during learning experiences and will also provide a basic understanding of processes as well as the importance of process management and integrating resources with processes. This early exposure will enable students to avoid the trap of focusing on the people-only view of leadership and will better prepare them for entry into the corporate sector.

Having already covered some humorous but all-too-real examples of poor leaders, we will begin the book with a serious discussion of our interpretation of the effective leader. There is a whole segment of leadership that has not been discussed before—a lack of awareness of the importance of process leadership, and a lack of focus on how process leadership can create the type of balance that's vital to maintaining a healthy, productive, and efficient organization.

We feel that people have been misguided to think of *leadership* as only leading people. This way of thinking has caused popular leadership and training programs to omit the critical element of process leadership. We feel strongly that this is a disservice to potential leaders, and we're here to change your perspective. We also feel that once leaders structure organizations properly through process integration, they will become more effective leaders of people as well.

Throughout this book we will insert personal stories from both authors that reinforce concepts presented in the chapters: Mike's stories are titled "A General's Reflection," and Chris's stories are called "Captain's Corners." Both are intended to provide examples where DPM concepts have been successfully used in actual leadership situations.

In the first section of the book, we will introduce you to each element of our Diamond Process Model. Many of you will be familiar with some of these elements, but we will define the different pieces so we can all share a common understanding. In the second half of the book, we will show you how to utilize the DPM as we highlight common problems with each element as well as the appropriate solutions to those problems. Finally, we will conclude by explaining how to optimize the model for your organization, as well as provide examples for some critical applications of the Diamond Process Model. We created this model as a tool to assist us in consulting and training leaders of all types. Many elements of the model are grounded in research, others in our past experiences both as leaders and trainers.

It is important to note that there is a close match between many of the requirements of the International Organization for Standardization (ISO) and uses of the Diamond Process Model. ISO standards are a foundational element for many organizations that represent safe, reliable, and good-quality products and services. The DPM facilitates uses of ISO-certified components.

This book is aimed at all levels of leaders, including first-level supervisors. In our opinion, the best way to learn as a first-time leader is to be thrown into a leadership position with an expectation to perform well. The lessons learned from this book will help you set the stage for having a better chance of succeeding when and if that time comes for you. The book will also help to fix what's not working within your organization. If your organization is squared away now, just wait; you will likely be put into a situation where you'll need the lessons from this book.

Other leaders will see things from this book that typify what they have been faced with either currently or throughout their careers. Our hope is that those leaders will be able to identify what isn't working correctly and to develop better ideas of how to fix their organization and become a better leader in the process. Having a sound, orderly, balanced organization can be a good first step in being a great leader. This book will help you reach that place.

Common responses from our students include "This makes good common sense," and "How did I miss that?" We are confident that at some point while reading this book you will also have that *Wow!* moment. We ask that you share what you learn with someone else, as our overall goal is to help others improve their leadership skills in order to make the world a better place.

CHAPTER 1

THE EFFECTIVE LEADER

In the introduction, we presented some examples of poor leaders. But what constitutes *good* leaders? What do they look like? How do they act? Who is best suited to be a leader? How can I tell whether or not I work for a good leader? If I am in a leadership position, what should I do? These are all fair questions to ask as we set out to create good leaders.

As you will hear from us time and time again, there is a process for everything, including the process to become a good leader. When we think of a person who is a good leader, we imagine someone with good character and a solid foundation of moral traits and ethical behavior.

On top of this foundation, a good leader also has a keen perspective and an eye for balance. Once you put all of this together in one package, you have yourself a *complete leader*. There is a process to becoming a complete leader, and we'd like to share that with you.

Since everyone has unique past experiences that give us all different perceptions, we need to start our discussion with a common understanding of terms so we can all play from the same sheet of music. There is a need here for a formal discussion, because there is a process to becoming a complete leader, and that process demands that we cannot simply do this "off the cuff."

In this book we refer to the term *leader* or *informal leader* as anyone who feels they are a leader. If you think of yourself as a leader, then we are talking about you. *Positional leaders* or *supervisors* are people who occupy formal leadership positions in an organization, such as a first-line supervisor or senior executive.

Anyone in an organization can be a leader, but most are informal leaders, meaning they do not get paid to supervise. The terms *worker*, *employee*, and *subordinate* refer to those individuals who work for the positional leader in an organization; those terms are used interchangeably in this book.

A GOOD LEADER NEEDS BALANCE

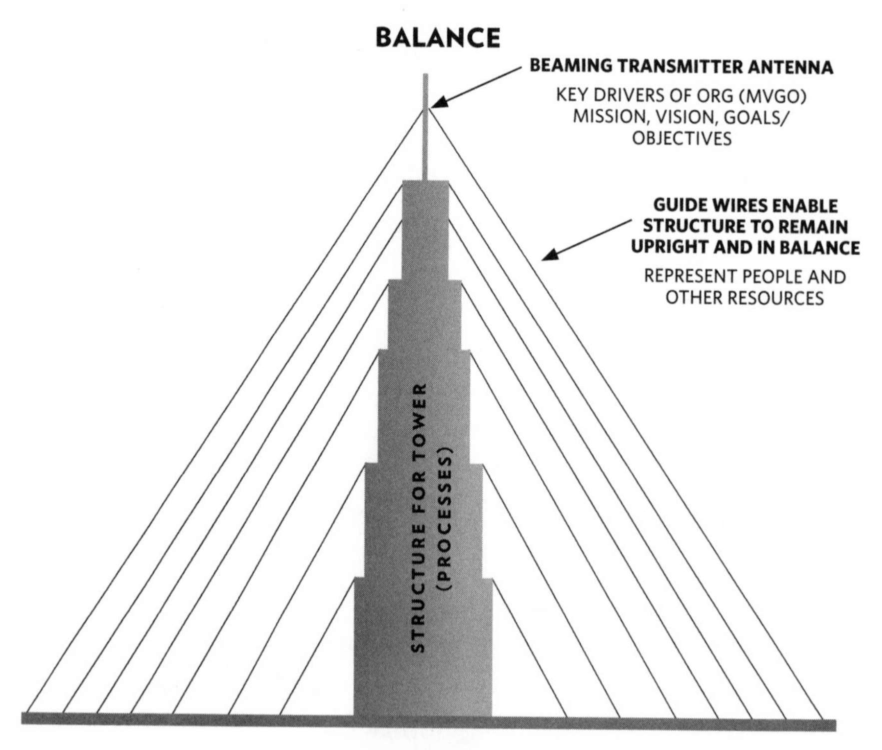

In order to transmit a signal, the structures (proccesses) must be well constructed and held in complete balance with guide wires (people & other resources) in order to be able to transmit (achieve their key drivers).

The first type of balance we will discuss encompasses the entire organization. A balanced approach to organizational leadership is crucial for anyone striving to be a complete leader. If a senior positional leader overmanages one area of an organization too much, the other areas will suffer from neglect.

Balance at the organizational level of leadership is also important for understanding both the present and the future of your company. Some leaders focus on current operations and fail to set goals for the future; this type of imbalance is dangerous because it is a nearsighted approach that can prevent the business from growing.

Leaders who are focused on the future of the company conduct strategic planning sessions, analyze external market conditions, and formulate visionary strategies. Without analyzing the future of a business, leaders will not be able to take advantage of opportunities that may arise. They will be more susceptible to external threats as they have never prepared for the future environment.

On the other hand, some leaders focus too much on what they want to achieve in the future and lose sight of the current state of their company. This type of imbalance is equally dangerous, because if a company fails to perform, it may not be around to see the future.

By maintaining proper focus on current operations, leaders will be able to identify the strengths and weaknesses of the company and understand why the organization is performing or lacking in certain areas. These insights will aid planning, both in the current state of the business as well as the future.

Ultimately the balanced organizational approach to leading ensures that leaders have the right information. This information in turn enables sound judgment and quality decision making. By maintaining an overall balanced approach to leading a company, a leader can ensure the organization is healthy in its entirety.

The complete leader also possesses a second type of balance at the personal level when dealing with subordinates: a balance of influence.

It is impossible to talk about influence without talking about power, so here goes.

There are two types of power we need to briefly discuss. The first is *legitimate power*, which is formal authority that comes with a position such as first-line supervisor (French & Raven, 1958). If you do something because your boss told you to, then your boss used legitimate power to influence you.

The second type of power is called *referent power*. Referent power emerges over time as you form positive, meaningful relationships with other people (French & Raven, 1959). Referent power is much stronger than legitimate power and can be acquired by anyone, not just supervisors. If you ask a coworker for help and that person aids you because you have developed a strong personal relationship with them, then you have influenced that person with referent power.

Although complete leaders rely more on referent power, they do understand the important balance between responsibility and legitimate power. Organizations legitimize positional leaders by empowering them with the authority, or legitimate power, to perform their assigned duties.

In order for organizations to be effective, positional leaders must then be held accountable for performing these duties or responsibilities within the position. Positional leaders must align their priorities with what is best for the organization. They must also make sound decisions based on ethics, morals, and company policy.

The complete leader also recognizes when there is an imbalance between the responsibilities assigned and the level of legitimate power or authority needed to perform his or her duties. Too little authority can undermine the positional leader and make them appear to subordinates as being weak or incompetent, as they do not have enough legitimate power to fulfill their normal duties as a supervisor.

For example, Chris was tasked by his Air Force senior leader to gain engineering approval to perform a critical flight test for an aircraft navigation device. His boss gave him only one week to gain the approval, which was quite a restraint.

The normal process for gaining this type of approval took at least six months. Chris recognized an imbalance between responsibility and legitimate power, even though he already had built a high level of referent power with other workers. In this instance, Chris did not have the legitimate power to reprioritize the work of his coworkers to accommodate his urgent need and work his task first.

Chris recognized that without a reprioritization of the other workers' tasks, there was no way to gain an engineering approval in the allotted time. Once he communicated this imbalance to his senior leader, the boss sent an email to the entire organization and informed them that Chris was personally working on his behalf; he also told them they should treat Chris as they would the senior leader himself. This one email gave Chris enough legitimate power to ask others to give his project priority, which allowed him to accomplish the task on time.

Leaders work best when they are assigned responsibility and legitimate power in somewhat equal amounts (Yukl, 2010). The more responsibility a positional leader has, the more legitimate power he or she will need. A complete leader will recognize an imbalance between power and responsibility, if one exists, and take steps to remedy the situation.

Complete leaders will also use their delegated authority to benefit the organization. They will use legitimate power when fulfilling the assigned duties of the organization and nothing more. The complete leader relies on referent power to influence others and leverages strong relationships to get things done.

Eisenhower's thoughts about leadership reinforce this concept:

"Leadership is the art of getting someone else to do something you want done because he wants to do it."[1]

BALANCING LEADER BEHAVIOR WITH WORKER EXPECTATIONS

Shows how organizational balances impact individuals and families.

---

1. The full quote is this: "Now I think, speaking roughly, by leadership we mean the art of getting someone else to do something that you want done because he wants to do it, not because your position of power can compel him to do it, or your position of authority. A commander of a regiment is not necessarily a leader. He has all of the appurtenances of power given by a set of Army regulations by which he can compel unified action. He can say to a body such as this, 'Rise,' and 'Sit down.' You do it exactly. But that is not leadership." Remarks at the Annual Conference of the Society for Personnel Administration, 5/12/54.

Subordinates expect positional leaders to use legitimate power to make necessary decisions. If a positional leader fails to do so, he or she creates a dangerous imbalance between leader behavior and worker expectations. If this imbalance occurs, supervisors can easily find themselves losing respect and morale from their subordinates.

Even worse, if the leader fails to make a decision that is necessary, workers may feel as though it is the responsibility of the workers themselves. This lack of action by the positional leader creates confusion, as no one is sure who should take the responsibility and make the decision. This scenario can result in power-jockeying if more than one person thinks they should be the one to act.

In his witty short called "A Responsibility Poem" about a four-person team, Charles Osgood characterizes this perfectly (quotation marks added):

> There was an important job to do and "Everybody" was asked to do it. "Everybody" was sure that "Somebody" would do it. "Anybody" would have done it, but "Nobody" did it. "Somebody" got angry because it was "Everybody's" job. "Everybody" thought "Anybody" would do it, but "Nobody" realized that "Anybody" wouldn't do it.

We have found that many positional leaders are continually asking themselves, "Should I, could I, would I?" when it comes to making decisions, accepting responsibilities, and leading people. The effective leader is usually more aggressive and asks for forgiveness rather than permission when it comes to responsibility. This approach usually garners more respect and esteem from their workers as a result.

Although exercising legitimate power is necessary for positional leaders to maintain balance and fulfill assigned responsibilities, the complete leader utilizes referent power to the maximum extent possible. For this reason, it is important for leaders to develop positive and meaningful relationships with workers.

It is impossible to be a complete leader by possessing only positional or legitimate power. Using only legitimate power, a supervisor can tell a subordinate to perform a task, and it will likely happen. But once the task is accomplished, the worker will stop any further activity. If the supervisor had strong referent power with the worker, then the subordinate would be more committed to the task, which would likely increase the quality of the work.

If the leader had strong referent power, the employee would also be more likely to provide feedback to the supervisor if there were any problems along the way. The worker would also communicate if there was a better way to accomplish the task or if the worker discovered new information that would benefit the supervisor or the organization. Without referent power, the positional leader would likely get no feedback.

☆☆

A GENERAL'S REFLECTION

Back when I was a one-star General, I was in charge of 27,000 logistics personnel from three different military service branches. We were stationed at an Army post in Kuwait, and we supported combat operations in the Iraq theater during OPERATION: Iraqi Freedom.

Early in my tenure I began visiting different units in my organization because I knew from past experience that the troops needed to see their senior leader engaged. I always took Archie, my Command Sergeant Major (CSM), with me because he was the senior enlisted leader and was a great second set of eyes. During these visits I would "kick the tires" by walking around and talking to the officers serving as unit positional leaders, and Archie would "check under the hood" by visiting some of the younger enlisted troops where they worked and slept.

I remember this one Friday when a new unit was assigned to my command. I immediately visited them, and during my nickel tour, as I talked with some of the leaders, I noticed that many of the officers who were positional leaders were in charge of other officers of the same rank. I found this odd, as usually the positional leaders would be higher ranking.

When examining the behavior of the positional leaders I got the impression that they were not acting the part; it was almost as if everyone was in charge, but no one was in charge. Also, when I asked probing questions I got the impression that they were "blowing smoke." Later, I compared notes with Archie and told him that I had the feeling that something wasn't right. He said, "Sir, I'm seeing the same thing."

I've never been one to sit on a "hunch," so I called in an outside inspection team and ordered an immediate health and welfare inspection on the unit. The inspection team did a deep dive into the unit and then reported to me later that night with their results. The commander of the inspection team brought some astonishing results that validated my suspicions. I felt like they would come back with something along those lines, but their findings actually overwhelmed me.

The results were three legal pages of violations—ranging from violations of General Order #1 (brokering alcohol and pornography in theater), to sexual harassment, fraternization, arson, and dereliction of duty.

The First Sergeant was recorded on video as having one of the female soldiers performing a lap dance at the mobilization station in front of dozens of members of the organization during a Christmas party. Every Friday night, the officers of the unit would replay the video during a party, which was how they got caught by the inspection team.

Continued

Several of the key leaders of the unit were running a pornography and alcohol ring. Mind you, both are illegal in Kuwait, as it is a Muslim country. They were selling pornography and alcohol to other inhabitants of the base they were living on, and jeopardizing every one of their customers.

Following the brief from the inspection team, I knew I had to make some immediate changes. I removed all of the leaders who were involved in the violations and placed them in other various units in nonleadership positions. I replaced them with other competent leaders and made sure they knew exactly what was expected of them in their newly assigned roles. All in all, I replaced five officers and five enlisted, which basically included every leader in the organization.

I feel I garnered a tremendous amount of respect and esteem from soldiers at all levels. I was able to sift through the negligence taking place and take the appropriate actions needed to replace the wrongdoers, reinstill the lost morale, and set the unit on a more correct path to success. The feedback I received following this event was much like, "It was about time some changes were made."

This change-out set a remarkable tone that resonated throughout the entire command. I began to see more responsive leadership from positional leaders, not only in that particular unit but also in other organizations. I saw more leaders buying in to my leadership philosophy of doing the right thing and living up to responsibilities and expectations. In time, more people would point out shortcomings in expected performance, not only in their own organizations but also in other organizations with which they conducted business.

I feel that this is why referent power is so strong. People didn't simply do what I asked of them and nothing more (as with legitimate power). I earned their respect and they committed themselves without limit because of the relationship we built through this experience.

Following this event, Mike garnered a tremendous amount of respect and esteem from members at all levels of the organization. He demonstrated balance as a complete leader by making necessary changes that were needed at that time for the organization.

He also showed courage for setting aside personal apprehensions in his willingness to make tough decisions. He led by example and illustrated for leaders throughout the organization the appropriate application of power as it relates to responsibility.

Mike also built referent power from subordinates as he showed the ability to lead in accordance with the best interests of the organization. His actions proved he cared deeply about the organization and its members, and people related to him on a strong personal level because of their shared commitment.

Subordinates tend to recognize the effectiveness of their leaders through actions and decisions they make. "Do as I say, not as I do" leadership tends to weaken a leader's rapport with subordinates. Complete leaders always lead by example. Failing to do so will ruin your credibility.

Overall, subordinates know what *right* looks like when it comes to leadership, and they know even more what *right doesn't look like.* Satisfying leader performance expectations from subordinates—such as being fair, walking the talk, and leading by example—is key to maintaining balance for a complete leader.

We have taken a moment to talk balance as it relates to the organization as a whole, balance with the individual leader's influence on other people, and balance between positional authority and responsibility. This was necessary because you can't be a complete leader without this understanding. But there is another critical aspect to the complete leader that we argue most leaders, both formal and informal, are lacking: the ultimate balance between people and processes.

PROCESS IS THE PATH THAT LEADS TO RESULTS

There is an age-old adage in the leadership community that states, "Leaders lead people and manage processes." We argue that complete leaders must lead both. Since people are involved in executing processes, the process itself must be led.

Positional leaders must define processes extensively, record processes, train workers to utilize the process, apply appropriate resources to the process, instill process discipline, and continually monitor the performance of the process. In our experience, most organizations fail to lead processes in one or more of these areas.

Some organizations simply do not have established processes whatsoever; this means the people *are* the process. Let's say at your current company you need to file a travel voucher from a recent business trip, and when you ask the finance department for assistance someone responds, "Oh, John takes care of that and he's not here today." In this organization, the process for filing a travel voucher is John. If there was a clearly defined process and people were trained on the process, then anyone in the finance department could assist you.

Lack of process leadership creates inefficiencies in an organization. In this scenario, you now have to take two days to process a travel voucher instead of one. What if John does not return tomorrow? What if John gets sick for two weeks? Who will take his place? The new "John" will have to establish his or her own process and "reinvent the wheel," or wait until John gets back to work.

If this is your organization, then you probably already know that filing a travel voucher is not the only process that lacks leadership. If there are fifty other processes like this one that have no process definition, the inefficiencies compound on top of each other and your organization is a breeding ground for chaos. This is why process is the path that leads to order, balance, and results. For that reason, we argue that when people think of leadership, they should be thinking *process* as well as *people*.

Leaders lead primarily two things: *people* and *processes*. If a leader wrote down everything he or she does on a daily, weekly, or monthly basis, most actions would fall under these two categories. We've found in our experience and formal leadership training that most people are taught to lead people but to leave processes to someone else.

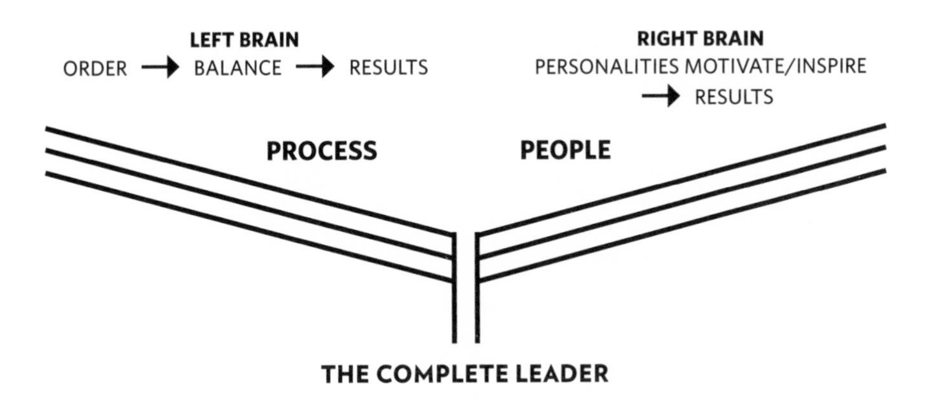

Before we delve into talking about why process leadership is lacking, we must pause to acknowledge that there are two types of leaders out there. Some of you (like Chris) are better at writing than math, are more extroverted, and have considerable social and people skills. If this sounds like you, then consider yourself a right-brained person for the purposes of this discussion. *Right-brained* is a term psychologists use to describe people with a predisposition to sensory-based activities and who prefer to do things because they "feel good."

On the other end of the spectrum are our left-brained folks. These are the analytical types of people (like Mike) who are usually engineers, technical experts, and are better at math than the rest of us. These leaders prefer calculated activities that result in an empirical answer, and they like to do things because they make sense or provide an absolute solution. If you like the fact that 2+2 always equals 4, then consider yourself a left-brained person for this discussion.

We do acknowledge that these are two ends of the spectrum and there are all sorts of people in between. But the basic premise of our argument is that people are predisposed in a certain way that makes them gravitate toward certain things and avoid others.

From our experiences, we've seen more right-brained types of people in positional leadership positions. This is likely due to several reasons, one of which is the fact that supervisors have to deal with people, and the right-brained folks out there tend to gravitate toward situations that include dealing with people.

Another argument is that left-brained types do not want to be in supervisory roles. People value different rewards. A cash reward is better for some than a time-off-work reward. Others would rather have public recognition in lieu of both.

People are different, and some left-brained folks out there consider a promotion as a form of torture. They prefer to be left alone to their work; they may have weighed the pros and cons of a promotion and simply decided it's just not worth the hassle. In other words, they could just be smarter than the rest of us.

Another explanation may be that since a large majority of supervisors are right-brained types, they may not appreciate the process skills or other analytical prowess that some of their left-brained employees bring to the table. So when it comes to promotions, they simply get looked over.

That being said, the lack of process leadership is understandable given the assumption that most positional leaders are the right-brained types. Many of the typical cookie-cutter definitions of leadership talk about motivating, inspiring, and ultimately influencing people. We are not claiming this approach is incorrect, but we offer that it is incomplete.

Second, leading *people* is the side that most folks gravitate toward, because it is more appealing and interesting to them and allows leaders to inspire, motivate, develop, coach, and mentor their team and individuals. People are the first thing these leaders focus on when moving into positions of authority or responsibility, because leaders want to meet everyone and begin developing professional relationships.

For right-brained leaders, leading processes is challenging and time consuming work that requires process definition, process mapping, flowcharts, defining and analyzing metrics, applying resources to processes, and making sure everything supports the strategic plan.

Since, to the right-brained majority, leading processes may not be as attractive as leading people, it makes sense that there is not a lot of focus on process leading, which is why many leaders simply don't want to do it.

For our left-brained readers who enjoy this type of work but avoid leadership positions because of needing to lead people, we intend to show you that the world needs your leadership, too. If people don't want to do process leadership, it often follows that they don't know much about it. But to understand it, we must begin with some definitions.

WHAT IS PROCESS LEADERSHIP?

We define process leadership as the iterative act of developing a process, applying appropriate resources to the process, and monitoring the performance of the process. Process leadership is more science than art, which makes it more appealing to the left-brained folks.

Processes can be visually depicted, measured, and refined over time, which provides characteristics suitable for quantitative analysis. Processes are inherently designed in systematic steps that can make them predictable and understandable (unlike people). Understanding processes can lead to process improvement and the attendant results of improved efficiency, productivity, and profits.

While serving as the Deputy Director of Logistics at CENTCOM, Mike was reviewing financial statements and realized the US government was paying $20M a month to lease shipping containers. He knew from being in theater that many of these containers were scattered around the bases and were not being used, but did not realize they were leased. When he began investigating the process for returning containers, he realized that the contractor responsible for their return had no process or authority to make it happen.

Mike spearheaded an effort to create a process to manage containers scattered in Iraq and Afghanistan. He developed a new step-by-step process, coordinated the process with all the stakeholders—from the government users to the owners of the containers—recorded the process in a mandatory military policy, and obtained feedback from each element to ensure the processes were being followed. This process leadership effort resulted in $140M cost avoidance for containers for the remainder of that year.

By taking the initiative to instill process leadership, Mike was able to increase efficiency and effectiveness, and to save significant unnecessary costs. He also empowered leaders at both the contractor and military levels by granting them the authority to lead as well as delivering them a defined process to follow. Although the exercise was quite painful, the rewards were just.

As we better understand the value of process-based leadership, we will also understand the value of those who are good at it. Only then can we uncover some hidden talents in our organizations, reward those individuals who excel at process-based leadership, and ultimately become better at it ourselves.

LEADING PEOPLE AND PROCESSES

We now understand balance as it relates to power and authority, and we know the overarching differences between process-based leadership and people-based leadership. We also realize that there are different types of leaders, some who gravitate toward leading process and others who lean toward leading people; both of which are equally important.

You may (or may not) have noticed that many of the dissatisfied worker comments we used in our examples of bad leadership tend to center around the lack of understanding processes that people use to accomplish work. By integrating the successful leading of both, a leader can learn to optimize his or her organization, accomplish goals and objectives, and eventually become a complete leader.

This book will show you how to achieve a perfect balance between leading people *and* leading processes through the Diamond Process Model (DPM). It does not matter whether you take a left- or right-brained approach, whether you are people- or process-oriented, or whether you are a positional or informal leader.

The DPM is a comprehensive integration framework that enables current and aspiring leaders to concentrate their focus into an overall approach toward leading their organizational resources (people, equipment, and capital) in an optimal manner. By utilizing the Diamond Process Model, leaders will help create the balance needed to keep the organization aligned—from senior leadership down to the lowest worker, and will maximize the efficiency and effectiveness of the organization.

Much (or all) of our work as consultants and trainers entails utilizing the Diamond Process Model to illustrate to leaders at all levels of an organization where they are failing to lead and achieve balance. Through the Diamond Process, the concepts in this book provide a holistic approach of simultaneously applying the DPM to all levels of an organization to properly align it and achieve what the military refers to as *Unity of Command*, whereby all members of an organization are striving to achieve the same purpose.

Regardless of where your position resides within an organization, we challenge you to find your place in the Diamond Process Model and understand how you fit into the organizational framework. By understanding your current position and what you should expect from leaders in other positions, you can become a better member of your organization.

Since we will be discussing the different levels of leadership, we want to ensure that everyone has a common understanding of terms. Simply stated, there are three main tiers of leadership in most organizations: top, middle, and bottom. Civilian organizations refer to these tiers as executive, middle management, and first-line. The military uses the terminology of strategic, operational, and tactical. We must make these distinctions, as within each level of positional leadership there are varying requirements for leading both people and processes.

COMPLETE LEADERSHIP IS NECESSARY

We've developed a process that will help you create a serious system to aid you in your journey to become a complete leader. We stressed the importance of reaching a balance between people and processes, since that is usually what is missing. But it is also important to note that being a complete leader requires more than simply achieving balance.

The complete leader is also someone who has developed essential character foundational traits such as integrity, courage, discipline, and a strong work ethic, along with setting standards, learning, listening, and taking the initiative. These traits are non-negotiable with subordinates and can mean the difference between earning their respect or losing out on it.

The complete leader must continue to hone and develop his or her leadership skills and focus on learning to become a decisive change agent and thought leader on emerging issues and concepts. Most importantly, a complete leader must understand the relationship between people and processes.

Once this learning has been acquired, complete leaders move toward the pinnacle of their tier by developing others, gaining wisdom, and exercising situational awareness of their organizations. Using all of this wisdom, knowledge, and experience, they should be prime candidates to help others become better leaders. This cycle occurs at each of the three tiers presented above. We feel that we are on the latter end of this spectrum and are here to practice what we preach.

Effective leadership is a result of balance at the organizational, personal, group, and process levels. Organizational balance sets the key strategic drivers that are only achieved by the processes supporting them. Processes are supported by people and other resources which, in turn, enable leaders to achieve key strategic drivers.

We have found through our experiences as leaders, trainers, and consultants that process leadership is most often overlooked. The lack of understanding the process level of leadership prevents positional and informal leaders from becoming complete leaders. However, working with the Diamond Process will allow you to overcome this limitation and enable you to be a better leader of people. The next chapter in this book will begin to introduce you to the elements of the Diamond Process Model (DPM).

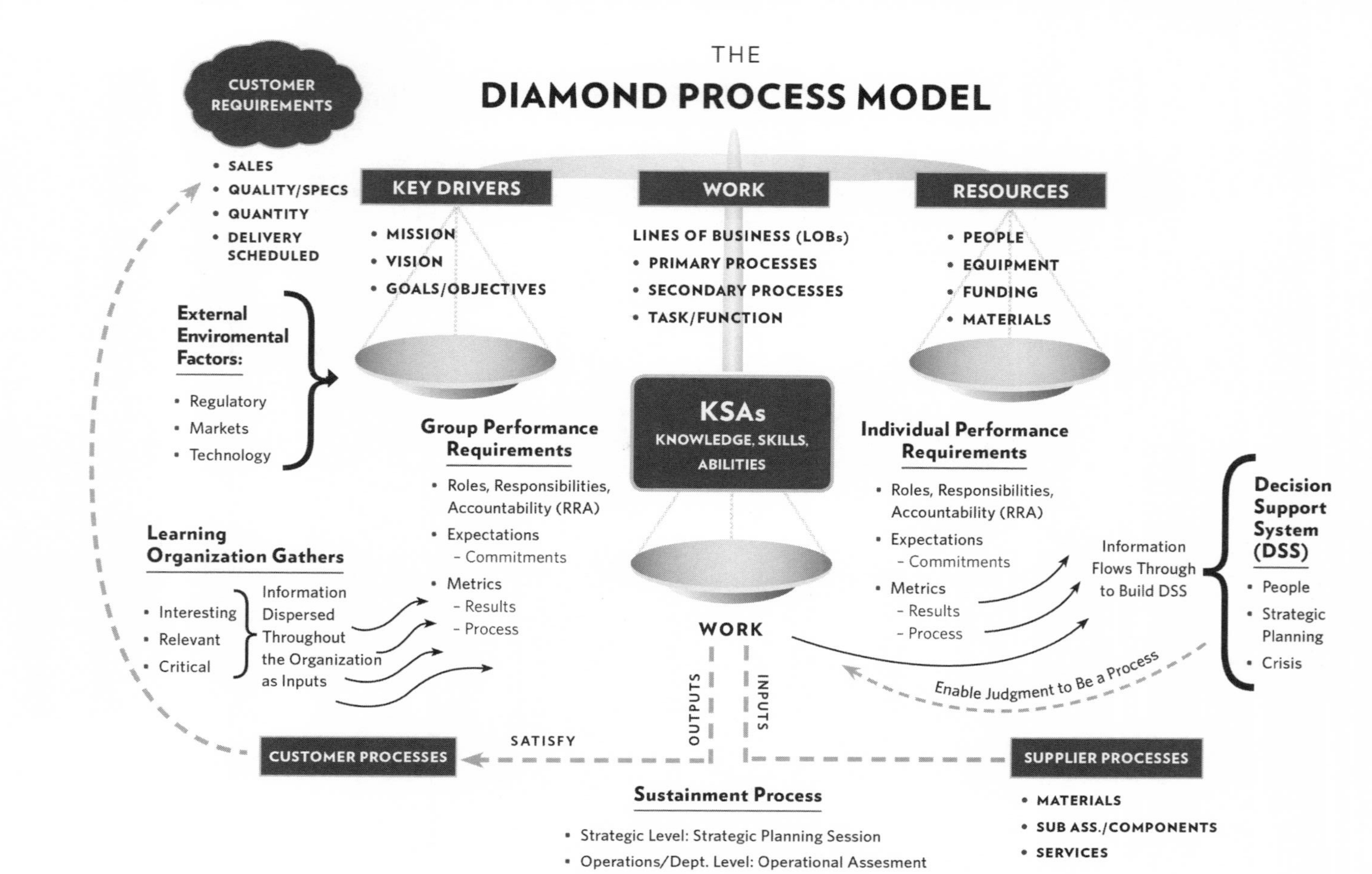
THE
DIAMOND PROCESS MODEL
CUSTOMER REQUIREMENTS
• SALES
• QUALITY/SPECS
• QUANTITY
• DELIVERY SCHEDULED
KEY DRIVERS
• MISSION
• VISION
• GOALS/OBJECTIVES
WORK
LINES OF BUSINESS (LOBs)
• PRIMARY PROCESSES
• SECONDARY PROCESSES
• TASK/FUNCTION
RESOURCES
• PEOPLE
• EQUIPMENT
• FUNDING
• MATERIALS
External Enviromental Factors:
• Regulatory
• Markets
• Technology
Group Performance Requirements
• Roles, Responsibilities, Accountability (RRA)
• Expectations
- Commitments
• Metrics
- Results
- Process
KSAs
KNOWLEDGE, SKILLS, ABILITIES
Individual Performance Requirements
• Roles, Responsibilities, Accountability (RRA)
• Expectations
- Commitments
• Metrics
- Results
- Process
Learning Organization Gathers
• Interesting
• Relevant
• Critical
Information Dispersed Throughout the Organization as Inputs
Information Flows Through to Build DSS
Decision Support System (DSS)
• People
• Strategic Planning
• Crisis
WORK
Enable Judgment to Be a Process
OUTPUTS
INPUTS
SATISFY
CUSTOMER PROCESSES
SUPPLIER PROCESSES
• MATERIALS
• SUB ASS./COMPONENTS
• SERVICES
Sustainment Process
• Strategic Level: Strategic Planning Session
• Operations/Dept. Level: Operational Assesment
• First Line Leader Level: Process Review

MAJOR SECTION
ONE:

ELEMENTS OF THE DIAMOND PROCESS MODEL

THE
DIAMOND PROCESS MODEL

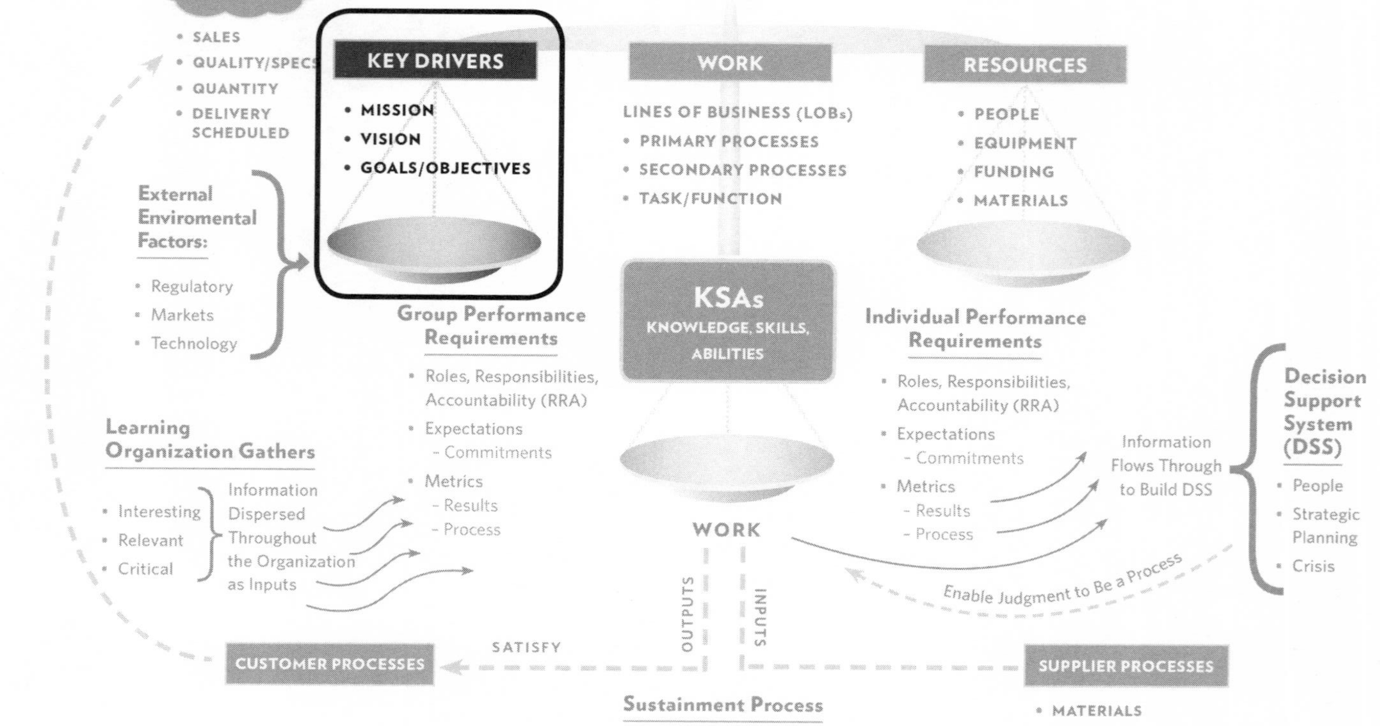
CUSTOMER REQUIREMENTS
• SALES
• QUALITY/SPECS
• QUANTITY
• DELIVERY SCHEDULED
KEY DRIVERS
• MISSION
• VISION
• GOALS/OBJECTIVES
WORK
LINES OF BUSINESS (LOBs)
• PRIMARY PROCESSES
• SECONDARY PROCESSES
• TASK/FUNCTION
RESOURCES
• PEOPLE
• EQUIPMENT
• FUNDING
• MATERIALS
External Enviromental Factors:
• Regulatory
• Markets
• Technology
Group Performance Requirements
• Roles, Responsibilities, Accountability (RRA)
• Expectations
- Commitments
• Metrics
- Results
- Process
KSAs
KNOWLEDGE, SKILLS, ABILITIES
Individual Performance Requirements
• Roles, Responsibilities, Accountability (RRA)
• Expectations
- Commitments
• Metrics
- Results
- Process
Learning Organization Gathers
• Interesting
• Relevant
• Critical
Information Dispersed Throughout the Organization as Inputs
WORK
Information Flows Through to Build DSS
Decision Support System (DSS)
• People
• Strategic Planning
• Crisis
Enable Judgment to Be a Process
OUTPUTS
INPUTS
SATISFY
CUSTOMER PROCESSES
SUPPLIER PROCESSES
• MATERIALS
• SUB ASS./COMPONENTS
• SERVICES
Sustainment Process
• Strategic Level: Strategic Planning Session
• Operations/Dept. Level: Operational Assesment
• First Line Leader Level: Process Review

CHAPTER 2

MISSION, VISION, GOALS, AND OBJECTIVES

In major section one, we will describe the Diamond Process Model with a top-down approach. The Diamond Process always starts with the highest levels of leadership and works down through the organization to the individual worker. This approach mirrors businesses themselves, since stuff always rolls downhill.

Each element will be introduced and explained in terms of the impact the elements have on both the model and your organization. By using elements of the Diamond Process Model as a leadership tool, we can achieve and maintain organizational balance, which is the key to success for any organization.

The DPM elements are grouped into three separate categories called *components*. Referring to components while discussing the model will make it easier to understand. The three components are the **key driver** component (Mission, Vision, Goals, and Objectives); **work process** component (lines of business; primary and secondary processes; tasks and functions); and the **resource** component (people, equipment, capital).

Let's begin with the key driver component, which contains the highest elements of the model: mission, vision, goals, and objectives (MVGOs). But before we begin defining the specific elements in the key driver component, we must point out that many organizations simply do not have or manage MVGOs, nor do they have a process to create or maintain them.

We find that there are many organizations that have no key drivers (or have only a pitiful excuse for them) to set a strategic direction. This equates to a rudderless ship flailing around in the ocean. Or as Chris and his Air Force colleagues say, "All thrust and no vector."

It is difficult to be a leader in an organization with no strategy. But unfortunately, that is the rule rather than the exception. Many organizations lack or fail to provide the discipline, time, or desire to have and maintain these key drivers. Instead, they simply focus on current operations.

In our experience, those who are most lacking in key drivers are our friends in small business. It is a shame because they could have the largest impact from focusing on a useful set of well-maintained key drivers such as strategic goals and objectives. Small businesses can gain a competitive advantage by having a strategy because most of their competitors don't have one. In this case, a little strategy can go a long way because it can help the small business focus its limited resources on processes that are needed most.

Yet most small business leaders just do not set aside the time, energy, and effort to perform strategic planning and do not realize they are missing out on one of the most important aspects of leading. If they were to put more emphasis on having MVGOs in place, they would realize much greater rewards for their time invested.

The most common reason that elements in the key driver component are absent in both small and large businesses is because the company does not have a process for strategic planning. This is a serious hurdle to overcome when you are striving for success in your organization.

A GENERAL'S REFLECTION

When I was a Colonel, I was assigned to command the 32nd Transportation Group in Tampa, FL. This was a reserve unit, which basically meant that most of its members were *weekend warriors*, and the core day-to-day operations were provided by a few select full-timers.

When I arrived at headquarters I found it was staffed with good people, but they lacked continuity, cohesiveness, and purpose. I knew I needed to understand the strategic vision of the previous leader so I could adjust the strategic plan.

When I asked, "What are you guys doing here?" and "Where are you all headed?" they just gave me that deer-in-the-headlights stare. They had been operating like most organizations do: living for today and taking things as they come.

I provided roles, responsibilities, accountability, and my expectations for subordinates. I then instituted a strategic planning session with my key leaders. During the session I outlined the key drivers to include the mission, vision, goals, and objectives. I then asked my subordinate leaders to develop the process and *resource components.*

A few weeks went by before I asked for feedback from our strategic planning session, and I was surprised that it was resoundingly positive. Most of the comments sounded like "Why haven't we done this before?" and "I feel like I know more of what I am supposed to do."

I could tell the team chemistry was coming together, as was the sense of purpose for what they were doing and why they were doing it. Since then I have utilized the strategic planning session in both military and corporate settings with amazing results in driving organizations forward. Thinking back to times when I did not use strategic planning sessions, I can easily recall how disjointed things were; I vowed I would never go back to those days again.

STRATEGIC PLANNING SESSIONS

Mission, vision, goals, and objectives—MVGOs—are the most important items to establish and to keep current in an organization. They are the key drivers for the entire organization and are the basis for balance, which enables efficiency, effectiveness, and unity. This is why MVGOs are contained in the *key driver* category at the top of the Diamond Process Model.

The formulation and review of all the key driver elements should be accomplished by top leaders during strategic planning. With the Diamond Process Model, the preferred method of strategic planning is to formalize the process with periodic strategic planning sessions.

These sessions can be game changers and are important for the health of all organizations, regardless of size. Since they are so important to the success of leaders, we are very surprised at the multitude of companies that do not conduct strategic planning sessions or any type of strategic planning.

Business leaders should develop a specific process for conducting strategic planning sessions. The process should define which key functional leaders should be present (executive, finance, information technology, marketing, sales, strategy, etc.), and what each leader is responsible for presenting during the session.

For example, the senior sales leader can provide insights as to how the company is performing in sales through different markets. This information, in turn, could influence the top leader's decision to modify goals or objectives in the strategic plan.

The process should also define who is responsible for conducting and organizing strategic planning sessions. Some large businesses designate one key leader and assign that person a staff of five or so people to assist in scheduling, organizing, preparing, and documenting the sessions.

Smaller organic organizations can delegate one or two people to be in charge of conducting strategic planning sessions to accomplish the same feat. The important thing to realize is that some dedicated person or group should be assigned to manage the strategic planning process.

EXTERNAL INFLUENCES ON STRATEGIC PLANNING

If you have never conducted a strategic planning session and are motivated to do so as you read this text, we want to give you a few more pointers. As you conduct these sessions you will want to look at the external environment surrounding your business and examine it for opportunities and threats.

There are too many environments out there for us to discuss all the possibilities. But what we can do is introduce you to the three primary external factors that affect almost everyone: regulatory (legal), technology, and markets. At a minimum, leaders will want to examine these three areas, as they can vastly affect the future viability of an organization, as well as the MVGOs in the strategic plan.

Some businesses, such as pharmaceutical or energy companies, are at the mercy of federal regulators such as the Food and Drug Administration (FDA) or the Environmental Protection Agency (EPA) respectively. These businesses likely review the external legal environment extensively during their strategic planning sessions in order to adapt to proposed changes in federal regulations.

Many companies are affected by federal, state, and/or local laws, but the ties are not as obvious. For example, in 2011, the state of California was considering a ban on a type of packaging foam, which almost put a container company out of business.

If the company identified this threat during a strategic planning session, they could have modified their strategic plan to either fight the ban through the legal system, change their business model to adapt to the new law, or a combination of both. Either way, it is essential to identify and analyze legal threats since they can affect the future of your organization.

Technology is another external factor that is constantly changing and should be examined during periodic strategic planning sessions. Increases in identity theft and emerging cyber threats like the incidents at the Veterans Administration and Target Corporation have highlighted the need for cyber security on a national stage.

Technological risks to your business should be presented and reviewed during strategic planning sessions so they can be managed at the executive (top) level of leadership. Risk identification should occur at the lower levels of the organization through processes in place to monitor trends and emerging technologies.

These same processes that identify possible risks can also identify opportunities, as some technologies may help your company tremendously. Regardless of whether you identify a risk or an opportunity, technology will continue to shape your organization's strategic plan.

The third primary external factor that can affect a strategic plan is markets. Competition shapes the way markets behave. It is necessary then for each organization to constantly be aware of their competitors—what they are doing and how it may affect their own strategic plan. You must also protect against other competitors by safeguarding your intellectual property and trade secrets in order to maintain your competitive advantage.

Strategic and contingency plans should be developed to look into potential markets for new products and services that may place you ahead of the competition. While some companies have specific departments devoted to researching products and markets, others have none at all—and I believe this is a mistake. We believe companies should always have someone pursuing these new opportunities.

While finding a new market can offer an opportunity for growth, it's also important to look for market segments that should be reduced or maybe even abandoned if they're just no longer favorable for the organization. This could be as a result of lost competitive edge, lost technological expertise, lost manpower, or other causes.

The often-quoted coach Yogi Berra once said, "If you don't know where you are going, you'll end up someplace else." For organizations, strategic planning sessions provide the venue for top leaders to figure out where they want to go. The mission, vision, goals, and objectives (MVGOs) tell everyone in your organization how to get there and provide the basis for their own strategic direction. It's time now to get an overview of the actual MVGOs.

MISSION, VISION, GOALS, AND OBJECTIVES

Leaders in successful companies establish key drivers during strategic planning sessions. Effective strategic planning sessions will produce a strategic plan that will include the following:

1. Clarification on why the organization exists (mission);
2. Strategic direction on the organization's current state as well as its desired future state (vision); and
3. Key steps the organization must accomplish to achieve the desired state (goals and objectives).

Let's look at each more closely.

THE MISSION STATEMENT

For many years now, research has been published on the importance of mission statements, and the market is flooded with books on how to write one. Here, however, we are simply going to explain how a mission statement is used in the context of the Diamond Process Model and what you need to know about it. Let's clearly define what a mission statement is, provide a good example of one, and make sure we discuss how important it can be.

The *mission* of the organization is its purpose for being in business.

The mission statement should articulate what you are in business to do and what you wake up to accomplish each day. The mission statement should be succinct, yet be general enough so as to allow the other levels of the organization to better interpret how it should be accomplished for the entire organization and what role they play. The mission is the "what" and the people decide "how."

Here is a great mission statement from the Anadarko Petroleum Corporation: "Anadarko's mission is to deliver a competitive and sustainable rate of return to shareholders by developing, acquiring, and exploring for oil and gas resources vital to the world's health and welfare." (MissionStatements.com, 2014)

After reading this mission statement, there is little doubt what the employees of this company wake up to do every morning. It is general in nature so that subordinate organizations can build their own missions around this corporate mission statement. Even if you are not a top-level national organization with subordinate companies, it is still essential to have your own mission statement. It will communicate to your employees why you are in business and allow them to keep their focus on what they are to accomplish.

The magic of a mission statement occurs when top leaders sit down to write one, because it forces the top level of leadership to ask themselves the question, "What is our mission?" The important answers that come in response to that question provide vital information that we use to begin populating our Diamond Process Model.

If top leaders never participate in the mission articulation exercise through strategic planning sessions, they can easily lose sight of why the organization exists and what it is supposed to accomplish. This was the case for a US Army unit that Mike was hired to help.

A GENERAL'S REFLECTION

Shortly after I retired from the Army Reserve, the Army contracted me and my four-person mentor team to consult Army commanders who were in charge of units that were getting ready to deploy in support of OPERATION: Iraqi Freedom.

For my first assignment I was tasked to consult the 561st Regional Support Group (RSG) as they were deploying to Baghdad to be the first Joint Area Support Group (JASG). The mission of the RSG in the US is to be trained and equipped to mobilize to any place in the world and to then set up and operate an Army base or installation.

Their new mission as a JASG was much more complex and expanded as they picked up the role of supporting not only US Army soldiers, but also the State Department and other US agencies as well as other military units in the Baghdad area. The new mission also required them to maintain and operate five separate bases instead of just one.

Prior to any Army unit deployment, there is a list of standard exercises that the unit must accomplish to demonstrate general competencies such as communication, logistics, intelligence, etc. After two weeks of observing these exercises for the unit, I remember their commander asking me to help bring the unit's members into a better focus for what they would be doing in Baghdad because, in his words, "They're just not getting it."

I conducted a short class for the soldiers and walked them step-by-step through figuring out the processes they would need to use in order to be successful in their new mission. Since my consulting process began with understanding the organization's mission, I discovered very quickly the reason why the unit was "just not getting it."

Everything they were set up to do was in support of a mission that had changed. Once I outlined their new mission and identified

Continued

the processes they needed to accomplish it, they were able to totally reorganize the unit. This resulted in a new organizational balance.

Through the exercise of defining the new mission and deciphering what it would take to accomplish it, I saw that the soldiers had all the answers they needed. They were very knowledgeable about their respective professions. The only piece that had been missing before was the process of defining the mission and interpreting what it meant for the unit.

The 561st became a successful organization due to this realignment because they were able to perform any mission assigned to them by higher headquarters. I received positive feedback from senior leaders in the Departments of Defense and State on the solid performance of the 561st while they were deployed in Baghdad.

The unit and its members were pioneers in establishing best practices that served the ensuing JASGs prior to their respective deployments. This was also a pioneering experience for me, because it forced me to write the materials that became the genesis of this book!

VISION

Once again, we are not going to spend too much time discussing vision, as it is one of the oldest topics in leadership. But, as with the mission statement, we need to define what a vision is and does, as well as provide a good example. We also need to communicate the importance of a good vision and talk about whose responsibility it is to write it.

The vision is where the organization as a whole wants to end up: the desired future state of the organization. We've found that a company's vision is often shortsighted as described by the key leader because of short-term thinking, laziness, ignorance, inability to think strategically, or lack of interest in looking toward a future state for the organization. We cannot stress the importance of a clear vision enough; it is arguably the most important element in the Diamond Process Model that is provided by top leadership.

The vision of an organization is a reflection of its visionary and its people. The visionary of the organization is oftentimes the Chief Executive Officer (CEO) or equivalent, since the person in that position sets the ultimate direction for where the company is heading. In smaller organizations, this responsibility is that of the owner or top leader.

What is important in business is that someone in the highest position of the organization communicates his or her vision to the company through a vision statement. It is only then your people will understand which direction you intend to go.

What is also important to the Diamond Process is the information that arises when this top leader sits down to write the vision for the organization. The process of writing a vision forces the leader to ask important questions. The answers to those questions will become critical information that will kick-start the Diamond Process.

A good vision statement will set the organization on a path for the "endgame" and provide the company with purpose. A clear vision will improve morale in the organization, as its members will feel they are headed in a positive direction. If the vision is expressed in a way that appeals to the values of the organizational members, it can prove to be an inspirational and motivational force.

An example of a good vision statement we've found comes from Habitat for Humanity: "A world where everyone has a decent place to live." This vision statement is simple and to the point. It shows the organization is headed in a positive direction because it implies that tomorrow people will have more decent places to live than today. This ideal also appeals to the moral values of many members of the organization and the volunteers who support it.

Notice the statement does not explain "how" or "by when." This allows subordinate organizations to develop **goals** and **objectives** that can work toward achieving this vision. More importantly, as both Mike and Chris understand by volunteering, the Habitat organization has processes in place in order to accomplish and support the vision.

GOALS AND OBJECTIVES

Goals and objectives provide the organization the key steps it needs to accomplish its mission and move further toward meeting the vision set by key leadership. These also provide tangible performance targets for subordinates as well as reference points through which success or failure can be measured. These elements are clearly leader-driven and serve as the pacemaker to the heart of the organization.

In order to be effective, goals and objectives should be realistic and prioritized according to the mission, vision, and direction of key leaders. Goals and objectives require much strategic thought, energy, planning, and time to develop. They must also be kept current to be most relevant. Goals and objectives are most effective when they cover short-, medium-, and long-term continuums.

Goals and objectives help coagulate and solidify the mission and vision, and they provide the foundation on which to build a formidable strategic plan. They also provide important quantitative information that can be used to create performance metrics for the organization. Each level within the organization should have metrics established that are tied to goals and objectives in the strategic plan and can gauge how well the organization is performing. We will discuss metrics in more detail in chapter four.

Goals and objectives should be formulated to strive for balance between achieving the mission (what we do today) as well as working toward the vision (what we want to be doing tomorrow). When an organization omits goals and objectives that measure progress, it usually fails to fulfill its vision.

It is the responsibility of top leadership to maintain discipline and resist the temptation to sacrifice the future of the organization in exchange for short-term success. The requirement to maintain a reasonable balance between mission/vision and related goals/objectives is nonnegotiable.

THE MOST IMPORTANT DPM ELEMENTS

If used properly, the Diamond Process Model (DPM) is a visual representation of the reality that is your company. If you have a mission but no vision, your business (as well as the DPM) will be out of balance, as both vision and mission are both focused on the "now." If you have a mission and vision but no goals and objectives, the Diamond Process Model will show that you have vector but no thrust.

With the Diamond Process, leadership starts at the top with the key driver component. Once we establish the mission, vision, and other elements through strategic planning sessions, subordinate leaders will then be able to develop their own mission, vision, goals, and objectives and align them with the key drivers of their top leadership. This *nesting* of key drivers will enable related organizations to stay synchronized and aligned to support the same cause.

When this is complete, we can all get focused on the work we have to accomplish. But we need a process to understand all the work that our business requires. The Diamond Process continues in the next chapter by introducing the **work process component,** which contains all the elements needed to organize the work that must be accomplished in any organization. The first element within the work process component is a **Line of Business (LOB)**.

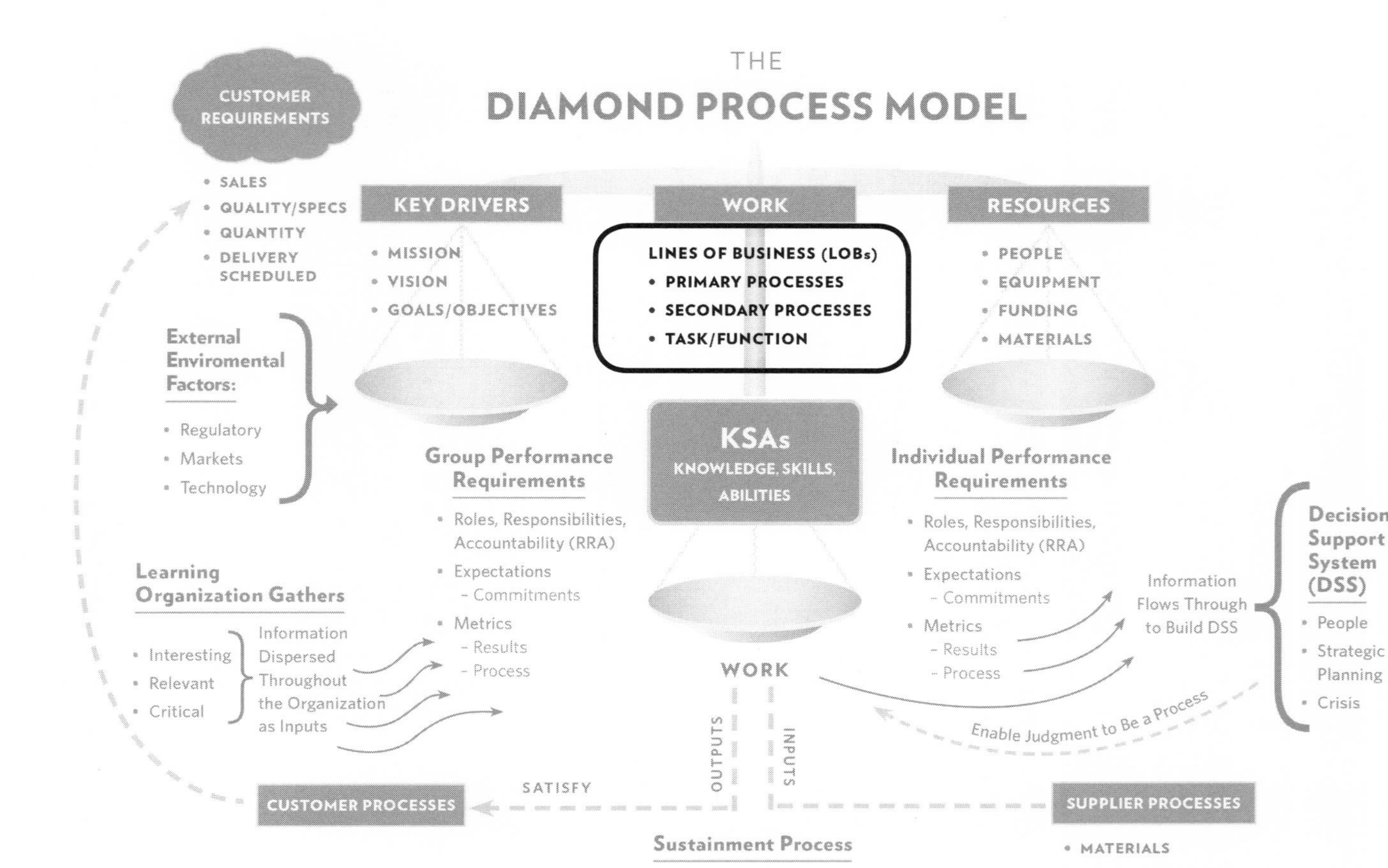
THE
DIAMOND PROCESS MODEL
CUSTOMER REQUIREMENTS
• SALES
• QUALITY/SPECS
• QUANTITY
• DELIVERY SCHEDULED
KEY DRIVERS
• MISSION
• VISION
• GOALS/OBJECTIVES
WORK
LINES OF BUSINESS (LOBs)
• PRIMARY PROCESSES
• SECONDARY PROCESSES
• TASK/FUNCTION
RESOURCES
• PEOPLE
• EQUIPMENT
• FUNDING
• MATERIALS
External Enviromental Factors:
• Regulatory
• Markets
• Technology
KSAs
KNOWLEDGE, SKILLS, ABILITIES
Group Performance Requirements
• Roles, Responsibilities, Accountability (RRA)
• Expectations
- Commitments
• Metrics
- Results
- Process
Individual Performance Requirements
• Roles, Responsibilities, Accountability (RRA)
• Expectations
- Commitments
• Metrics
- Results
- Process
Learning Organization Gathers
• Interesting
• Relevant
• Critical
Information Dispersed Throughout the Organization as Inputs
Information Flows Through to Build DSS
Decision Support System (DSS)
• People
• Strategic Planning
• Crisis
WORK
Enable Judgment to Be a Process
OUTPUTS
INPUTS
SATISFY
CUSTOMER PROCESSES
SUPPLIER PROCESSES
• MATERIALS
• SUB ASS./COMPONENTS
• SERVICES
Sustainment Process
• Strategic Level: Strategic Planning Session
• Operations/Dept. Level: Operational Assesment
• First Line Leader Level: Process Review

CHAPTER 3

LINES OF BUSINESS

Now that you have a mission depicted in your strategic planning session by senior leadership, you know why you wake up and go to work every morning. But how do you complete that mission? What type of work do you perform? How does your work relate to the success of your company? What work processes do you drive to help your organization achieve its mission? How do these processes need to change over time to meet the company's vision?

To answer all of these questions, we need to move into the *work process component* of the Diamond Process Model. There we will begin to understand all the work that needs to get accomplished in your organization to achieve the key drivers in the strategic plan. But since there is usually so much to be done, we need a way to organize it. This is why we use *Lines of Business* (LOB).

Lines of Business (LOB) is the first element in the second major DPM component of *work processes*. An LOB is a process container for all the primary and secondary processes that a business needs to perform in order to conduct daily business and meet its mission. In order for a company to organize work processes, LOBs must be determined and analyzed from a process perspective.

Since many organizations do not focus on process leadership, they do not have LOBs to contain and organize work processes. Without process organization, leaders lose sight of what workers are doing and where resources are going. Without this oversight, many leaders are reduced to running around "putting out fires" instead of leading effectively.

Even worse, without LOBs there is no way to connect the work that people perform in your organization back to the key drivers in the strategic plan. As a result, you can have purpose and direction, as well as goals and objectives, but no way to get where you decided to go in the strategic plan. You will also lack process measures to tell you if you are on track. Basically, you have "all vector and no thrust."

But before we show you how to determine, create, and manage LOBs, we must first explain how they came about. This is a best practice used by the military that we've modified so we can apply it to any organization.

LOB ORIGINS

During high-level military strategic planning sessions, senior officers in the US military subscribe to a strategic planning process that includes discussion on different *Lines of Effort (LOE)*. When planning for potential military action, it is very important to plan each element individually and completely, regardless of whether it involves logistics or combat engagement. Once each LOE is planned accordingly, all the LOEs should be aligned in order to complete the mission and its objectives.

Inspired by LOEs, a line of business (LOB) is a key high-level element determined as a result of senior-level strategic planning sessions that describe the major processes that a business or organization needs to perform in order to meet its mission. LOBs are usually short, so don't let the length of the definition mislead you. For example,

Toyota's LOB may be "sell vehicles." Wal-Mart's LOB could be to "sell household items."

To be most effective, LOBs need to be general in nature, yet distinct and mutually exclusive. The LOB must be general because its name must be able to correctly relay the overall effort, which contains a multitude of related processes. An LOB is a general classification that is similar to a parent directory in a computer. For example, in Microsoft Windows, the parent directory "program files" contains all the supporting files (processes) necessary to execute the specific program application.

LOBs must also be *distinct* because businesses may have more than one. To use our Wal-Mart example, aside from the LOB "sell household items," they may also have another LOB to "provide personal auto care."

Markets, supply chains, supporting personnel, and other necessary business processes are likely different when providing auto care versus selling household items. Therefore, formulating a distinct LOB for each is necessary to organize a company's efforts. If they simply had one LOB of "sell stuff," it would not be specific enough to separate and optimize their different lines of business.

LOBs must also be *mutually exclusive.* The whole purpose of designating LOBs in the Diamond Process Model is to categorize and bundle the high-level processes needed for your business to perform a specific function well. Once each function is separated you can examine the LOBs independently and integrate each of them with people, processes, and resources, which will do lots of cool stuff like increase efficiency, save money, and increase profit.

LOB DETERMINATION

Now that we know what an LOB is, we can learn how to make one. LOBs must be defined by senior leaders in strategic planning sessions.

Otherwise, each supervisor would have his or her own interpretation of what an LOB should be, and your organization would be really confused.

During these strategic planning sessions, senior leaders must ask the following two extremely important questions:

1. "What are we in business for?"
2. "What are the high-level processes that need to be performed to enable us to accomplish our mission?"

The answers to these questions should be the basis for an in-depth brainstorming session through which the highest organization-level processes are recorded. Someone in the room should write down every high-level process that is mentioned on a whiteboard or paper so they are visible to everyone in the room.

Similar to other brainstorming sessions, there are no wrong answers, and the senior leader should ensure the environment is one that enables people to speak out. Once everyone in the room has exhausted every possible process they can think of, it is time to apply the litmus test.

☆☆

A GENERAL'S REFLECTION

In 2008 while I was a two-star serving on active duty, I was assigned a new position as Director of Coalition Coordination at US Central Command (CENTCOM) in Tampa, FL. With this new position, I inherited an organization of forty or so US joint military members (AF, Army, Navy, and Marine) and several foreign-coalition military members representing sixty-two allied countries.

Keep in mind that the US was in full swing in Iraq military operations; but Enduring Freedom had kicked off, so most of our troops were supporting efforts in Afghanistan. One of my responsibilities as Coalition Coordinator was to travel to countries like Georgia and negotiate their committing more troops to the cause.

We supported nearly 50 separate military units with over 9,000 coalition forces that operated in our Area of Responsibility (AOR), which included Iraq, Afghanistan, and the 27 countries surrounding them.

This support included logistical items such as uniforms, weapons, vehicles, gas, and basically anything that the people needed to fight. We also were on the hook for resolving diplomatic issues in cases where some countries had restrictions on missions they could or could not perform due to religious or other conflicts.

We provided administrative support for contractual documents that needed to be approved through the State Department, NATO, or any country that allowed for their participation. Most importantly we coordinated the capability to train for combat operations so we had a way to train coalition members once they arrived in-country to support wartime operations.

We were a force multiplier, which means that once a combatant commander identified the need for additional forces or follow-on forces, our organization had the ability to come together and coordinate with other agencies to meet those requirements with personnel from our coalition member nations.

When I got in the swing of things I noticed my folks were always in "firefighting mode." They were good people doing great work but they were not strategically organized to handle the future requirements and the coordination it took to make those requirements reality.

I started asking my subordinates about how they provided support to our coalition brethren and was told that they did it on a case-by-case basis. I knew right then we were not organized properly to efficiently respond to our customers, which was why we were fighting fires.

I pulled all my subordinates together and we had a strategic

Continued

planning session. I started with my two questions and asked, "Why are we in business?" and "What are the high-level processes that we need to perform so we can accomplish our mission?" Everyone knew why we were in business; but something was missing when we examined our high-level processes and our lines of effort (LOEs).

I asked where most of the countries that we supported came from and was told Europe because most were members of NATO. I recognized this as a high-level process, so I asked what kind of coordination took place with the US European Command (EUCOM). I was told whenever we needed to secure logistical items we coordinated with EUCOM on a case-by-case basis.

As I asked more and more questions about the processes we used to support all of these coalition forces, it became apparent to me that we were missing a major line of effort (LOE) for my military organization: that of having a coordination team that worked directly with EUCOM to support our coalition forces in the CENTCOM theater.

This became a win-win because everyone came out a winner. First, the customer (coalition force) got the best service they had ever had because of the new LOE and the resources we committed to perform that part of our mission. My staff developed a much closer working relationship with all parties involved, which improved efficiency and lowered coordination time to fill new requirements. EUCOM was better prepared to take care of the coalition forces that deployed; and the combatant commander got the troops he needed to continue to meet his combat mission in theater.

LOB LITMUS TEST

As you will recall, LOBs must be mutually exclusive to optimize analysis and avoid confusion. Therefore, it is time to analyze the processes that were written down and determine if two of them have overlap or share subordinate processes. If they do, then these two processes are not mutually exclusive and should be listed next to each other since they are related in some way.

When you put two processes together, put the higher-level process on top of the lower-level process and label the top one as a **primary process**. Continue organizing these high-level processes until you are confident the board is showing vertical categories of processes that are mutually exclusive from the other categories. When you are finished, the highest primary process in each column is likely the LOB. But before we make that determination, we have one more test.

In a successful organization, LOBs support key strategic drivers that are derived from the organization's Mission, Vision, Goals, and Objectives (MVGOs). Therefore, before we classify a primary process as an LOB, we must allow senior leaders in the room the opportunity to ensure key drivers are supported.

First, examine the primary processes to ensure they capture everything needed to conduct daily business (mission). Next, ensure those primary processes capture everything you want to do to move the organization toward the desired future state (vision). Finally, ensure the primary process supports and encompasses the goals and objectives of strategic leaders. This will ensure the organization is aligned with the strategic intent of its leadership.

If your primary processes pass the LOB litmus test, you can safely classify them as your company's lines of business. However, if you are like most organizations we've consulted, at this point you probably have a roomful of strategic leaders staring at a whiteboard with puzzled looks on their faces. At this point in the LOB determination process, it is common for strategic leaders to realize they have too many or not enough LOBs.

WHAT IS MISSING WITH MY LOBS?

One point of confusion is when strategic leaders look at their list of LOBs and realize there is a critical function of their organization that is not supported in some way or another. This happens because sometimes people *think* they know why they are in business, but in all actuality they made a simple miscalculation that threw off the strategic direction of their company. This was the case when Mike consulted with a small software company.

Mike consulted with a software development firm that specialized in intranet-type software designed to establish greater connectivity and communication throughout various schools and churches. Before conducting a site visit, Mike gave them the two LOB determination questions and instructed their strategic leaders to formulate their LOBs. During the company's independent LOB determination processes, they had originally identified two LOBs: churches and schools.

When Mike reviewed the litmus test, he discovered that they really had only one LOB, and that was software development. What they did was confuse their LOB with the markets they actually served—schools and churches. Despite having only one LOB with these two distinct markets, they are now very successful in the software development for their two current markets and are postured for yet a third market: healthcare.

This firm was small and organic, so the damage was not vast. But they were confused, and if left to continue down the path they were on, they would have set-up many redundant processes. Clarifying they had only one LOB enabled the leaders of this firm to correctly organize their processes, which then aligned their people to enter a new market and support their mission.

Sometimes a company is missing an LOB needed to accomplish a vision. This is quite common when strategic leadership defines a vision for the first time and then conducts LOB determination in the same strategic planning session. Since the company hadn't previously declared a concrete vision for the company, it makes sense there was no supporting LOB.

This scenario presents a great opportunity for senior leaders to discuss what type of future LOB they need to incorporate to support the new vision for the organization. They can use the strategic planning session to record details of the LOB, develop an implementation plan, and outline goals and objectives so they can posture the organization to incorporate the LOB at a future point.

LOB QUANTITY

When some organizations complete the LOB determination process during a strategic planning session, they discover there are way too many LOBs. We've found that organizations are most effective when they have between three and eight LOBs. This is because lines of business are primary processes that are at a very high level; having too many makes an organization vulnerable as it spreads scarce resources too thin.

Having too many LOBs also makes strategic planning very intensive and confusing, and we've not found many organizations capable of executing this type of strategic thought. This is why the US military is separated between multiple components, with each specializing in air, land, sea, fast-response, or intercoastal.

If you discover you have too many LOBs, you should revert back to your mission and vision in order to seek clarity. Understand what you do well *now* and what you want to do well in the *future*. Then, condense your lines of business in order to leverage your company's resources to support those key strategic drivers. Also, use the strategic planning session to detail a plan with time-sensitive goals and objectives to execute the change of strategy for your organization.

Some companies are highly specialized and have only one line of business. We want to communicate that there is nothing wrong with this type of organization and we've seen many that are very successful.

It is common for a business to diversify as it grows and as new markets present opportunities. Considering this, if you grow your business you may develop more LOBs. If you do intend to grow, then utilize strategic planning sessions to formulate a *plan* to grow. The strategic plan should include which lines of business you need and when they should be incorporated to accomplish the vision of growth.

HOW TO MANAGE CHANGES IN YOUR LINE OF BUSINESS

Conducting effective strategic planning sessions early and often is important when integrating people, processes, and resources. Strategic planning sessions help to maintain organizational balance and establish unity of effort. When you are reviewing your strategic plan, you should also examine your lines of business to determine if they need any attention. There are several reasons why your LOBs may change.

The most common reason for LOB change is growth. Sometimes a process becomes so large it turns into a primary process or a completely separate line of business. This occurred with the Hewlett-Packard (HP) company in the 1990s.

HP started with an overall line of business to produce *complete personal computer systems*. As part of this LOB, they had a primary supporting process to produce various pieces of hardware to support their main product, the complete personal computer system. At some point, customers in the external market increased demand for computer system components rather than complete systems.

HP responded to this demand and began specializing in printer manufacturing and distribution. At this point, *printer production* became its own LOB, with the personal computer system a separate LOB for a different market segment. Had they not recognized this emerging market change in their strategic planning, HP would have missed a great opportunity for growth.

OUTSIDE-IN

Regularly scheduled strategic planning sessions are great for giving yourself an opportunity to analyze changes in the external business environment. But sometimes there are internal changes in the organization, which should trigger a strategic planning session in order to analyze your LOBs.

The first of these internal changes is a reorganization. When companies consider a re-org, which include actions such as an acquisition or merger, LOBs must be examined strategically to determine the best course of action. It would be wasteful to keep every process with both organizations and the accompanying resources committed to those processes.

Having already determined clear and concise lines of business for your organization will help you when determining how to make changes. You can examine the other company's LOBs and processes and pit them against your own to see what is extra or what is missing if you are adapting a new business model.

This exercise will also help you determine what kind of resources (personnel, equipment, capital) to apply to which process and in what quantity. Ultimately this review will help you ensure your key strategic drivers (MVGOs) remain focused and supported with people and processes, which creates balance for your organization. This process will also promote synergy among the different organizational elements and therefore ensure the new processes and resources are integrated properly.

Another internal change that should trigger a strategic planning session (and ensuing LOB review) is when considering outsourcing. Since LOBs are core functions of the organization, they should seldom, if ever, be outsourced. If they are, you are basically telling your stakeholders, "What we do is so easy, anyone can do it."

On the other hand, primary (or secondary) processes under each LOB can be outsourced or subcontracted to a third party if the business model makes sense. Before these processes are deferred to an outside entity, it is critical that senior leadership examine the affected lines of business and the secondary effects on other LOBs and the organization as a whole. This will ensure that the remaining lines of business and processes have synergy and the organization remains balanced with key strategic drivers.

The same is true for insourcing or reshoring. As strategic plans change, some organizations want to bring a primary process back into the organization, or develop a primary process that was previously accomplished by a third party. This often happens in companies that are not well versed at strategic planning. Sometimes they outsource a primary process to save money, only to realize that once the process is gone they suffered intangible losses that are crucial for the organization to thrive.

A 2013 survey by Deloitte shows that 48% of respondents have terminated an outsourcing agreement due to one of three primary reasons: the need to improve customer service, gain better control over processes, or reduce costs. This appears to be a trend by many companies as they do further research and find that the outsourcing strategy did not meet their original expectations (Deloitte LLC, 2013).

THE LITTLE GUYS

Small- and medium-size organizations may not have a strategic planning staff, or even a strategic plan. We just want to remind you that this is not okay. LOB determination and planning are as critical to the success of small organizations as they are for larger ones. It is vital that someone have the overall responsibility to accomplish the strategic planning process; otherwise the organization falls prey to the lack of strategic direction that is needed to thrive and grow. Being one of the little guys does not exempt you from this threat.

WORK WITH A PURPOSE

LOB analysis enables the organization to align processes with key drivers (MVGOs) in the strategic plan. This effort is necessary since LOBs determine downstream processes that can become out of balance, out of sync, and can cause the organization to unravel.

At this point you may realize you have not identified the LOBs in your organization or have identified them incorrectly. This is okay because now you have the awareness of the meaning and significance of an LOB, and you can take this knowledge to your next strategic planning session.

The LOB element on the Diamond Process Model is simply a container to organize work processes. What is essential now is that we continue our journey to becoming a complete leader. The next step on this journey is to continue down the Diamond Process Model and look at the processes contained in our LOBs. This is where we begin to characterize the work that enables us to complete our mission.

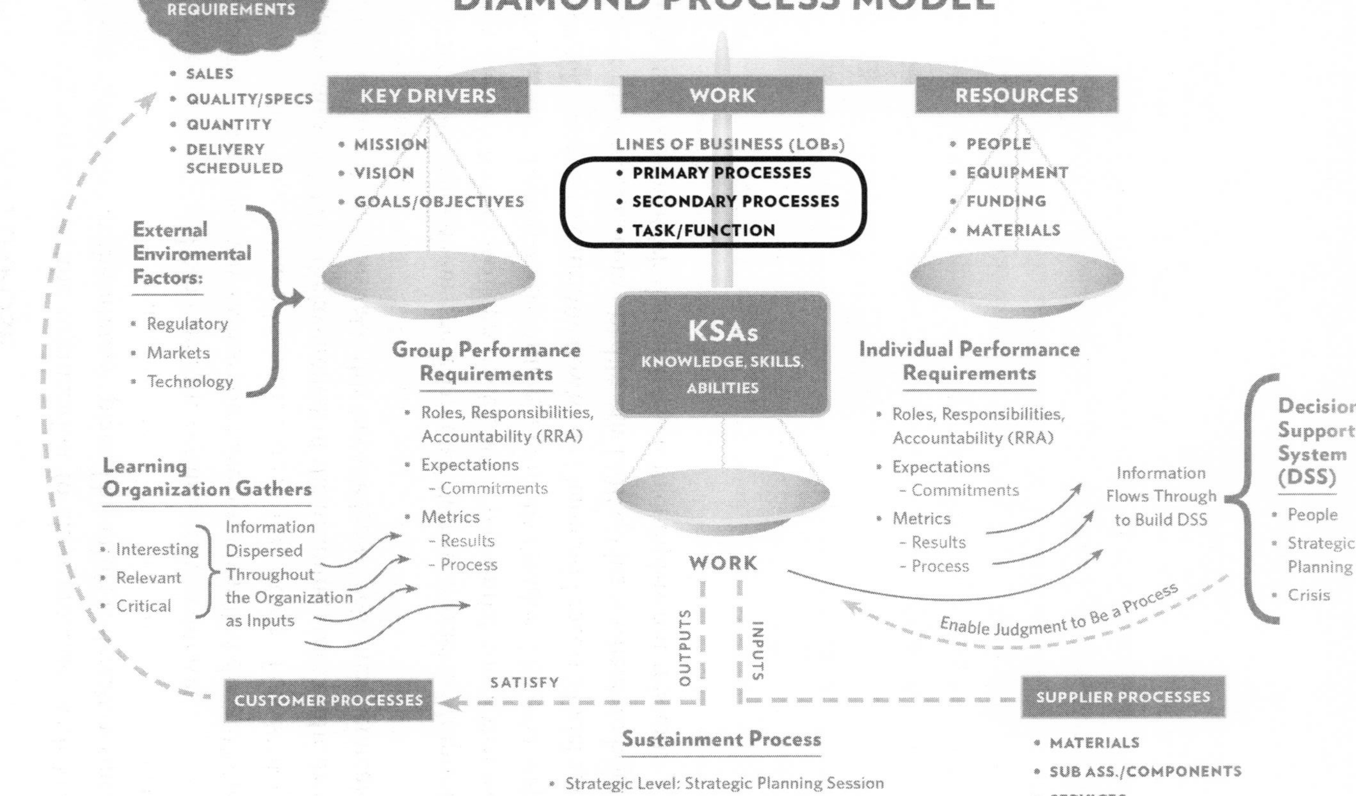
THE
DIAMOND PROCESS MODEL
CUSTOMER REQUIREMENTS
• SALES
• QUALITY/SPECS
• QUANTITY
• DELIVERY SCHEDULED
KEY DRIVERS
• MISSION
• VISION
• GOALS/OBJECTIVES
WORK
LINES OF BUSINESS (LOBs)
• PRIMARY PROCESSES
• SECONDARY PROCESSES
• TASK/FUNCTION
RESOURCES
• PEOPLE
• EQUIPMENT
• FUNDING
• MATERIALS
External Enviromental Factors:
• Regulatory
• Markets
• Technology
KSAs
KNOWLEDGE, SKILLS, ABILITIES
Group Performance Requirements
• Roles, Responsibilities, Accountability (RRA)
• Expectations
- Commitments
• Metrics
- Results
- Process
Individual Performance Requirements
• Roles, Responsibilities, Accountability (RRA)
• Expectations
- Commitments
• Metrics
- Results
- Process
Learning Organization Gathers
• Interesting
• Relevant
• Critical
Information Dispersed Throughout the Organization as Inputs
Information Flows Through to Build DSS
Decision Support System (DSS)
• People
• Strategic Planning
• Crisis
WORK
OUTPUTS
INPUTS
Enable Judgment to Be a Process
SATISFY
CUSTOMER PROCESSES
SUPPLIER PROCESSES
• MATERIALS
• SUB ASS./COMPONENTS
• SERVICES
Sustainment Process
• Strategic Level: Strategic Planning Session
• Operations/Dept. Level: Operational Assesment
• First Line Leader Level: Process Review

CHAPTER 4

THE NATURE OF WORK

One of the most important things you can do on your journey to becoming a complete leader is to understand work processes. Many leaders fail to realize you cannot effectively lead people without also leading processes. If you commit yourself to understanding processes and leading them properly, you will find yourself in a productive situation where you are delivering what your workers *want* and what your boss *needs*. Process leadership is very time consuming and requires much effort, but the rewards make it all worthwhile.

Mike recalls during his tenure of commanding all logistical forces in OIF that he was blessed with senior leaders who understood the processes that logistics performed in order to make combat forces successful. If they did not understand something, he was asked to explain it in *process detail* so the leaders could readily understand the impact it would have on their ability to accomplish their missions.

The term *process detail* took him back to his early days in the Army when he was required, like all junior officers, to learn about the processes he led using the Mission Essential Task List (METL) process. The METL required him to identify and record the company tasks and then further break them down for all levels within the company, even including platoon and squad levels. This level of process detail nested the processes for work tasks to be accomplished, and it forced leaders to understand organizational processes.

A GENERAL'S REFLECTION

Back in 1999 when I was a full-bird Colonel, I took command of the 32nd Transportation Group, which was responsible for moving people and cargo via land and sea both inside the continental US as well as overseas in times of war. I immediately began making my rounds and conducted initial site visits to the seven unique units that were assigned to my group.

One of the last units I visited was the 824th Transportation Company, which was a highly specialized transportation unit that provided ship-to-shore transport using U-boat-type vessels. There were only three organizations in the entire US Army inventory that performed this function, which meant this particular unit was responsible for one-third of all waterborne transport for the Army both in war and peacetime.

The military refers to these types of units as *low-density high-demand* (LDHD), and usually they are treated as critical assets. Therefore, I was always of the mindset that managing a LDHD unit was a critical process in and of itself.

Upon arriving at this unit, I asked the unit commander my favorite two questions: "What are the single points of failure in your work processes and why?" and "Who could you least afford to lose and why?" Her oversimplified answer was, "We need more money to train our personnel."

I knew from her half-hearted answer she had not performed the work to understand her critical processes or to understand what her single points of failure were. So I performed a critical review of the unit's processes and uncovered a shortfall in their training program as they had failed to accurately project the manpower needed to perform the mission.

To give the commander some credit, she did identify that her younger soldiers needed critical training. In order to gain certification to pilot these types of vessels, you had to perform coursework, attend a class, log a certain amount of hours of on-the-job training (OJT), and demonstrate the skills on an actual mission. The entire certification process took nine to twelve months per soldier, so it was a critical process to manage these certifications. But training young members of the organization wasn't the real problem.

IDENTIFY CRITICAL PROCESSES

The first step to becoming a process leader is to identify the **critical processes** of your organization as well as the people who support them. In order to determine which processes are critical, you should ask yourself the following question: "What are the single points of failure in my work processes and why?" The answer to this question will provide you information on process threats that could break your organization. Oftentimes there are several processes that can hinder an organization, so you should list each one in great detail.

The next step in process leadership is to understand priority. Even though there are several critical processes of your organization, some are always more important than others. By listing and prioritizing each single point of failure, you can begin to analyze each process and make decisions on where you, as the leader, should apply appropriate resources to mitigate the process threats.

We see many leaders who have a hard time helping subordinates because they do not understand the processes of their organization. Without critical process identification, leaders cannot know what resources to apply, and more importantly, where to apply them.

It is very important to document your process of identifying critical processes and record your answers. You can also ask your subject-matter experts for their inputs if you do not fully understand a critical process. The most important thing is *that* you get the right answer, not necessarily *how* you get the right answer.

The information you receive when answering these questions should also culminate in a *plan of action*. This plan should be very detailed and list action items (AIs), including who is responsible to complete the action and when the action should be completed or implemented. Documenting this plan in great detail is even more important if your work processes are technical.

The second question you should ask is this: "What person in your organization could you least afford to lose and why?" This is a loaded question that will likely dump all your dirty laundry on the floor when it comes to process leadership.

First, if you have someone in your organization that you cannot afford to lose, that person is likely driving a critical process. Several organizations do not have detailed processes, so in the absence of the process, often the person becomes the process. This is a dangerous scenario because if the critical process *person* is run over by a truck, then the process becomes a truck with no driver.

The way to resolve this situation is to create and document a process to achieve what this individual performs routinely. Once that's recorded you can have that person train others to the process as a way to mitigate risk in the absence of the primary worker.

This exercise also creates a critical process that is owned by the organization rather than the individual. When documented, this critical process can be analyzed by leadership in order to assess whether the process has the resources it needs to produce desired effects for the organization—the desired effects being to support the LOB and to enable key drivers in the strategic plan.

Sometimes the answer to the question about which person you can least afford to lose reveals other vulnerabilities within an organization.

The person driving a critical process is not always an expert. There have been numerous times we've seen critical processes driven by inexperienced workers. Whether it happens because of sudden turnover or poor planning, having critical processes driven by inexperienced and untrained workers puts your organization at risk.

If you have a new worker driving a critical process, by asking yourself this question you can identify that individual. You can help them develop a process if one does not exist and also monitor the risk to the company. If needed, you can apply resources such as training, equipment, or support personnel from other functional areas. By identifying the risk and applying the right resources, you can protect the critical processes of your organization and eliminate single points of failure.

Gaining accurate knowledge based on the answers to these questions can go a long way toward helping a leader elevate his or her skill level and performance. Leadership is about decision making, and this exercise helps ensure leaders will make accurate decisions as to when and how to apply critical resources.

Be mindful that it takes great effort and detailed analysis to identify critical processes accurately. There are also grave consequences for taking shortcuts. Instead of putting in the work, we've seen leaders in the past provide their *best guess* on identifying critical processes. This can cause the leaders to drive unnecessary changes and begin applying resources in the wrong direction. It can also cause them to misdiagnose the problem.

☆☆

A GENERAL'S REFLECTION, CONTINUED

When I conducted a demographic study of the 824th Transportation Company, I uncovered what I deemed to be the "Tale of Two Cities." While on my visit I noticed there were a lot of older Warrant Officers

Continued

(WO). I asked the commander, "How many of your WOs are over the age of fifty?" She replied, "Sir, I don't know."

Upon further investigation, we learned that 40% of all the soldiers in the unit were above the age of fifty, and the other 60% below the age of twenty-five. This meant all the certified people, the "over-fifties," were on the verge of retirement, and all the younger people, the "under-twenty-fives," were nowhere close to certification. In essence, the unit was about to be completely broken, as they would not have anyone certified to pilot a vessel. In the Army Reserve if a unit is unable to perform its core mission, they are erased off the master list and dissolved.

True enough, the unit's single point of failure was the lack of training and certification for their "green" newbies before the over-fifties retired. The over-fifties were instrumental in the training and certification of the under-twenty-fives, especially during the OJT portion.

Through months of emergency management, we were finally able to identify the critical steps required to get all the training and funding resources needed to certify the younger soldiers of the organization. We also had to closely manage retirements to ensure we did not lose the ability to meet our mission. It took two years to remedy the shortfall of certified boat leaders and engineers to properly crew the vessels and to bring this unit back to a healthy state. If we had not vetted our critical processes at that time, this unit would be extinct today.

Four years later, when I was a Brigadier General in command in the Iraqi theater, I had one of the other two of these units returning back to the United States. I remember coming out of a meeting early one morning while on my way to the helipad to take a hop and visit another unit along with my staff. I saw a familiar face walking down the hallway toward me and I realized it was the training manager for the 824th. He approached me proudly, saluted, and said, "Sir, Sergeant Carter and the 824th Trans Company reporting for duty."

HAVING A BALANCED WORKLOAD

You've probably heard someone refer to the "80/20 rule," wherein 80% of the work is accomplished by 20% of the people. Unfortunately, this is prominent in most organizations because they do not use processes to lead their personnel appropriately. Unfair workload distribution can cause dissention in the ranks, jealousy, increased perceptions of favoritism, worker frustration, turnover, and unhappiness.

Leading critical processes enables organizations to meet the key drivers established by their senior leaders. In other words, they give the bosses what they *need*. Another important enabler with leading processes is it gives the workers what they *want*. We've already seen how we can use critical process leadership to apply resources to enable success. We can also use this process to balance workload among subordinates.

Workers really do want their supervisors to know exactly what they do, how they do it, and what it takes to accomplish the necessary process needed to perform work. By identifying critical processes and becoming a process leader, supervisors can meet worker expectations.

We've seen that workers are more eager to communicate with leaders if they feel they are understood and appreciated. These increased lines of communication can benefit the organization greatly. The supervisor can understand the processes, apply his or her personnel to those processes, balance the workload with the right personnel, and support them with the right resources.

Now that we understand how to identify *critical processes*, we can move down our Diamond Process Model further inside the LOB container and examine other types of processes.

PRIMARY PROCESSES

Not all processes are critical, but some are more important than others to perform the work needed for your organization to thrive.

When we formulated our lines of business, we listed all of the processes necessary to perform work. The highest-level processes were deemed as the LOB. Inside each LOB for your company reside **primary processes** at the top and the ensuing **secondary processes** below them.

Processes are the manner in which groups or individuals in an organization perform their work. The highest element of work under the LOB is referred to as the *primary process* on the Diamond Process Model. There is no limit to the number of primary processes within an LOB. Keep in mind that processes drive the requirement for personnel needed to accomplish the work and its attendant supervision.

It is also important to consider that some processes, even primary ones, are not wholly contained and performed within one organization on the org chart. Initially processes should be detailed without regard to the organizational hierarchy, as we are primarily concerned with how work gets done, not who does it. To help identify primary processes, you should ask yourself questions such as these: "What are the processes that need to be done to accomplish this particular LOB?" and "Are there any other steps needed to accomplish this LOB?"

A good rule of thumb for evaluating whether you have arrived at determining your primary processes is to examine whether you can combine two processes into one. If it is possible to do so, you are not there yet. You should continue to try consolidating before settling on the remaining ones as your primary processes. Once you arrive at these, you will begin to break down the primary processes further into *secondary processes*, *tasks*, and *functions*.

SECONDARY PROCESSES

Secondary processes describe the steps that need to be accomplished to facilitate the primary process. The Diamond Process Model uses the element of secondary processes to organize work that can be further broken down into the smaller DPM elements—*tasks* and *functions*. We use the model in this way until the steps required to perform work are described at the lowest level. Once this breakdown is complete, you should be able to see, in a structured format, which steps are performed in a particular process and, consequently, how the process enables the primary process and the overarching line of business.

In order to get a vivid description of *how* the work gets done, you should develop *flowcharts* and *process maps* for each of the simple tasks and functions within the secondary process. The flowcharts and process maps can then trace the tasks and functions back up the Diamond Process Model all the way to each primary process.

We realize it is very time consuming and laborious to organize work in this way. But if you put in the time, you will be able to visualize the volume of work that gets accomplished in your organization. These flowcharts and process maps will become the basis for performing any process improvement or change management that will improve *how* the organization functions or executes its LOBs and achieves its mission.

FLOWCHARTS

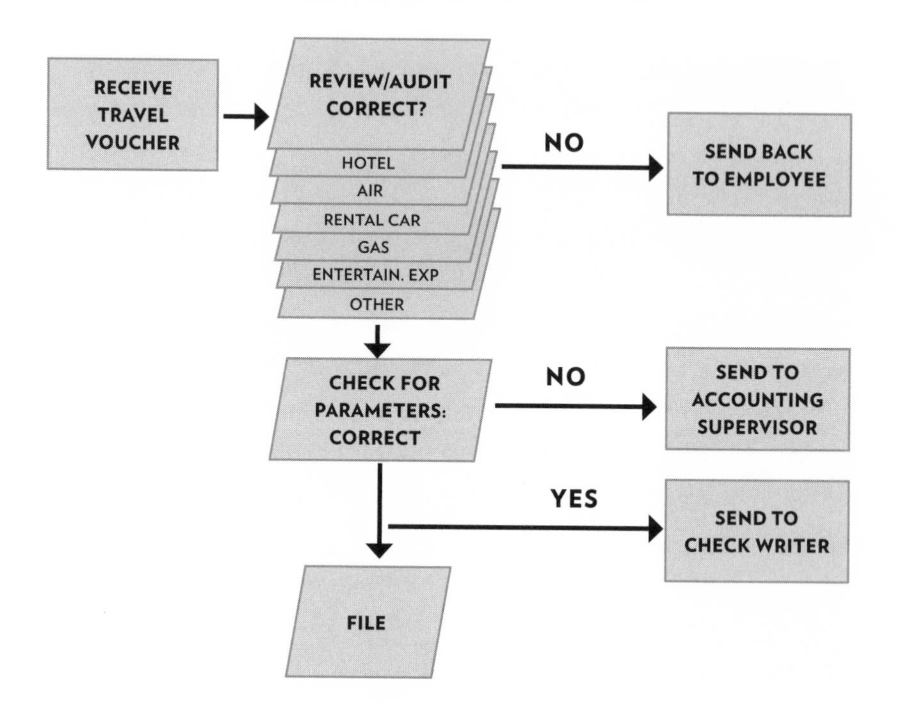

Flowcharts should be accomplished with assistance from the subject-matter experts or the individuals in the organization who perform the work. Flowcharts should capture the steps needed for workers to accomplish a particular task, function, or process.

The task or process itself should be recorded step-by-step for what is done inside your organization, without regard to what others perform from outside your organization. Those members outside your organization should go through the same process of recording, step-by-step, those tasks they perform related to the same process. It is important to keep the organizations separated so you can analyze the *handoffs* between them later.

Flowcharts can get quite complex when there are numerous steps involved in achieving a task or process. So be very careful to clearly outline what is needed to perform the work. Do not be tempted to shortchange the flowcharting process. Incomplete flowcharts can leave out important pieces of the process and provide leadership with inaccurate data on which they make important decisions such as where to apply scarce resources.

Flowcharts can become tremendous visual aids to help and train workers who are new to the established process. They can also be used to cross-train employees from other functional areas and show workers the process relationships between offices. Good flowcharts provide leaders a common understanding of how their organization operates, and they provide critical information that can aid decision-makers when determining where to apply resources.

Our flowcharts should also contain integration with our customer's work processes and our supplier's processes, as depicted on the DPM chart.

PROCESS MAPS

Process maps are created using the inputs from flowcharts. Process maps are normally drafted with the left-hand column populated with individuals and/or organizations that have a role in the overall process. Each of these individuals or organizations are provided their own row or "swim lane" to depict their steps or roles in performing or supporting the whole process.

The process map should then be flowed with appropriate symbols, step-by-step from left to right, depicting from start to finish what work is done and by what organization/individual. Once populated, the process map will contain the entire process and will show each individual or organization's part in the process.

Where the process flow crosses from one swim lane to another, there occurs what is called a *handoff*. These handoffs are important

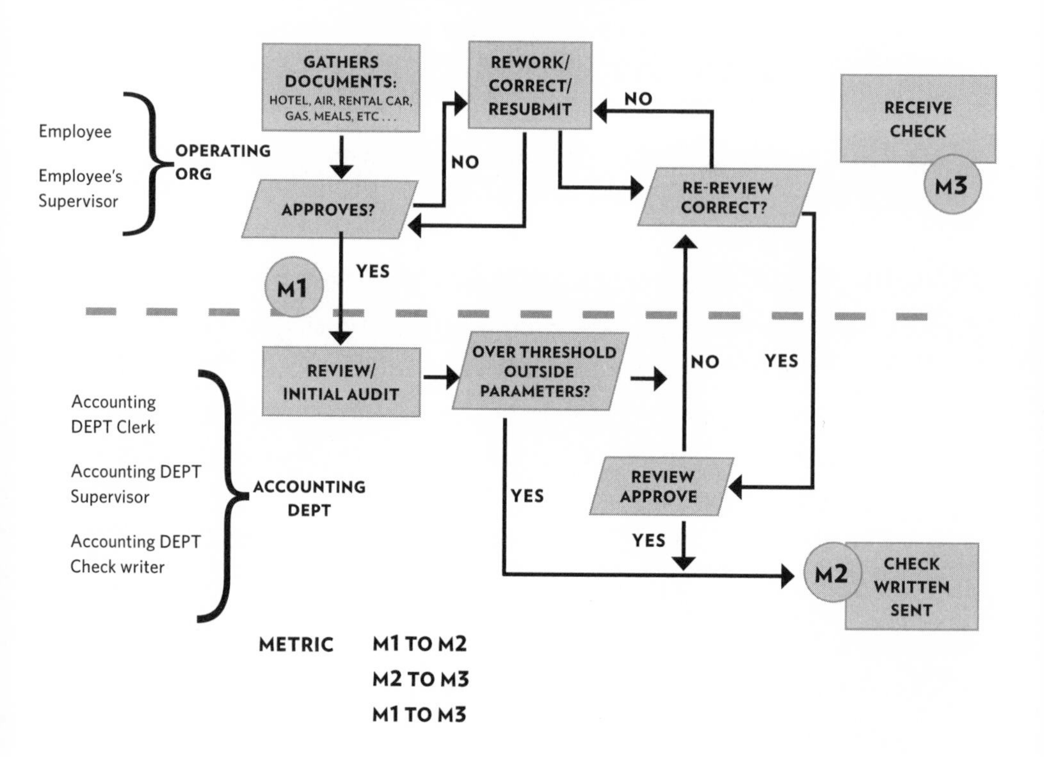

because they represent prime locations for process failure, as you will see later in this chapter when we talk about measures. Handoffs are the reason flowcharts are created without regard to outside organizations.

By compiling flowcharts into an overall process map, you can enable leaders to visually see and understand how the work is accomplished during a process. The map also shows who performs the work and where the potential pitfalls could be that become single points of failure for the organization.

Unlike flowcharts, process maps present more comprehensive information to leaders as the maps relate processes accomplished by a collection of entities rather than just a single entity. Also, every handoff in a process map presents an opportunity to install a process measure.

Mike once advised a client in the gas-exploration industry and found the company had a single process map that was so large it wrapped around all four walls in their training room. Believe it or not, that was not one of their more complex process maps! But the client knew from experience that process maps were so valuable to leaders in the organization that they were willing to put in the time so they could readily see what was taking place to accomplish that particular process.

☆☆

A GENERAL'S REFLECTION

When I was a one-star commanding all logistical forces during OPERATION: Iraqi Freedom, we had to prepare for a unique mission: we were tasked to plan and execute the first rotation of forces in the history of the US Army. Our mission was to take 125K soldiers and 20K pieces of equipment in Iraq and replace them with the same number of personnel and equipment from the States. Oh, by the way—this had to be done while combat operations were in full swing throughout the entire theater of operations.

There was no guidance or "doctrine," as we call it in the service, to recommend a way forward. There was also no recent history that helped: During the Vietnam conflict, the US Army rotated individuals and small units, while leaving large units and equipment in-country. WWII and Korean War forces were reinforced after initial deployment, but everyone came back at the same time.

To get a handle on what needed to happen, we had to have flowcharts and process maps from each unit involved in leaving or entering the theater for every step of the operation that was going to take place. The process maps had to be fully synchronized and

Continued

understood by everyone who had a role in the force rotation operation, including all outside support organizations that enabled these moves to happen.

So that everyone could get on the same page, we did what the military calls a Rehearsal of Concept (ROC) drill—a dry run with all the players. I needed a visual representation of the battlefield, so I asked my folks to build a "sand table." We brought in dump trucks filled with sand and dumped them in an aircraft hangar until I had a 2000-square-foot sandbox that was six inches deep.

We constructed all the nodes, routes, and unit locations we needed to use for the operation. With process maps and flowcharts in hand, we walked through a day-by-day enactment of personnel and equipment movements for both inbound and outbound units. Although the ROC took two full days in 125-degree heat, it proved to be very fruitful for us.

We started the force rotation within three weeks of the ROC. Our plan was to implement the operation over ninety days, and we didn't deviate by a single day. We successfully completed the first force rotation for the US Army during combat operations, and it went off without a hitch. We had zero fatalities during the entire operation, and we used our process as a benchmark to conduct future force rotation operations.

I credit the people for pulling off a successful operation. But I also feel the flowcharts and process maps were critical pieces, as they provided the underlying tools that enabled each unit to understand their part in the overall operation. To this day, the US Army uses the process we developed for force rotations; they even formalized the flowcharts and process maps on a single fifteen-foot color-coded diagram that is now affectionately referred to as "the Horse Blanket."

REDUNDANT WORK PROCESSES

Once flowcharts and process maps are complete, leaders should review them with their workers to identify any redundancies. A redundancy is any process or task/function that happens more than once but is actually needed only once.

We have found that most redundant work is done by two or more different workers in one or more different functional units within the same organization. Sometimes when we detect redundancies it becomes quite comical, as the workers usually have no idea the other is performing the same task. Once identified, leaders can combine the redundant efforts of these two workers under one process and assign the responsibility to one of them. This often frees up the second individual to drive other needed processes.

A common example we often discover is two different organizations or units that create a report with the same information and provide it to the same supervisor or higher-level organization. Without process mapping and flowcharting, no one would likely identify the redundancy. Repetitive, redundant, and unnecessary work steals vital resources from your organization. It is imperative to identify these inefficiencies so you can free up scarce resources and eliminate waste.

Due to the common redundancies with reports, we suggest that your organization perform a reports review wherein they take all the reports being produced by the organization and validate that each report is actually needed. It seems as though once reports start being generated, they continue endlessly, whether or not they are actually needed. This is often because the person receiving the report has the "better safe than sorry" mentality and fails to stop the reports from being generated. The resources it takes to generate these reports can be a significant burden on the company and could be applied to other critical processes.

We also want to communicate that not all redundancies are bad, and sometimes they are essential. If your organization is producing a critical report that is delivered to a very high strategic leader in the parent organization, you may want to insert some redundancy (share it with lower-ranking leaders) for quality assurance. This is a good technique as long as the redundancies are intentional and serve a purpose. You don't want them just because you don't know they exist.

PROCESS IMPROVEMENT

Process improvement is a leadership buzzword that looks good in performance appraisals; thus, everyone is quite willing to blindly jump on the process improvement bandwagon without having any idea what they are doing. You must realize that if you do not have defined processes, there is nothing to improve upon.

Since leaders typically know very little about process leadership, they often have inaccurate perceptions of what process leadership entails. Using the Diamond Process Model to create unity of effort in a company, from the key strategic drivers down to the smallest task and function, is much more than *process improvement*. But if you do these things, you can enable process improvement.

The topic of process improvement is located strategically at the end of this chapter because it is something you can accomplish only after you put in the work to detail your LOBs and primary/secondary processes. However once this work has been accomplished, a process leader can utilize this information to vastly improve the performance of his or her organization. The two most common forms of process improvement are remedying *redundancies* and *gaps*.

Redundancies involve more than just simply identifying two people who do the same job. If your flowcharts and process maps are accurate, you can utilize them to identify tasks and functions that can be consolidated. You can also move tasks and functions around to different individuals so those workers can specialize and focus on tasks that have less breadth and more depth. By focusing on specialization, you can increase your economies of scale and get more out of each worker.

The second most common area to execute process improvement is to analyze your *handoffs*. As described earlier in the chapter, this is the point on your flowchart or process map where one employee passes work to another; or where one organizational unit passes the work to another unit.

Handoffs, and any coordination for that matter, are usually accompanied by some sort of time delay. Unnecessary handoffs increase these time delays, which expound on each other and create serious lags in your process. By making minor adjustments to the steps of your flowcharts, you can increase the number of tasks that are performed within a specific office area before moving the task to another functional area.

Another good way to find areas for process improvement is to establish feedback channels. One common method is to provide your customers with feedback forms or give them access to a system through which they can file complaints. Another common feedback channel is to establish a quality-assurance (QA) office. QA inspectors and leaders can file monthly or quarterly reports and brief leadership on areas in the organization that are not meeting quality standards.

If you have detailed maps and flowcharts, it is much easier to improve your processes. As a leader, if you receive negative performance feedback regarding your functional area, you will be able to quickly begin troubleshooting which area of your process or task may be causing the issue.

Even better, you can delegate this troubleshooting to your experts and allow them to analyze their own process and make recommendations. This exercise will also help workers understand the intricacies of the process they own. Leaders should be involved but not overly involved; this is worker territory so leaders should be careful to avoid micromanagement.

METRICS

The most powerful (and underutilized) feedback channel is performance metrics. We will discuss metrics in great detail in chapter 13, but here we need to communicate how important metrics can be to maintaining healthy processes. Metrics are critical in order to measure the ability of your processes to achieve goals and objectives set forth by leadership. They also provide key indicators as to how you have performed in the past, and how you may perform in the future. Additionally, they drive behaviors, both good and bad, that affect the performance of your workers.

There are two types of metrics: *results* and *process* measures. Most organizations are at least aware of *results measures* and use them to manage their business. A result measure is the end result of what is recorded at the end of the process. For example, if you are a sales organization, a results measure could be the total dollar amount of sales for a certain period such as a quarter or year. Results measures are useful for measuring a company's past performance over a period of time, but they have some inherent flaws.

First, since they show only past performance, they may come too late to allow you to make necessary process changes. This is why military organizations refer to these types of metrics as *lagging indicators.*

Second, results measures alone cannot communicate vital indicators needed for assessing an organization's complete health. This is because results measures are relative in nature. Whether the result is "good" or "bad" is subject to the person viewing the metric.

In order to be utilized effectively, results measures should be designed and reported in relation to the strategic goals and objectives of your organization. One successful strategy is to define a minimum, maximum, and optimal value for each result measure.

By creating these parameters, senior leaders can all share a common understanding of the company's past performance. Another good management technique is to review performance measures on a monthly or quarterly basis. This will illustrate trend information so you can determine whether your organization is gradually improving, declining, or staying the same.

Every organization is prone to the *business cycle* phenomenon where performance naturally improves or declines based on conditions of the external operating environment. For this reason, you should be careful not to make rash decisions based solely on performance measures on a month-to-month basis.

Due to the inherent flaws of results measures, it is a good idea to also use *process measures* when evaluating the health of your organization. Process measures are created to indicate the effectiveness of the flow for each process.

For example, you can identify a process that contains multiple handoffs and measure the time between each handoff. You can then compare the actual process times to the estimated process time that was independently calculated before you started measuring the process. Similar to performance measures, once leadership agrees on minimum, maximum, and standard times, you can utilize the information to evaluate the effectiveness and efficiency of your process.

Process measures are what the military refers to as *leading indicators*. That is because they give you real-time information, which can indicate the future performance of your organization. Unlike results measures, process measures afford you the opportunity to make changes to your processes that can improve your results measures.

From what we've experienced, most organizations, if they have metrics, utilize only performance-based measures, and they focus on the end-result only. The proper way to instill an effective metrics program is to start at the beginning with process measures and work your way to the end with results measures. By working through the process maps from start to finish, applying process measures at each handoff, and concluding with performance metrics, you can optimize the utility of your metric program.

Process measures can be game changers for an organization. They can increase efficiency, productivity, and profitability by enabling leaders to make changes to a process and view the effects on that process to determine if the changes were effective. Process measures are very strong because they warn you before you deliver your final product or service. Therefore, they allow you to make changes *before* something bad happens.

REPORTING METRICS

When and how to report metrics are as important as the metrics themselves. Metric reports should be designed with the intention of enabling leaders to better lead their organizations. Metric reporting does this by enabling leaders to make changes to the processes that need it and to reinforce good results.

When determining the basis of metric reporting, the most important question is, "What information do we need to provide our leaders so they can make critical decisions?" The answer to this question is the requirement to your metric reporting, and you should stay disciplined in your attempts to meet this requirement. More is not always better. It is about getting the right information and reporting it at the right time to the right person. Thus, another critical piece of information to identify is *to whom* the metrics should be reported.

When to report metrics depends on your organization. As a general rule, process measures should be reported more frequently than performance measures. Remember, process measures tell you when something bad is going to happen in the future, so you need that information in order to make changes.

Performance metrics should be displayed on a twelve-month display so strategic leaders can make determinations on the long-term trends of the organization's performance. Performance metrics should be reviewed at least quarterly, but not more than on a monthly basis. Leaders should be weary of making important strategic decisions on a month-to-month basis, as *business cycles* are normal and performance usually varies slightly due to the external business environment.

Many successful leaders in this day and age use computer software, slide shows, or other *dashboards* as a quick reference for metric reporting. These dashboards are a compilation of results measures that currently replace what reports did in yesteryear. We have designed our own version of a dashboard that we will introduce you to later in the book. Our version, called the *Balometer*©, is centered on the Diamond Process Model and ties in all the elements of your organization to provide you important information on whether your organization has the right balance.

CHANGE MANAGEMENT

Process leadership is crucial to enable effective change management. Without putting in all the work we've outlined above, you cannot successfully tell whether your changes are having a positive (or negative) effect on your organization. By having completed process maps, flowcharts, and process improvement reviews, the stage is set to effectively manage change. Trying to perform change management in any other way can be counterproductive. Some organizations attempt to do change management without having performed any flowcharting or process mapping or any of the other items contained in the Diamond Process Model. This can become less fruitful than what it should be from using the DPM.

Work is where the rubber meets the road in your organization and should be where you spend most of your time leading. Process is the path that leads to results, and you cannot effectively lead your people without also leading your processes. You must take the time and effort to understand the nature of your work and the processes and people that create that work. If you don't, you won't know what you don't know; and in this case it will hurt you.

FROM PROCESSES TO PEOPLE

Now we understand how to characterize the *work* we need to accomplish in an organization through process leadership. We understand how all work can be taken from the smallest elements of tasks and functions and build them into processes within each LOB. All of the processes in the LOB container are focused on supporting the key drivers from the strategic plan.

All of our effort up to this point has been organizing *what* work should be done and *how* the work should be organized to create unity of effort in an organization. The next step is to introduce you to the Diamond Process Model element, which serves as the fuel which drives the processes in your LOB—*groups and individuals.* We must understand people if we are to successfully integrate them with our processes.

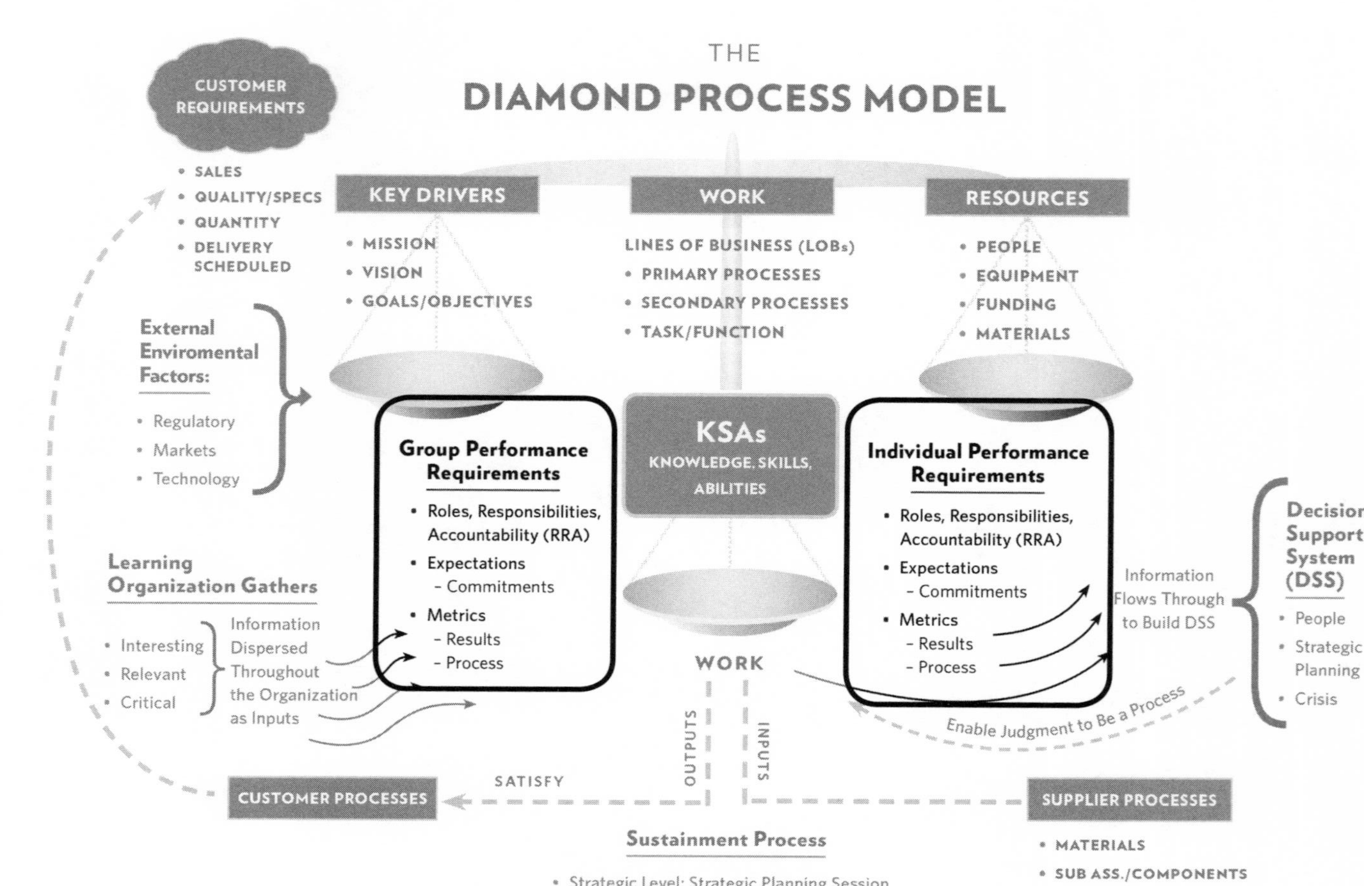
THE
DIAMOND PROCESS MODEL
CUSTOMER REQUIREMENTS
• SALES
• QUALITY/SPECS
• QUANTITY
• DELIVERY SCHEDULED
KEY DRIVERS
• MISSION
• VISION
• GOALS/OBJECTIVES
WORK
LINES OF BUSINESS (LOBs)
• PRIMARY PROCESSES
• SECONDARY PROCESSES
• TASK/FUNCTION
RESOURCES
• PEOPLE
• EQUIPMENT
• FUNDING
• MATERIALS
External Enviromental Factors:
• Regulatory
• Markets
• Technology
Group Performance Requirements
• Roles, Responsibilities, Accountability (RRA)
• Expectations
- Commitments
• Metrics
- Results
- Process
KSAs
KNOWLEDGE, SKILLS, ABILITIES
Individual Performance Requirements
• Roles, Responsibilities, Accountability (RRA)
• Expectations
- Commitments
• Metrics
- Results
- Process
Decision Support System (DSS)
• People
• Strategic Planning
• Crisis
Information Flows Through to Build DSS
Learning Organization Gathers
• Interesting
• Relevant
• Critical
Information Dispersed Throughout the Organization as Inputs
WORK
OUTPUTS
INPUTS
Enable Judgment to Be a Process
SATISFY
CUSTOMER PROCESSES
SUPPLIER PROCESSES
• MATERIALS
• SUB ASS./COMPONENTS
• SERVICES
Sustainment Process
• Strategic Level: Strategic Planning Session
• Operations/Dept. Level: Operational Assesment
• First Line Leader Level: Process Review

CHAPTER 5

GROUPS AND INDIVIDUALS

To effectively integrate people with processes, you first need to correctly develop processes. Now that we have this general understanding of process management, we can turn our focus to the people who perform work for your organization. Once we understand both, we can successfully integrate them to support each line of business, which, in turn, executes the MVGOs of your organization.

People are the most valuable resource of an organization. Workers that understand where your company is (mission), where it wants to go (vision), and how to drive your processes will be better armed to help you meet your goals and objectives. Without people driving processes, your business is just a pile of worthless equipment.

To be literal, people are also very valuable because of the capital a company must invest to recruit, hire, and train them. Oftentimes the initial human resource investment for a new employee is significantly more than the starting salary for the accompanying position. This is why employee turnover is so problematic; if people leave, it costs valuable resources to rehire and retrain someone else.

Since people are so critical to the organization, it is surprising how many companies look to cut people in order to solve a short-term financial crisis. Whenever we see a headline to the effect of "Quarterly earnings down, X company to cut 10,000 jobs in Y facility," we realize company X has not integrated people with processes. This headline represents a "knee-jerk" reaction that is absent critical thinking. The decision to randomly cut workers will likely hurt company X in the future because they will probably need to rehire and retrain replacements at a future date—which will cost more. Essentially, this strategy is a quick fix and simply delays a larger underlying problem to a future date.

If company X had successfully integrated people and processes, they would know what resources to trim in an emergency situation to save money. Instead of simply cutting 10,000 random jobs at a random facility, an integrated company could have several more options, such as postponing training, combining secondary processes, eliminating non-essential equipment, etc.

If company X followed the Diamond Process Model, they would already own a contingency plan (drafted in a strategic planning session) outlining what resources to cut in this situation. This plan would already contain details of a cutback, which still enables critical processes that support the LOB. They would simply have to dust off the contingency and review it for any changes since the last strategic planning session.

Successfully integrated organizations tend to have longer-term strategies and are less prone to take a short-term measure for perceived cost savings. They understand that doing so can cause severe impacts to the future success of the organization. Sometimes unexpected external conditions such as the economy, technology, or dissolving markets can create a short-term crisis. But to be prepared for these crises, we must know how people integrate with our organization. To do so, we must first define the next element of our Diamond Process Model: groups and individuals. Then we can examine how to successfully manage expectations so we can set up groups and individuals to integrate them into processes. Finally, we will look at how to successfully manage Knowledge, Skills, and Abilities (KSAs) for optimum process integration.

THE GROUP

A group can be a section, department, division, or any type of functional subunit that is formed to accomplish the work tasks/functions and processes required for the group's mission for a particular line of business. For the purposes of this book, the terms *groups* and *teams* are the same. Also, the Diamond Process Model assumes that companies at least have an organizational chart and that work has already been accomplished.

As an element on the Diamond Process Model, each group should be assigned roles, responsibilities, and expectations. For the DPM, groups should also have related performance measures (metrics) to show to what extent they are meeting established expectations. The metrics should be linked directly to the mission of the larger organization as articulated via the MVGOs contained in the strategic plan.

When reviewing metrics, supervisors can have a quick visual reference to gauge group performance. If group performance is lagging, the functional supervisor can look into the problem and see if any changes need to be made. Future performance metrics can then indicate whether the change was successful.

Sometimes a group will easily meet or exceed expectations, and those successes will be recorded through the performance metrics. Leaders can take the opportunity to evaluate resources the group has to meet expectations; if the group has too many resources, they can be reallocated to other groups in the organization. If the group has just the right amount of resources but is still performing well, it can take that opportunity to record best practices for the company.

It is the leader's responsibility to monitor group performance and provide the resources and tools the group needs to achieve its functional expectations, just as it is the leader's responsibility to monitor individual performance and do the same.

THE INDIVIDUAL

An individual is any single person in the organization, regardless of whether they are in a stand-alone position or a member of a group. For the purposes of this book, the terms *individual*, *worker*, *subordinate,* and *employee* are the same.

Individuals are also elements on the Diamond Process Model and must be managed separately from groups. This is because not all individuals belong to a group within the organization. If we did not treat individuals as a separate element, we would not be able to manage their function, as their role is not performed by a group.

One example is an executive assistant or secretary; although this is an administrative position, a secretary could be an important part of a process. Administrative and executive assistants often control the flow of information or have the important role of sending out an email or meeting invite that would initiate an important secondary process for the organization.

Second, some individuals are either members of more than one group or perform multiple functions that support separate processes or groups. It is vital to track these types of individuals separately, as they can fill gaps in a process.

Third, when examining what *knowledge*, *skills*, and *abilities* (KSAs) are needed to successfully execute processes, the KSAs must be examined both on the group and the individual level. By treating individuals as a separate element, we can examine shortfalls and overages when it comes to training or desired skills for the position (whether stand-alone or in a group).

With groups and individuals it is essential to communicate

performance expectations. This is a lesson Mike learned long ago, as presented in the following story.

A GENERAL'S REFLECTION

As a junior officer, I learned the value of using expectations in process management quite early. In the '80s I had a Battalion Commander named Colonel Inge Waddle. Inge was a man who was small in stature but had a very large presence. Even though he was a personable leader, you always knew deep down he was all about business.

One of my early encounters with Inge was when he walked in my office and told me that he might have to fire me. Even though I was a relatively new commander in the unit and was already making changes, he informed me that we were not meeting his expectations. He followed this encounter by sending me an updated expectations letter that outlined everything he expected of me and my unit. I knew what I had to do; now I just had to do it.

When I asked other officers in the unit about Inge, they told me he had a "two-strike" policy and I had already burned my first one just by showing up. Needless to say, I was motivated to work my tail off to meet his expectations.

A month later, when it was obvious I was making the right changes and getting with the program, Inge paid me a special visit. It was a Saturday morning on a drill weekend, and he came in especially to let me know he was very happy with my performance. He gave me feedback, let me know that I was meeting his expectations, and encouraged me to continue.

I really admired Inge because he was a very results-oriented person. I later found out that he always put his expectations in writing and delivered the letter to all his subordinate leaders. By doing this,

Continued

each of his commanders knew exactly what was expected of them, so all they had to do was go out and do it.

I adopted Inge's process of using expectations to establish a baseline of what subordinates were expected to do in order to drive individual and group performance. I have used these written expectations for my subordinates in every leadership position I have since taken.

I feel my success as a leader in the military largely stems from the fact that Inge taught me about expectations management. In fact, I still have the original letter that he delivered to me as a reminder of its importance.

GROUP EXPECTATIONS

Leaders should communicate clear expectations to each group for how the leader wants the group to perform. If clear expectations are not communicated, individuals in the group, or the group as a whole, will set their own standards of performance. These performance standards may not be in line with what the leader desires, and this can lead to conflict.

Since many different workers make up a group, the expectations for a group tend to be more generalized and less specific than individual expectations. Also, group effectiveness is not necessarily dependent on an individual's success.

Supervisors ultimately derive group expectations by analyzing the key driver elements of the organization. Once the leader understands the goal or objective, he or she should determine what processes the group needs to execute in order to meet the target. To achieve balance and unity, MVGOs should drive all work in the organization. Setting expectations for performance is a way that leaders can ensure this happens.

When looking at these processes, the leader should communicate clearly to the group which processes are more critical and have the higher priority, such as a process which is a single point of failure. The leader should train each group on the primary and secondary processes and communicate his or her expectations for each. Expectation management will aid groups and individuals in deciding where to prioritize their time, energy, and resources.

INDIVIDUAL EXPECTATIONS

Without expectations, an organization loses an important link in its alignment from key strategic drivers to the people. From the more generalized group expectations, leaders assign individuals their specific expectations so that each employee should know what is expected of them when they show up for work in the morning.

Some studies show evidence that supervisors can have significant influence on workers, especially new employees. Specifically, if a supervisor clarifies what is expected from an employee, they can create a positive effect on worker performance (Bauer & Green, 1998). Leaders will typically be required to clarify expectations to individuals more often than groups; and new employees will require the most frequent intervention.

Unlike group expectations, which are derived directly from the MVGOs, the basis for most individual expectations is the job description for the individual position. Position descriptions should already be aligned with the strategic plan for the company. Supervisors should review position descriptions prior to advertising a job to ensure that it does not need updating.

There are some derived position expectations if an individual belongs to a group. If this is the case, leaders should express these expectations to the individual in order to link the new employee to group goals. Without doing so, the leader could jeopardize the success of the group.

Expectations are the basis for the development of commitments for individuals. A commitment is a signed agreement between the individual and a supervisor wherein the worker certifies he or she understands what is expected of them for a particular job.

Commitments become the baseline for employee performance and can be an effective tool to measure individual performance. Since supervisors are normally required to evaluate subordinates on a periodic basis, commitments can come in handy. Performance can also be gauged from individual performance metrics calculated to report what percentage of the total commitments the member met over the reporting period. A worker's performance can also be derived from group performance metrics if the employee belongs to a group.

The logical cycle of group expectations, metrics, individual expectations, commitments, and evaluations bring continuity, consistency, and efficiency to the Diamond Process Model. Linking each of these from individuals to groups, and from groups to the established MVGOs of a company, will ensure balance and unity of effort.

We have worked with numerous organizations that do not have either group or individual expectations, and this creates problems. If no one has informed the individuals and groups what is expected, then they cannot be held accountable for failing to meet those expectations. An organization without accountability is one sailing through the seas of uncertainty. No one is really in charge, yet it may seem that everyone is in charge.

CAPTAIN'S CORNER

While serving as an aircraft maintenance officer in the Air Force, I had the opportunity to lead a large number of airmen. Since I received my commission late in my career, I often find myself mentoring some of my younger peers.

Another young officer sought my counsel one day and asked if

I would help him. We sat down in my office and he explained how he was struggling because one of his troops kept showing up late for work. I asked if he had verbally counseled the individual, and he responded, "Yes."

So I told the officer if I were in his position, I would write the individual a letter of counseling and document the corrective action. He said, "That is the problem. I don't want to be the bad guy and ruin his career by giving him paperwork." To this I replied, "You're only the bad guy if you tolerate bad standards and poor behavior."

I've found it's quite effective to look at the situation objectively instead of personally. When I am assigned to a new position, I always communicate my expectations to groups and individuals. In the Air Force, we refer to these expectations as "standards" of performance. If someone shows up late to work, I will pull them aside and verbally counsel them to ensure they understand the standard. If the worker shows up late again, I simply award them what they earn—disciplinary paperwork.

The most important aspect of this situation is to hold the individual accountable to the standard. If supervisors do not hold subordinates accountable or enforce standards, then the tolerated behavior becomes the new standard. Then, if you selectively enforce standards, you can be rightfully accused of favoritism and unfairness. Complete leaders are driven to be fair to their subordinates, and also set the standard and live by the expectations they set for subordinates.

As you can see, I did not "give" anyone anything. It was not my personal decision to punish someone or jeopardize their career. As a leader, I simply recognized a situation and acted accordingly. This is important to remember: Once you communicate the standards (expectations), worker behavior dictates leader response. This is also true for rewards. If a leader communicates expectations, and workers exceed those expectations, the leader can (and should) recognize the worker's performance appropriately.

GROUP ROLES, RESPONSIBILITIES, AND ACCOUNTABILITY (RRA)

Once a group has clear expectations, then the stage is set for leaders to assign the group organizational Roles, Responsibilities, and Accountability (RRA). Unlike expectations, which communicate *how* to perform, roles and responsibilities communicate *what* to perform.

Senior leaders should provide a *role* to each group for the function they are assigned to perform in the organization. The senior leader will determine group roles based on analyzing what the line of business (LOB) demands for each group of processes. Once the senior leader determines group roles, he or she should communicate them to the operational leader who is the senior member of a group. The process through which this communication is made (verbal, written, etc.) is not as important as long as the message is clear.

Next, the senior group leader will assign *responsibilities* to the group outlining the products and services they are required to provide. Most group leaders communicate RRA in weekly staff meetings, but this communication is only limited to the creativity of the leader. Most importantly, leaders can then communicate to the group that they are *accountable* to fulfill the set roles and responsibilities.

Sometimes leaders in strategic planning sessions identify opportunities based on examining the external environment of a company. These leaders will often devise a plan to take advantage of new opportunities which, in turn, affects group RRAs. We will explain strategic change in detail in chapter 8, but it is important to realize that RRA will not remain constant.

It is necessary for you to develop your own process through which you communicate group RRA effectively. This will ensure you can support not only the current operations of a business, but also incorporate changes throughout the organization when needed to support a new strategic direction.

INDIVIDUAL ROLES, RESPONSIBILITY, AND ACCOUNTABILITY (RRA)

From the group RRA, group leaders should assign individuals their own specific roles and responsibilities to support the group function. This affords the leader the opportunity to decide which employee fulfills certain roles and functions to support the group as a whole.

This flexibility is important, as the supervisor can balance overall needs of the organization with the needs of individuals. For example, the leader can decide to train a new group member by teaming them up with an experienced member of the group. This provides critical training for the new employee while still protecting a critical role for the organization.

Along with individual roles and responsibilities, the supervisor should also let the member know they are accountable. This accountability should be documented in the form of individual commitment and signed during a feedback session to avoid confusion. *How* accountability is communicated is not as important as *that* accountability is communicated.

The accountability for each individual, when compiled, should sum up to the total accountability for the group. If this is accomplished for each group in the entire organization, the sum of all commitments and evaluations should ensure the achievement of all the key driver elements and performance targets in the strategic plan for the organization.

We refer to this alignment process as *linking* because it connects people to the key drivers in the strategic plan of the organization through work processes. Each individual in the organization should know specifically what element, such as a goal or objective, they are contributing to and also be aware of the single leader, or *champion*, who is ultimately responsible for ensuring success of that specific key driver. We will discuss key driver champions further in chapter 10.

Although it may be an initial administrative burden, you should begin to see the value in having this linkage. It is important to note that all of this accountability serves to keep the groups and the larger organization in balance. Roles and responsibilities also keep an organization focused on its key strategic drivers (MVGOs), which is the primary purpose of the Diamond Process Model.

Processes enable leaders to maintain positive control over an organization. But processes are driven by people. To gain positive control over the efforts of groups and individuals that drive our processes, we must communicate and document individual and group roles, responsibility, and accountability. But if your people are ill-equipped to meet the RRA that are assigned, then all this work is for naught.

KNOWLEDGE, SKILLS, AND ABILITIES (KSA)

KSAs are the knowledge, skills, and abilities required to perform work processes at the proficiency level needed to meet the key drivers of the organization (MVGOs). Employees increase KSAs through reading, participating in formal training classes, and most importantly through relevant past experiences. It is important to understand which skills or abilities subordinates require to perform their duties, and what experience levels are needed for various leader positions in the organization.

Depending on the role or responsibility assigned to it, each group should have clearly articulated Knowledge, Skills, and Abilities (KSAs) identifying those core member traits that are needed to facilitate the work done in a subunit. It is extremely important that leaders identify skill requirements strategically in accordance with the key drivers in the strategic plan.

To accomplish this, leaders must understand what is needed both now (mission) and later (vision) for the organization to thrive. When crafting KSA requirements, supervisors should plan for the optimal solution to accomplish the vision. That is, plan the KSA requirements for the "ultimate employee."

If you really want to develop a championship team, it starts with strong KSA requirements. Leaders should ask themselves, "What optimal traits should an employee possess that will guarantee we meet our goals and objectives in the future?"

The group may lack certain knowledge, skills, or abilities needed to fit the "best-case scenario," or even worse, they may lack the skills to perform the work assigned in the current state. This situation is a serious challenge for leaders; when KSA gaps exist, leaders are confronted with the difficult task to fill the gaps with available resources, seek new resources, or change the functional unit that performs the work.

On a positive note, KSA gaps identify critical areas where you can apply resources. Supervisors can internally examine their own groups to identify members who have the largest KSA gaps. Leaders can then decide which employee has priority for the training needed to fill the current position. Supervisors can also use this exercise to safeguard critical processes or to reassign employees who exceed the required KSAs for any particular role.

When formulating the required KSA requirements for a position, supervisors should list the individual knowledge, skills, or abilities in intricate detail for what is required to fulfill the expectations, roles, and responsibilities assigned to the group. The level of KSAs required depends on two conditions: the performance expectations of the group, and the goals and objectives in the strategic plan.

If performance expectations are low, then the KSAs needed to perform a role or function are also low. An example might be a data entry person supporting a secondary process. This position requires limited job knowledge with a focus on typing skills needed to input data into a system. On the other hand, a sales lead who manages several customer accounts may be driving more critical primary processes; this position will have a variety of KSAs needed to perform the function.

The second condition that determines the level of KSAs needed for a position is the goals and objectives outlined in the strategic plan. Operational and first-line supervisors should review the strategic plan when developing KSA requirements for their assigned groups and individuals. KSA management changes drastically depending on which strategic direction is set by key leaders.

If the vision in the strategic plan is one for growth, leaders must ensure KSAs for positions are in the same realm of expertise, but a greater KSA proficiency level is needed. This is because if your business will grow, your current workers will likely assume a future role for training newer members. Current employees must develop a higher KSA proficiency to fill the new role.

If the vision in the strategic plan is to grow a new line of business, leaders will need to develop a new set of KSAs and hire workers with relevant experience to fill new positions. Leaders can also examine the KSAs of current employees in order to decide if some of them have the capacity to develop their individual knowledge, skills, or abilities to support the new line of business and the goals or objectives that come with them.

If your company's vision is a complete departure from current operations, such as changing an assembly line in a packaging plant from manual workers to robotics, then your attendant KSAs may need a complete overhaul. The important thing to remember is that when the strategic plan changes, so do KSA requirements needed to meet the new strategic direction.

As you can see, the KSA strategy you employ as a leader can undergo vast changes, if required by the scenario. But it's important to remember, as with every element in the Diamond Process Model, that every decision or action you take as a complete leader must be tied to the strategic direction of the organization. Only then can we strike a balance and provide unity of effort.

The largest variable to consider when determining KSAs for different performance expectations is *experience*. When considering KSAs for leaders and workers supporting primary processes, experience will likely be more important. The same is also true for technical positions such as engineers and IT personnel. The more technical the work, the greater degree of knowledge and experience required for the group.

From our experience consulting with organizations, we realize they only advertise positions based on general job requirements. Companies do not usually take the time to develop individual KSA requirements for a job or position. A job requirement for a first-line supervisor in an engineering field for oil production may be 1) a technical undergraduate degree and 2) five years of relevant experience.

A better approach is to have human resources work with the leader hiring that position and develop KSAs for the position to go along with the job requirement. A KSA requirement would state, "five years of experience in general oil production," "three years of hands-on equipment operation of the various equipment used in the process," "certifications from petroleum associations," "experience in leading a team," "experience in leading processes and/or projects," "ability to work as part of a team and build his or her own team," "basic computer skills," and "specific software skills in design, graphic programs, etc."

As you can see, the KSA approach is more specific for what is actually needed to perform the work, as well as what may be needed in the future. Realistically, job applicants may have only some of the important KSAs or experiences needed; but this will yield better information for decision makers seeking to hire the best candidate. Leaders can vet applicants on what they have versus what they will need once hired.

Organizations that hire based solely on the job description often acquire workers that are under-experienced and ill-equipped for the challenges they face as leaders or workers supporting primary processes. The job-description-only approach starts with low expectations, inadequate job description requirements, and consequently low KSAs. This all translates to low performance for your organization. If you really want to develop a championship team, start with strong KSAs!

Occasionally when you hire a new worker or if the strategic direction changes, your organization may find itself in a position where individuals supporting a primary process may be under-qualified. When the position expectation exceeds the KSA level of the employee filling that position, you have a situation we call a *KSA gap*. KSA gaps represent operational risks to your organization, as they are an internal weakness. It follows that we need to discuss handling strategies to mitigate the effects of these risks.

HOW TO HANDLE KSA GAPS

If you do not identify KSA gaps and mitigate them, it becomes difficult to elevate the capability and performance of an organization. But when you address the problems that KSA gaps present, you can raise many things to include expectations, capability, and performance. There are several ways to mitigate these KSA gaps, most of which involve Human Resources (HR) functions.

Generally, HR has the overall responsibility for the organization in terms of hiring, training, and skills upgrade or enhancement. They can work with the different operational departments to mitigate the KSA gaps once they are identified. HR may be able to hire a person with the skills required that can, in turn, train others in the department to mitigate other gaps.

HR can also acquire training for selected unit members that could most benefit and enhance group performance. If only one positional

KSA gap exists, then you can send that member to a formal class. If a group KSA gap exists, you can send one member to a formal class who can then come back and teach the rest of the group as the subject-matter expert.

If another functional subgroup within the organization has a worker who already has the KSAs needed, you can temporarily move a single worker to the other unit for training. Once proficient, that member can return to the original group and train others if needed. Inversely, another technique is to temporarily remove the expert and bring them in the unit that needs training. Once that individual trains the group, he or she can return.

If the skills are for something that is not available, workers could be allowed to research ways to gain the skills needed. This happens when you are breaking new ground on a process that no one else does and it becomes a support mechanism for the company's vision. Highly skilled workers can be segregated and provided resources for research and development purposes.

Companies also use a process known as "benchmarking" to improve a group/individual skill in order to elevate the organization's operating posture. Most companies who use this practice look for a "best of breed" or another organization that does a task, function, or process at an exceptionally high level that they can pattern their own processes after. Customer service is one of those functions that gets benchmarked a great deal due to the impact it has on productivity and profits.

The 824th Transportation Company (see chapter 4, "A General's Reflection") is a good example of mitigating KSAs. Upon our arrival, numerous members in the unit did not have the requisite level of expertise needed to allow the organization to execute its mission of providing specialized ship-to-shore transportation. The key to our success as leaders of that organization was to identify these shortfalls in the knowledge, skills, and abilities to perform the mission.

Once we identified the KSA gaps, we were able to increase the performance of the unit by selecting choice individuals and providing them with timely outside training according to a detailed integrated plan, enabling us to mitigate some KSA gaps that existed. We then brought those members back into the unit and empowered them to train other boat skippers and engineers so they could develop the skills the overall groups needed to meet their mission.

KSA development and analysis does not always bring bad news. Sometimes, instead of uncovering weaknesses in an organization, we instead find that individuals or groups have knowledge, skills, or abilities that far exceed the job requirements. If the individual has KSAs above and beyond what the position requires, you have what we call excess KSAs.

To identify excess KSAs, we strongly suggest that you develop a process whereby you can canvass your organization for the total skills that your people possess. Excess KSAs may be utilized for numerous activities that you probably are not doing currently. Some of the skills can be used in other segments of the larger organization, and possibly to support different or new LOBs.

You may have to consider whether the people are best utilized in that other area of the larger organization or whether to leave them in the same group. You may find that these skills could enable the larger organization to start a new LOB, support a change in strategic direction, or identify individuals that are promotable to leadership positions.

☆☆

A GENERAL'S REFLECTION

When I was a one-star General, I was deployed to command all logistical forces in Iraq to support OPERATION: Iraqi Freedom (OIF). In the early days of OIF I was faced with an interesting dilemma where I had to seek out excess KSAs to fulfill a much-needed requirement.

An individual assigned to one of my units was the logistician who managed food for the entire Iraq theater and was responsible for providing a half a million daily meals. One day he came up missing, and the only thing anyone could tell me was that he had recently gone to sick call with some sort of illness. For two weeks we searched for this man while "putting out fires" and trying to keep the flow of food coming in for my hungry soldiers and civilians.

Come to find out, this soldier had been transported back to the States after experiencing severe headaches attributed to excessive heat and dust. Well, that kept him from ever coming back to a desert environment, but I had a much bigger problem. I had no way to account for him or other soldiers in his situation, because my personnel, finance, and medical data systems were broken and I could not count on these systems to accurately track people transitioning and living in a combat zone. When I reported this critical vulnerability to my superiors, I was told the Pentagon had a fix that would be available in six months; the problem was, I couldn't wait six months.

One night when I was making my rounds, I came upon a young officer, adequately named Captain Smart, working fastidiously on what appeared to be a database of some sort. I asked him what he was working on and he said, "We are working on a database to track thousands of individuals in the rear." I said, "What do you mean 'we'? Do you have a mouse in your pocket?" He said, "No, sir, I have two other guys in my unit that are database managers and programmers." I discovered that he and his accomplices had excess KSAs. They were reservists and, in their civilian jobs, each had rather distinguished IT backgrounds.

I saw this as an opportunity to fix my accountability problem, so I informed Captain Smart he no longer worked for his Colonel, but for me personally. I made him the lead of a special team, enabled them with resources, and gave them an objective to fix the accountability gap between the three local administrative systems.

Continued

Captain Smart and his team developed and produced a field-expedient integrated fix to the personnel, medical, and finance accountability systems and employed the changes in less than ninety days. We extended the scope of our project and identified, analyzed, and fixed other software vulnerabilities that previously had no other resolution.

As it were, our six-month fix promised by the Pentagon never came to fruition. In fact, that program, named "Defense Integrated Military Human Resources System (DIMHRS)," was cancelled in 2010 by the CJCS Admiral Mullen, after at least twelve years of work and several billion dollars (yes, with a "b") wasted. Needless to say, that program was an astronomical failure.

Hence, I learned a valuable lesson from having excess KSAs within my organization; with excess KSAs, wonderful things can come to pass if you know about them and act. Peg this as another one of those 'you don't know what you don't know' items. You will be immensely surprised what skills you find that members of your organization have in the way of hobbies, past jobs, church work, degrees, and many others.

Now, some of these skills cannot be utilized anywhere in your larger organization or for future LOBs, but you will still find some that can be game changers for you and the larger organization. And you may find another way to get to know your people better and develop a better rapport with them.

Groups and individuals are an integral part of your organization (and the Diamond Process Model), and they power the processes within your lines of business to meet the MVGOs set for the larger organization. You should see again the logical linkage of the elements in the model, but don't lose sight of the ultimate end-result for which we are striving: balance. Work among groups should be balanced as well as work among individuals within a group.

Now we understand the importance of communicating roles, responsibilities, and accountability with groups and individuals. Most importantly, we realize that communicating clear expectations is what is usually left out of the equation. But if your people are to be empowered to meet your expectations, they need resources. Without providing the appropriate manpower, equipment, and capital, you cannot expect your people to deliver.

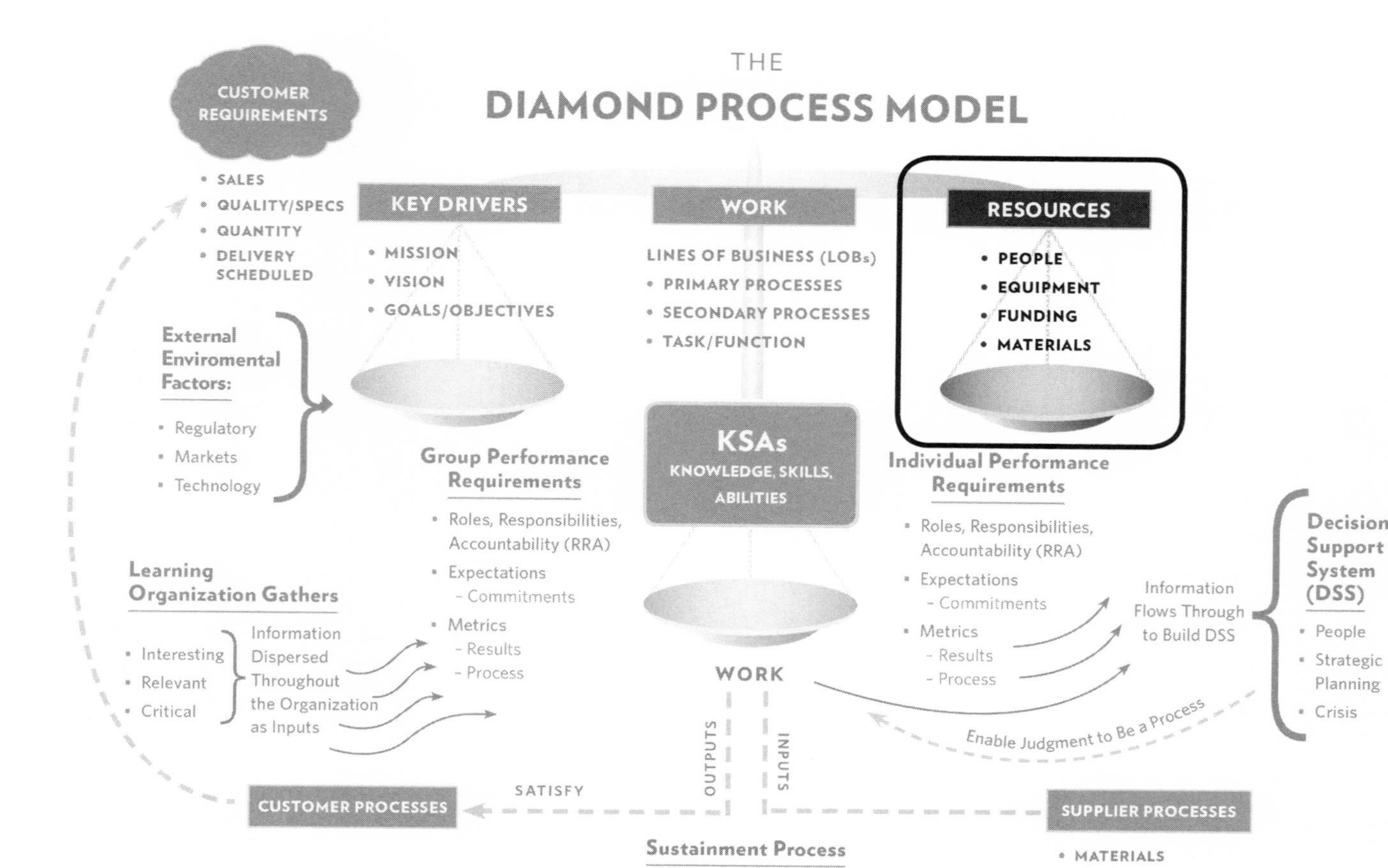

THE
DIAMOND PROCESS MODEL
CUSTOMER REQUIREMENTS
• SALES
• QUALITY/SPECS
• QUANTITY
• DELIVERY SCHEDULED
KEY DRIVERS
• MISSION
• VISION
• GOALS/OBJECTIVES
WORK
LINES OF BUSINESS (LOBs)
• PRIMARY PROCESSES
• SECONDARY PROCESSES
• TASK/FUNCTION
RESOURCES
• PEOPLE
• EQUIPMENT
• FUNDING
• MATERIALS
External Enviromental Factors:
• Regulatory
• Markets
• Technology
Group Performance Requirements
• Roles, Responsibilities, Accountability (RRA)
• Expectations
- Commitments
• Metrics
- Results
- Process
KSAs
KNOWLEDGE, SKILLS, ABILITIES
Individual Performance Requirements
• Roles, Responsibilities, Accountability (RRA)
• Expectations
- Commitments
• Metrics
- Results
- Process
Learning Organization Gathers
• Interesting
• Relevant
• Critical
Information Dispersed Throughout the Organization as Inputs
WORK
Information Flows Through to Build DSS
Decision Support System (DSS)
• People
• Strategic Planning
• Crisis
Enable Judgment to Be a Process
OUTPUTS
INPUTS
SATISFY
CUSTOMER PROCESSES
SUPPLIER PROCESSES
• MATERIALS
• SUB ASS./COMPONENTS
• SERVICES
Sustainment Process
• Strategic Level: Strategic Planning Session
• Operations/Dept. Level: Operational Assesment
• First Line Leader Level: Process Review

CHAPTER 6

RESOURCES

At this point, you should have a good understanding of the top two components in the Diamond Process Model, which are the key driver (MVGO), and work process components (LOBs/processes/groups/individuals). Before we can show you all the great uses for the model, we need to explain the *resource* component, which consists of people, equipment, and capital.

Resources are quite different from any of the previous elements we have discussed. This is because all of the other elements in the Diamond Process—from the key strategic drivers through LOBs and processes—all represent *requirements* for an organization. Once applied, *resources* are the fuel that turns these requirements into capabilities.

We will also introduce a new term called *Life-Cycle Management* (LCM), which is the acquisition and management of equipment during its expected serviceable life and retiring/replacing it at the appropriate time.

☆☆

A GENERAL'S REFLECTION

When I was serving as a General Officer in Iraq as a logistical commander, I had a lot of folks running convoys. I always like to go out and get hands-on so I can understand the full array of processes people are executing. It always served me well to experience what my soldiers deal with from their perspective.

Since convoy operation is one of the most dangerous businesses out there, you can imagine I had to provide a little justification to my boss. He knew what I was trying to do, so our compromise was for me to take a shorter trip.

The convoy I was assigned to that day left out of Navistar, which was the last base in Kuwait before going over the Iraqi border; we were headed to Baghdad. My orders were to get off at the third stop in Scania, but it took us a couple of days to get there. After a long day on the road, we pulled off and bedded down so the maintenance folks could take care of the convoy vehicles.

The next day while we were on the move, I kept noticing lots of water pallets lining both sides of the road. I wondered if we had a training issue with folks not knowing how to secure cargo or an equipment issue with not being able to tie down our supplies.

When I asked the convoy commander why we couldn't hold on to our stuff, he explained to me that the Iraqis were digging trenches in the road. Apparently the locals realized if they made the roads rough enough, then we would lose supplies off the deuce-and-a-half trucks, and then the kids could scavenge what fell off.

We finally arrived in Scania, about ninety miles south of Baghdad, so I had to get scheduled for a ride back to Navistar. I walked in the scheduler's office and she was quite surprised to see the star on my helmet. I'm actually glad she was surprised because I didn't want to advertise that there was a 1-star riding on a convoy.

She informed me that there was a "white" convoy headed back in the morning, so I told her to sign me up—but to keep quiet about it. White convoy is the term we used for contractor convoys. I thought this would be a different, but informational, experience.

When we headed back the next day, we came around the same area where we had lost water pallets the day before. It was rough as all get out, so the contactor was also losing supplies; but I heard a radio call that one of the trucks blew a tire.

I was quite shocked when I heard the civilian convoy commander radio back and say, "Blow it up!" I looked at him and said, "Excuse me? What did you say?" He confirmed he gave the order to blow the truck up.

I asked him how far the maintenance personnel were from our location and he told me they were only about eight miles down the road. I promptly informed him that they were to "circle the wagons," set up security, and wait for the maintenance personnel to come change the tire.

When I got back to Kuwait, I walked directly into the office of the commander who was responsible for overseeing this contractor and demanded to see his records for lost vehicles. To date, the contractor had blown up over 100 vehicles at $250K each. Needless to say, this was not my idea of life-cycle management. And, by the way, I also remedied the practice of blowing up "injured" vehicles by defense contractors. Following my visit to the Battalion Commander, there were only four more vehicles destroyed for the rest of my tenure, all of which met the criteria for that particular tactic.

There are three types of resources we will cover in this chapter; people, equipment, and capital. These are the three resources that represent elements in the Diamond Process Model because any resource you need to drive a process can be captured in one of these three categories. Before we begin explaining these elements we must take a moment to communicate our approach of dealing with people as a resource in the Diamond Process Model.

PEOPLE ARE A VITAL RESOURCE

In our discussions, we will look at people objectively as a resource to power processes. We are not arguing you should treat your people like you would a printer. We just feel that leaders typically lead people and forget processes. Therefore, we want to focus on people leadership only as it pertains to process integration.

When managing people as a resource in the Diamond Process Model, there are two main questions you need to answer: "Which ones?" and "How many?" In chapter 5 we discussed the importance of adopting the KSA approach to hiring the individual with the right qualifications for a job. What we did not discuss is hiring the right people to fit the culture of an organization.

Organizational culture includes the shared values and beliefs among people of a company and is expressed through awards, symbols, ceremonies, slogans, and events. There are many different types of cultural climates within organizations and too many traditions to speak of. But what is important when considering people as a resource is that the individuals you hire need to fit the cultural climate of your organization.

If you hire someone that does not "buy in" to your organizational culture, you run into two significant problems. First, the new hire could jeopardize the vision of your company. The corporate climate is often driven from strategic leaders in the organization. These are the same leaders who create the vision and strategic direction of your company. If new employees do not believe in the direction of your organization, then they may not be motivated to drive your processes to meet goals and objectives in the strategic plan.

The second problem is cost. If new employees are not a good fit with your organization, they could leave prematurely after you've invested time and money into their development. As discussed in chapter 5, high turnover is costly and depletes capital, another important resource in the Diamond Process Model.

The next major question you need to answer when objectively looking at people as a resource is how many people to provide. A complete leader provides the resources needed to meet expectations and deliver processes to meet the key drivers in the strategic plan. If you do not provide adequate personnel to meet these expectations, you are setting your company up for failure.

Determining numbers in an organization is a tricky business—and a subjective process. Since each situation is complex and unique, we will provide some general guidelines to help you determine the right number of people to drive your specific processes. The first major guideline is to understand that the act of determining manning requirements is a bottom-up process.

When using the Diamond Process Model, we start strategically in the key driver component, drive down through the process component with LOBs, and review resource elements at the end. This is because we want to make sure every process supports the strategic plan. But what we are left with is a bunch of requirements that always need resources.

When we need to figure out how to apply resources, we start at the bottom levels of an organization because that is where the work happens. Group leaders should be intimately familiar with processes. If they feel there is a shortfall, they must communicate that requirement up to a mid-level manager.

Once the requirement is identified, leaders need to vet the requirement. Sometimes leaders can assign multiple roles, move existing personnel to different jobs, or realign process assignments to overcome a shortfall. If none of these options are viable, you may be forced to hire a new employee.

Using the bottom-up method allows leaders to get in tune with their organizations. Leaders can identify requirements and determine how to balance scarce human resources to protect those processes that are most critical. Most of all, this exercise creates balance in an organization, which is why we're here.

Another guideline when determining how many people to drive processes is to use the tools you have available. When following the Diamond Process Model, we perform lots of great work in LOB and process management. We even build detailed process maps that outline each work process performed by the organization. These process maps can be valuable tools when determining manning requirements.

It is also a smart idea to have a prioritization structure for personnel. Some people are more important to an organization because they drive one or more primary processes. Your organization cannot let these processes go unsupported. This prioritization can be used to develop contingency plans in strategic planning sessions in case your company must temporarily lay off some workers or perform cutbacks. Prioritization can also demand that a position be filled sooner rather than later.

For every resource, including people, we need to discuss life-cycle management (LCM). Your people have a life cycle with respect to working as a viable asset for your organization. This is not meant to be a cold approach toward people, but just like equipment, people have a work expectancy.

Whether or not we want to admit it, people get old and retire. It is necessary to be mindful of the characteristics of the people who drive our processes. Some people will want to retire from your organization, while others have bigger aspirations and will want to transfer for career development. We need to understand our workforce is never stable, and we should have plans to replace workers when they move on. We also need to protect our critical processes so we can continue to support the key strategic drivers of an organization.

EQUIPMENT

Once the organization is staffed with the right work force, they will need to be equipped with the best tools available to produce high-level products and services for customers. Equipment should enhance people's ability to produce and enable them to meet roles, responsibilities, and expectations from leadership.

Work processes should drive the requirement for equipment used in the workplace and should be linked in whatever fashion you use to link people. Equipment shortages or obsolescence can plague otherwise efficient processes and lower the productivity of work units. Outdated equipment can impact the KSAs for the people that are using the equipment and cause them to become obsolete as well. To operate efficiently, people need to be trained and equipment needs to be maintained.

Similar to hiring people, establishing appropriate resourcing requirements for equipment can be difficult as it is tough to tell how much and what type of equipment is optimal for a job. It also should be managed from the bottom-up so mid-level managers have the opportunity to vet requirements against known processes. These requirements are different for each organization, but there are some best practices to live by to optimize your company.

Whether you are in a high-tech manufacturing organization or running a widget-repair business, if you intend to lead the competition in your market segment, you will not accomplish your goals with outdated and dilapidated equipment. The same is true for software.

If you are using old operating software on your workstations then you are accepting certain risks, as the competition can gain a competitive advantage if they are more technologically sound. Old software becomes outdated and can decrease worker productivity and increase worker frustration because simple tasks may require much more time to complete.

It is solely the leader's responsibility to ensure that people have the correct equipment to perform their jobs, which also includes making sure the equipment is not obsolete. One best practice to ensure this happens is to use life-cycle management (LCM).

There is a place for LCM in your organization as it helps to improve the utility of your equipment and, consequently, your workers. As equipment ages, it gets harder to use and requires more capital resources to keep going. Managing the life cycle of your resources helps to manage these tradeoffs; at some point, the continued use of older equipment becomes more costly than purchasing new equipment. LCM can also help you consider other factors, such as salvage value, that can aid in the decision to change resources.

In order to employ an effective life-cycle management strategy, you must have an accurate way to record the depreciation of equipment. Proper depreciation management processes should record a standard depreciation over the usable life of an asset. They should also contain a cost-benefit threshold, where the equipment becomes unusable from a business case standpoint. Improper depreciation will throw off the LCM process and cause ripple effects in capital funding as well.

There are smart ways to extend the service life of equipment to alleviate the need to constantly replace assets. A workable, systemic maintenance program and processes to execute it can extend the serviceable life of equipment. The maintenance plan should include management of all warranties, recalls, and updates. It should also have detailed measures to perform preventive maintenance. Having detailed processes can also provide critical information to use in times of crisis, as in the following story provided by Chris.

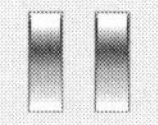

CAPTAIN'S CORNER

In 2010 I was deployed to Kandahar, Afghanistan, in support of OPERATION: Enduring Freedom. I was in charge of an aircraft maintenance unit and was responsible for maintaining two dozen MQ-1B Predators that were flying daily combat air patrols (CAPs) in Afghanistan.

This was my first deployment as a maintenance officer, and I was amazed at not only the talent of the Airmen performing maintenance, but also the sophistication in the detailed maintenance plans used by the Air Force. Each aircraft had standard preventive maintenance and inspections whose frequency was based on hourly usage, so we knew exactly what equipment, personnel, and consumable resources were needed and when.

Around my fourth month down-range, we experienced a bit of a crisis. Since we had so many aircraft, we used quite a bit of engine oil. We could forecast our demand with great detail so we knew exactly how much to keep on hand, and we kept all of our oil in crates staged in a certain location in our area of the airfield. One day when we opened a new crate, we discovered that the brand of oil was different from what we were used to using.

A crisis emerged when we used the new oil to service an aircraft and it caused the engine to overheat. We tested the oil on another aircraft and the same thing happened, which meant that we could not use the new oil that we had stocked up and also could not use the two aircraft we had just filled up.

I immediately got on the phone back to the States and got an emergency shipment of the old style of oil sent our way. The problem was it was going to take three days to arrive at our location, and I still had to support the combat sorties with serviceable aircraft. The

Continued

other problem was that our maintenance plan was going to change, and aircraft that were scheduled to be down now had to fly. What followed the presence of this crisis was undoubtedly one of the most impressive problem-solving exercises that I will ever be a part of.

I gathered my expert maintainers and communicated our tactical objective to devise a plan to be able to fly for three days without using any additional oil. This was quite tricky because one aircraft could fly only three times before the oil had to be changed. Two aircraft were already disabled because they were filled with new oil; some aircraft were already airborne, and others were undergoing heavy maintenance so they had no engines installed.

Having identified the problem, we were now ready to gather resources so we could list and test possible solutions. We pulled together our best minds, most experienced personnel, the extensive spreadsheet we used to track maintenance, a whiteboard, and started brainstorming.

We began sorting aircraft by tail number and how many hours they had left before the next scheduled hourly maintenance cycle. We then started arranging the tails into the flying schedule we needed to support. We rearranged the chart several times until we finally arrived at a schedule that would satisfy mission requirements with no additional oil.

We then had to record the washout of rearranging the flying schedule and also record all the changes to the new maintenance schedule. After three hours, we were finally able to craft a new maintenance plan that allowed for us to support the flying plan. The only reason we were able to achieve such a feat is because we insisted we had the training and expertise to succeed. We took a disciplined approach to solving the problem while still remaining within the limitations required by our maintenance plan. Our efforts were rewarded, because we did not miss a single combat sortie and did not break any procedures in doing so.

Having a detailed maintenance plan, a system to track it, and skillful Airmen allowed us to be successful that day. We were so familiar with our maintenance plan and our life-cycle management strategy, we were able to manipulate it to avoid a crisis. Without this system (and the people who knew it) we would not have been able to succeed. Escaping this predicament while under such great pressure to deliver air assets to our combatant commander made for a great Air Force day.

Similar to our customer service example in chapter 5, many organizations use benchmarking to adopt community best practices in maintaining equipment. Many academics, businesses, and practitioners have studied Toyota Motor Company because of their well-known maintenance practices and quality control expertise. Sometimes there is lower risk when adopting the practices of other companies, especially if the practices are proven.

Equipment and process improvement have an interdependent relationship. While conducting exercises in process improvement, you may find that these efforts highlight the need for a tool or piece of equipment that may improve how work gets accomplished in a more efficient way. There are times when replacing a machine will eliminate the need for other people or equipment.

When this occurs, your organization should use an established process to reallocate saved resources. Just because you eliminate the need for one worker in a certain area does not mean you have to get rid of the worker. You can analyze the employee's KSAs and place them in another area of the organization.

The opposite is also true; sometimes the acquisition of a new piece of equipment drives the need to improve a process. This is the case if a piece of equipment fails and you purchase a newer replacement.

The new piece of equipment may have capabilities above the older machine, which drives the need to improve and adjust your processes.

Equipment management and utilization make the most of your people and processes. It can also save money. Good asset management programs save costs and increase capital in the long run. This extra capital can be used to invest back in equipment or in new employees or employee training. Higher-trained employees can improve processes and better manage equipment. As you can see, each of these three resources complement each other.

CAPITAL

We do not intend to get into the intimate details of high financing here in our book. But we do want to emphasize the part that capitalization plays in the Diamond Process Model. Capital funding is always a critical resource for every organization. What is most important is that companies invest these resources in a way that provides the greatest benefit—getting the biggest bang for the buck.

In order to do this, leaders must identify which priorities within the organization warrant funding over other requirements. These priorities, as everything throughout the Diamond Process, should be established in strategic planning sessions where key leaders drive the strategic helm of the organization. The vessel that propels the strategic plan is the budget.

Your financial group will be the shepherds for the organization's budget. Most companies we've seen get into a chicken-egg dilemma when addressing budget priorities: Is it the requirements that drive funding needs, or is it the availability of funding that allows them to derive requirements? Or, is it markets and competition that drive both? Depending on the sector in which you operate, it could be one or all three.

It usually makes most sense for organizations to have requirements already developed from the strategic plan to determine what and how much funding they need. Keep in mind, we are striving to meet the key drivers for the organization to include the mission, vision, goals, and objectives. But we also want to maintain balance, and funds are critical in doing so.

On the other hand, if your organization is able to generate more-than-expected income from internal operations or external opportunities, then your key leaders may want to obtain more resources (people or equipment) to enable key drivers. Seizing these opportunities could bring unexpected advances toward your company's vision, so it pays to be prepared with a plan.

Markets and competition can dictate mandatory investments if you want to remain a player in your sector. This is common in the tech industry, especially highly competitive markets such as that for the mobile phone. If a competitor reveals a bigger screen, a higher resolution, or an operating system that attracts a larger customer base, you will be better off if you invest instead of doing nothing.

RESOURCES: THE FINAL DPM ELEMENT

If you recall from chapter 4 when we began to characterize work processes, we asked two important questions: "What is your single point of failure in your work processes?" and "Why?" The answers to these questions often call into play resources and how the resources get prioritized in your organization. It could very well be that the lack of people, equipment, or capital could represent your single point of failure.

It is critical for leaders to identify the work processes that could be that single point of failure and demand a higher commitment or allocation of the people, equipment, or capital resources needed to resolve them. How these challenges are addressed can be a game changer for many organizations.

For most organizations, resourcing is the most critical element of their tailored Diamond Process Model. Focusing on how to excel at each of these three resources is important because they often mean the difference between success and failure. The people you have staffed in the company will need the tools and capital to shape and produce the high-level services you intend based on your MVGOs. Again, we strive for balance.

Too many resources can lead to waste, inefficiency, or misuse. Too little can lead to an idle workforce, fewer products or services rendered, and customer dissatisfaction. Budgets will play an important role in this balancing act, not only for resources but for the Diamond Process Model as a whole. The inability to resource properly puts the strategic plan and its key drivers in jeopardy and sends the model, and organization, into an unbalanced death spiral.

IN SUMMARY

We have now covered the first major section in the book and have introduced you to all of the elements on the Diamond Process Model. But before we show you how to use the elements to optimize your organization, we need to remind you of some necessary measures that all of the elements share.

First, it is imperative that all the DPM elements, and the data they represent, are kept updated. Only with current and accurate information can you get the best results from using the Diamond Process. We've found it helpful to make changes to your model immediately following each strategic planning session, since the DPM is greatly affected by that process.

Next, remember all the elements are interdependent and exist to maintain balance. Understanding the balanced logic behind the model helps you on your journey to become a complete leader and helps provide unity of effort to the organization on its journey to achieve the mission and vision set forth by strategic leadership.

MAJOR SECTION TWO:

USING THE DIAMOND PROCESS MODEL

CHAPTER 7

THE DIAMOND PROCESS MODEL

Now that we've identified each element of the Diamond Process Model, it is time to put them to use. In section two of this book, we will show you how to use the DPM as a complete leader in order to optimize your organization and achieve balance and unity of effort. This chapter will cover most of the situations we've encountered as consultants and trainers and should translate directly to your current organization. This chapter will also show you different methods to apply the model and provide remedies for several common problems.

One of our favorite "demotivator" statements from despair.com states: "Always remember that you are unique. Just like everybody else." Even though businesses are unique, we've found that, like people, all organizations have fundamental similarities. The Diamond Process Model is designed using these commonalities in a way that applies to each organization.

But before jumping into specific DPM applications, let's take the time to explain some critical relationships between the Diamond Process Model's elements and components. Instead of treating each DPM element as a stand-alone entity as described in section one, we need to understand the relationships between the elements and how they interact to affect your organization.

Each element is interdependent, which means if one is out of balance, it affects the rest to varying degrees. But this also means if you get them integrated properly, you will reap the rewards of a balanced business that is driving toward strategic goals and objectives; better yet, you will be marching down the path to be a complete leader.

CRITICAL DPM INTERDEPENDENCIES

It is best to look at the model in three distinct components to analyze the components' interactions and the ways they interconnect and eventually integrate. The Diamond Process Model illustrates the relationship between each component. The first elements are on the left side of the scale, which make up the key strategic driver component and include the mission, vision, goals, and objectives from the strategic plan.

Key drivers are the ultimate reason an organization exists. To ensure balance and unity of effort, all work and every element of the Diamond Process Model must satisfy these key drivers. If everything in your organization is not supporting key drivers, the result will be an out-of-balance organization that will need to be corrected. Specific corrective actions will be discussed in chapter nine.

The second component of the model is *work processes*, and it resides in the center of the chart. Work processes represent lines of business (LOB); processes (primary/secondary/task/function); group roles, responsibilities, and accountability; group expectations; and group metrics. The work process component is the pivot point of the entire model (and your company) because it connects everything from top to bottom in your organization.

The work process component should be in balance with accomplishing the key driver component. Where they are not balanced, meaning work processes do not adequately support key drivers, the leader should be alerted that there is an out-of-balance situation that requires active resolution. We will discuss specific process leader actions in chapters 10–13.

The first two components of the Diamond Process Model represent your organization's operational requirements that need to be resourced. The third component, *resources*, represents the people, equipment, and capital that provide the capability to meet those requirements. The resource component fuels the work process component, which in turn enables the key driver component.

In the Diamond Process Model, the resource component links with the process component to visually represent the relationship between resources and the work process it supports. From a bird's-eye view, leaders look for the aggregate of resources (people, equipment, and capital) to fulfill the aggregate of all work processes. When these two are not equal, the model is out of balance and the leader should once again be alerted that corrective action is required to achieve balance in the organization.

WHEN RESOURCES AND WORK PROCESS COME TOGETHER

CAPITAL BUYS
People
Equipment
Capital
LIFE CYCLE MGMT
GETS INTEGRATED INTO
WORK PROCESSES
WHICH
ACHIEVE MEET EXCEED
KEY DRIVERS
Mission
Vision
Goals

To illustrate the interdependencies between the resource and work process components, let's take a moment to reflect back on chapter four when we discussed process maps. Remember, process maps show a visual depiction, from left to right, of each member or functional subunit that controls a particular process. Once process maps are developed, leaders have the opportunity to integrate resources individually against each process shown, and collectively for group processes.

Process allocation, or *loading* resources to support each of these processes, requires careful planning by leaders as it is essential to maintain balance. Each process must have adequate people, equipment, and capital in order to ensure success. We point this out because we've found that most organizations establish some sort of key drivers, few companies establish processes (below high-level ones), and hardly any integrate resources. Such was the case in the following story:

A GENERAL'S REFLECTION

After I retired from the military, I ran into an active-duty Brigadier General at a function. We conversed about leadership, and he asked me if I was interested in reviewing his strategic plan process. He was in charge of developing a strategic plan for a major defense command and wanted a second set of eyes. I told him I would love the opportunity to help him out.

I began our mentoring session by using the Diamond Process Model and started at the top. The General had done a good job outlining his key drivers and had articulated a mission, vision, goals, and strategic objectives. Unlike many leaders I've mentored, he even had developed high-level processes and had assigned group roles and responsibilities as well as expectations. Through this process he felt very good about what he had done with respect to what he called his *vertical integration*.

When I continued with the Diamond Process Model planning and showed him the process to fully integrate resource components, his attitude changed. When I talked specifically of assigning people, equipment, and capital to each one of his processes, his jaw dropped to the floor. It was apparent that he had not expanded his thinking to include resource integration in his vertical integration approach.

This individual was a good leader and was well educated, so I knew exactly how to show him the impact of resource integration. I simply asked, "What would happen if these resource steps were not accomplished?" After a long pause he responded emotionally, "The whole organization will implode!"

The General made the realization that without integrating resources individually with the group processes, he would not have the balance required to be successful in meeting his key drivers. Therein lies the importance of performing the necessary integration piece that separates the leaders from the "wannabes."

Alignment of the top two components is only the first half of the battle; resource integration is where the ends meet the means. You must do both to have complete organizational balance and succeed!

Through component relationships, the Diamond Process Model will enable you to see where your organization may be out of balance with the various elements and fall short of meeting your key drivers. Conceptually, resources should be able to adequately cover all of the processes you have designated to be accomplished. If you do not have enough of whatever resource, you will not be able to achieve that particular process, and your MVGO will be jeopardized.

HOW PEOPLE RELATE TO WORK

Up to this point we have viewed people as an element that belongs to the resource component in the Diamond Process Model. This is handy from the bird's-eye view for DPM integration, but we all know people are more than simply an objective element; we are dynamic individuals with talents, emotions, perceptions, and values. Considering these more humanistic qualities, we need to look at balance in a slightly different way and consider the interdependency between people and processes.

Leaders need to balance workload so that employees are sharing responsibilities somewhat equally. This way we enhance each process to which a worker is assigned and optimize the overall effort of each individual—and all individuals collectively. A balanced workload approach will help the organization become more efficient, effective, and successful.

The plight of many workers is that the organization will load more work on those that are *workhorses* and ride them into oblivion. This is where the 80/20 rule comes in, whereby 80% of the work gets accomplished by 20% of the people. This strategy will work for a while until the workhorse gets his fill of an imbalanced workload and unfair compensation for that additional work. This particular balance discrepancy is at the core of many people issues that managers are confronted with each day. This imbalance can inhibit communication between leader and worker, increase worker frustration, decrease productivity, and even drive higher turnover.

The only reason the 80/20 rule exists is because leaders allow it to. Instead of communicating roles and responsibilities and holding people accountable, some supervisors tolerate low performance and take the easy road by assigning extra work to the overachievers. Once tolerated, low performance becomes the new standard for the low performers.

As consultants, we are always leery when a client informs us that they have "people problems." This is because, whether or not they realize it, many of these personnel issues can be traced back to poor process development and/or lack of integration of resources to processes. We have compiled a matrix that shows how many common issues workers experience can be tied back to unsuspecting causes.

Many of these problems can be a result of people and/or equipment not being linked correctly to processes. This lack of integration also hampers leaders from being able to perform leadership behaviors such as coaching, developing, mentoring, motivating, and inspiring because they are spending all their time dealing with personnel issues.

From an individual's perspective, they also need to know how they fit into the organization's work processes. Supervisors can communicate roles, responsibilities, accountability, and expectations during periodic operational reviews so subordinates know not only *what* they are expected to do but *why*.

If leaders explain the "big picture" to workers, oftentimes employees will be more motivated because they will realize what they do is important to the organization as a whole. Subordinates who understand the overall integration of a process can also help in process improvement, as they will become the subject-matter experts and will have the most technical knowledge concerning processes.

Do you recall the janitor who worked at NASA in Houston back in the early days of the space program? A visiting dignitary asked him, "What do you do here?" He replied, "Sir, I am helping to put a man on the moon!"

WHEN RESOURCES MEET PROCESS

We've briefly explained that the key drivers and work process components determine requirements, and it is our job as leaders to match those requirements with resources to turn them into capabilities. But we must take a balanced approach when applying resources to our processes so that we can keep those processes balanced and support the entire line of business, not just part of it.

We've found that when applying resources to process, it is essential to start with people first. We do understand that nothing happens without money, so you must apply capital as needed. But people can affect equipment and processes, since they serve not only as resources but also process leaders, which means the people need to come first.

Since different workers can determine which or how much equipment to use, or how much pay is needed, we need to support our processes with people first. Remember to take the KSA approach when applying a person to a process. Always plan for the ultimate employee who will help achieve the vision in your key drivers.

Usually the ultimate employee is not available, is too expensive, or simply does not exist, which means there are likely to be KSA gaps. If gaps exist between the knowledge, skills, and abilities of what is expected for the position and those inherent with the person filling the position, begin to formulate your mitigation strategy early so you can achieve balance. KSA gaps may force you to initially apply more than one person to a process for training, so make sure you have a long-term plan.

PEOPLE AND THEIR EQUIPMENT

Once the right person is matched against the work process, then you can resource the worker with the proper equipment to ensure the process is supported. If this is a new, technical, or highly skilled position, it sometimes pays to give the employee a vote in which equipment is needed for the job.

A well-trained worker who is properly equipped will perform optimally, which is what the supervisor wants and what the organization needs to meet key drivers. This means we need to achieve balance when equipping our personnel and be mindful that providing sufficient quality equipment can optimize worker performance.

Sometimes, higher-quality equipment can mean you have fewer people to drive a process. If this is the right approach for your situation, keep in mind that you need a higher-skilled worker to operate more sophisticated equipment. The opposite is also true; sometimes higher-quality workers result in less equipment, or better use of consumable equipment resources such as oil, because the higher-skilled worker will have the ability to conserve and make fewer mistakes, which results in less waste.

People also play a key role in extending the service life of equipment. They can be trained to perform preventive and scheduled maintenance and conduct life-cycle management practices to protect equipment resources. Workers can also signal to leaders when the equipment is reaching the end of its service life and will need replacing.

When acquiring new equipment, skilled technicians can serve as subject-matter experts during the acquisition process. They can provide leadership with key insights from a technical perspective that can help aid buying decisions.

The final interdependency between equipment and people is operational risk. Safety programs are paramount to protect all three resource elements, as equipment can hurt the people who operate it. Safety incidents are costly because you lose employees and productivity, damage equipment, and increase costs associated with insurance, medical bills, and worker's compensation.

FUELING PROCESS WITH MONEY

Capital is needed throughout the resource allocation process because everything you do has a monetary cost assigned. It costs money to formulate processes, hire new workers, purchase equipment, perform process improvement, and cover overhead administrative costs. When looking at capital as an element on the Diamond Process Model, there are two things to remember.

First, nothing happens without money. On the Diamond Process Model, capital is a *critical enabler* that ultimately brings capability to all your requirements. When planning, make sure you budget appropriately so you can fund a process to a level that at least initially supports the process. It is a waste of resources if you develop a process, purchase the equipment for the process, and then cannot afford to pay someone to drive the process. This oversight turns assets into liabilities.

Next, make sure you track capital at the process level. It is quite costly to establish a new process, purchase equipment for the process, and hire workers to drive the process. Oftentimes, you are forced to plan for the minimal solution in order to ensure the process supports your line of business. Similar to a KSA gap with people, this often creates a capital resource gap.

When this occurs, make sure you keep detailed records on where you have resource gaps that need capital to optimize your processes. It is also a good idea to prioritize the processes based on which are most critical to your organization. By doing this, if and when capital resources become available, you will know where to apply them to optimize your organization.

REQUIREMENTS VERSUS CAPABILITIES

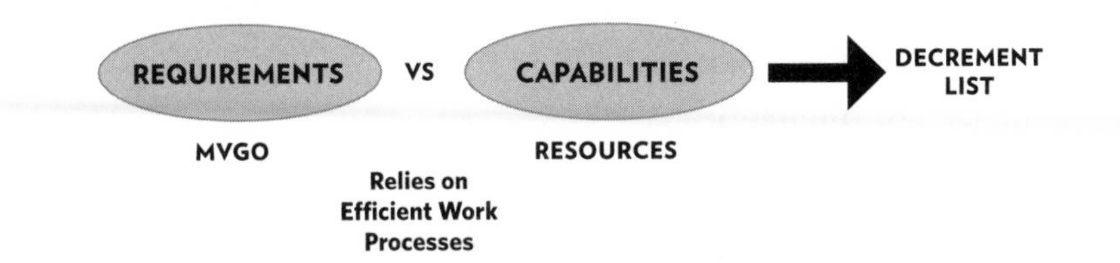

Requirements and capabilities present yet another balancing conundrum for the leader that resembles that of our Diamond Process Model balance scale. Requirements are derived from the key driver component (MVGO) and are represented downstream in the work process component (LOB). The total requirements for your organization are comprised of both the key drivers and process components.

Some may argue that external factors (markets, technology, and legal) also present and adjust requirements for the organization. Although this is true, when utilizing the Diamond Process methodology we assume strategic leaders capture these additional requirements in a strategic planning session and document them as part of the key drivers. Therefore, these external requirements will always be included.

Capabilities to meet requirements are represented through resource elements (people, equipment, capital). The one characteristic that is shared among all resources is that they are available only in limited quantities. The success or failure of organizations often occurs because limited resources are applied incorrectly.

The entire existence of the Diamond Process Model and the reason for all the process work and balancing is to identify which processes are most critical. In other words, we identify which requirements most need capabilities. There will always be unfunded requirements that will not be filled. But these unfunded requirements cannot be critical processes that enable the work processes that maintain and satisfy key drivers in the strategic plan.

A CALL TO ACTION

Sometimes you don't know what you don't know. Many organizations go through workdays not knowing they lack a certain resource element to accomplish a goal. The company's performance suffers because leaders do not realize the organization is out of balance. Diamond Process Model planning illuminates the interdependencies among all the elements while supporting the key drivers of the organization. It identifies which resources are needed to provide the capability to meet the requirements of each process area. Ultimately, the DPM makes sure you know what you don't know.

The Diamond Process Model is an important tool to help leaders identify when there is an imbalance in their organization. Whether this imbalance occurs with a process not supporting MVGOs, or an unfair workload, identification is only the first step. Once the Diamond Process Model output informs the leader of a problem, it is time for action. The following story is a good example of the problems imbalance can create and how a leader can take action to resolve issues once they are identified.

☆☆

A GENERAL'S REFLECTION

In the fall of 2003, when OIF forces had been deployed for just under a year, I realized there was a need to send in new units to replace the currently deployed force. Since I was in charge of the Theater Support Command, I knew the responsibility for planning and executing the 125k-person force rotation was mine and mine alone.

I had a four-person Deployment/Redeployment Coordination Center (DRCC) team on my staff that was developing all facets of this rotation of forces by interpreting guidance from the Pentagon. I quickly went from overseer of this process to leader of this process when my DRCC team informed me that the troop rotation was not going to be "tit for tat." Instead of a one-for-one swap, we were exchanging different types of units—which completely changed the rules of the game.

We developed a planning process and directed the work be accomplished in two phases. The first phase was to develop unit mission requirements for work that had to be continued in theater. Some missions were going away, so we needed to rule them out. Other missions were going to be replaced by defense contractors: The remaining missions were not all going to be replaced by US Army personnel. In some cases, an Army Military Police (MP) unit was replaced by a Navy Shore Patrol (SP) unit and assigned to perform an Army mission.

In the second phase of the planning process we had to capture individual skill sets that were assigned to the units. We had to list the skills that we were redeploying back to the States and reference them to the individual skill sets of the deploying members to ensure that all group work processes could be continued once the exchange had occurred. Where there were not complete matches, I had to acquire individual replacements to round out the KSA gaps for the arriving unit.

This two-step planning process was an expedient-type Diamond Process Model application and was critical to the success of the first force rotation in OIF. The critical integration process we created became standard procedure for joint force rotations. This process has since been used for every follow-on rotation by the US Army during the Iraq and Afghanistan campaigns.

If the initial integration of resources with processes was not balanced, then the force rotation would have been at severe risk and could have cost the US government countless dollars and potentially the lives of our service members.

THE BALOMETER©

Correcting imbalances is just as important as identifying them. But often the corrective action becomes much easier and more precisely targeted once the identification has taken place. Both identifying and correcting imbalances will enable leaders to stay on top of the processes they are vested with leading and will make them a better leader of people.

Since imbalance identification is so critical, we've created a software tool called the Balometer to assist. This software tool is associated with the Diamond Process Model and identifies where the different elements in your organization are out of balance; it will show you what needs to be addressed if you are to meet your key drivers. The Balometer also provides a menu of corrective actions that can be executed to bring the organization back in balance.

APPLYING THE DIAMOND PROCESS METHOD

Now that you have a good understanding of DPM fundamentals, be assured that your investment of time is about to pay major dividends. It was essential that we develop a shared understanding of DPM elements—the relationship between elements, and the interdependencies of components—so we don't have to do any backtracking when we start applying the model to your business.

Now that you are prepared, we'll address how you can apply the Diamond Process Model to your organization. More importantly, you can begin to view your organization using the Diamond perspective. Equipped with your new "DPM Goggles," you will begin to see obvious areas of improvement for your organization that you may have overlooked in the past.

Next, we will present the two methods for applying the DPM.

They are quite simple: The first method is for businesses that do not yet exist. The second is for transforming existing organizations.

CHAPTER 8

DPM: THE METHOD TO THE METHOD

Now that we understand the Diamond Process Model elements, components, and how they relate to each other, it is time to put this knowledge to good use. We have created two methods for applying the DPM to your company. The first, called the *blank sheet* approach, is for organizations that do not exist. The second method, *conversion*, is used for existing companies.

The blank sheet approach is most useful if you are starting a new enterprise and are designing the organization and its work processes for the first time. Using this systematic process will be better than simply allowing your company to evolve sporadically.

STARTING FROM SCRATCH

We designed the blank sheet approach under the assumption that, at the start, a company will at least have a single leader and a business plan. Some entrepreneurs who are well-versed at start-ups may even have a team and some financing. But how do we get started correctly to build that well-balanced organizational empire? The answer is to start with the *what*.

Based on our experiences, we've found that most leaders begin

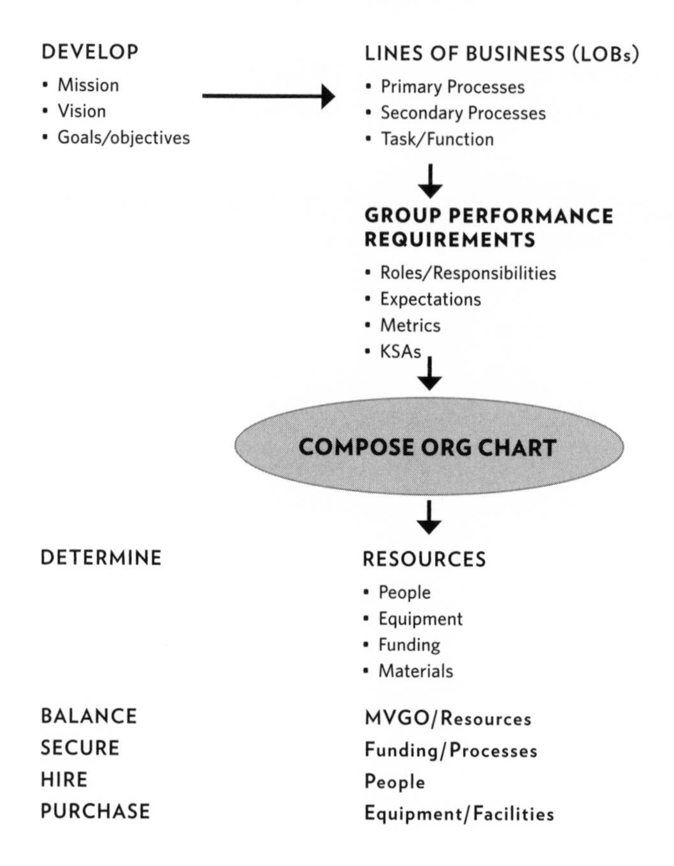

structuring an organization based on *who* the players are going to be rather than *what* work must be done. Aside from your start-up team, the *what* is much more important in establishing the foundation of a new organization and its attendant processes than the *who*.

Mike worked for a software development company whose leadership was trying to promote a growth strategy, or so they thought. There really was no strategy to it; they were just into growing. One of the business owners would continuously solicit new work; when he landed a new customer he would come back to the office and tell the other owners. They would then pick a middle manager and say "go do it."

The middle manager would put together a team to fill positions for the new segment. The company moved the workers into a new office together and told them to make it happen. Each time this occurred, the people in the new section did not understand *what* needed to be done or who needed to do it. This created a very chaotic situation, which made the workers unsettled.

This leadership approach produced two kinds of workers in the company. The first were the apathetic long-term employees who took the "here we go again" attitude. The second were the newcomers who would simply quit within their first year.

The problem with the people-first approach is you are starting at the bottom of the Diamond Process Model and working up. People are resources that drive work processes, not the other way around. You must understand what work you need to accomplish before you decide what resources you need to enable the work.

We feel this fundamental flaw is tied to our core argument that people think of *leadership* as the art of leading *people* only. When starting an organization, it is crucial we think of process up front. We must identify what we want to do (key drivers), how we are going to do it (work processes), and what we need to make it happen (resources).

We must start organizing a business with the top-down DPM approach. As we explained in chapter 2, this starts by setting key strategic drivers in a strategic planning session. Once the mission, vision, goals, and objectives have been established, you have started defining the *what*. The mission identifies *what today*, while the vision identifies *what tomorrow*; goals and objectives are your path to get from here to there.

Next, we will go through each of the steps in the process component, which include defining lines of business (LOBs) and your primary/secondary processes. Once you organize the process work in the LOB, you can determine requirements for group roles, responsibilities, and expectations.

While following the Diamond Process, you should always ensure that your processes support your strategic plan. This exercise will ensure you are maintaining balance between the key driver component and the work process component. Don't be surprised if it takes several iterations to get it right.

Once your work processes are aligned with key drivers, you can apply resources to fuel the process requirements. This is where you bring in the people to drive your primary and secondary processes. Remember to take the KSA approach, discussed in chapter 5, to plan for the *ultimate employee.* Also, pay close attention to KSA gaps once you assign someone to fill a role or position, since shortfalls in knowledge, skills, or abilities can create process weakness.

Initially assigning people to processes can be a daunting exercise. It is best to start with the number and types of workers you need to fill the highest-level primary processes. This allows you to start fueling your organization with human resources and will enable you to start turning those requirements into capabilities. Also, your first hires can help you navigate the rest of the work requirements if they are equipped with the proper KSAs.

Once people are assigned, you must decide what training and equipment they need. Keep in mind that training and equipment varies depending on who you hire. So consider what we talked about in chapter 7: the relationship between *people* and *equipment* elements in the *resource* component.

The last stage of the blank sheet approach is to determine the initial capital investment you need to fund the people and equipment that drive your processes. Again, you need to ensure that all of the resources are balanced with the processes they are supporting. Once you execute the blank sheet process step-by-step, you will have a good handle on what the organization will look like and what resources are needed to fuel your process requirements.

A GENERAL'S REFLECTION

In 2003, several weeks after the ground campaign in OPERATION: Iraqi Freedom, I took charge of the Theater Support Command. My predecessor left me with a headquarters (HQ) staff of 75 people that were left over from his original staff of 475. I also had 27,000 soldiers under my command whom this limited staff was supposed to manage. My orders were to clean up the leftovers and get ready to redeploy back to the United States by Christmas. After all, we had won the war, right?

As history has taught us, the OIF campaign was just getting started; we just didn't realize it at first. I was expected to be sending units home, but it seemed like everyone was staying and we were busier than ever. Then I noticed our coalition partners showing up with new units, which increased my support requirements, and I realized we were in this thing for the long haul.

When the mission changed from "draw down forces and come home" to "build and secure Iraq," so did our requirements. Essentially I was a deployed commander in need of a blank sheet approach. I had a new mission without a complete staff organization to support it. I had not established a new vision or goals and objectives to get there.

I immediately grabbed my key strategic leaders and began conducting strategic planning sessions. Our objective was to develop a new strategic plan that would establish requirements and allow us to get the additional resources needed to meet our new mission.

We followed the blank sheet approach and hammered out all the processes the command staff would perform based on the work required with the new mission set. We created flowcharts and process

Continued

maps for all the primary and secondary processes we needed. We then identified all the resources we would require to fuel the processes to meet our key drivers.

We came up with 250 positions needed to accomplish the work. I notified my senior leadership in theater that I needed another 175 HQ staff. After meeting with some colorful resistance, I showed him the requirements; and the positions were filled over the next three months. In the meantime, we turned focus to supporting our primary processes until our reinforcements arrived.

Over a decade later, the new 250-person HQ staff we created is still being used. The blank sheet approach proved to be both timely and productive for my staff and me in developing the processes and resources needed to command a logistics theater of operations during a time of war. The blank sheet approach enabled us to be successful as it allowed us to identify the necessary resources needed to accomplish key drivers during combat support operations.

TIMING

After you complete the blank sheet approach, you should have a framework of the work that needs to be accomplished and the people who need to perform it. Another critical factor is to decide *when* to execute your plan. Applying resources too early can create waste and increase cost. Applying them too late can cripple your processes.

We recommend a carefully planned time-phased approach. Phasing allows you to regulate the flow of resources in smaller chunks, which eases the management burden. This also helps promote balance because you can take more time to make sure the resources are applied correctly in accordance with your plan.

Phasing allows you to enliven your primary processes with much-needed resources. It is also easier on the budget since you won't need as much initial capital. You can execute your plan over a period of time and spread out the capital resource burden.

When phasing in resources, be mindful of changes. Sometimes reality presents unknown challenges that were not captured during the planning stages. When this occurs, make sure you keep your Diamond Process Model updated so your documentation continues to mirror what is actually going on in your organization as well as its changing dynamics.

MERGERS, ACQUISITIONS, AND RE-ORGS

Aside from starting a brand new company, there are other situations that require the blank sheet approach such as mergers, re-orgs, or new acquisitions. In all of these situations, leaders are challenged with taking what they have and creating something new.

Starting with something is oftentimes more difficult than starting with nothing. With mergers and acquisitions, you are forced to combine processes and resources with contrasting organizational constructs. The terms "merge" and "acquire" both suggest you must combine what is there. A better way to approach the situation is to "create" something entirely new.

Similar to our approach for hiring someone based on KSAs, you should create the new "ultimate" company. Use the blank sheet approach to formulate your strategic plan, develop work processes, and identify requirements to drive those processes.

This approach will provide leadership with an unbiased and objective view of how the organization should be set up. It will also capture the work processes that need to be accomplished to adequately support your lines of business and, ultimately, the strategic plan. Once the blank sheet approach is accomplished, the right resources, including people, can be assigned to ensure support of your key drivers.

This process also gives a rationale to decision makers. Mergers, acquisitions, and re-orgs can often be political events riddled with stress and emotions because the natural feeling is that someone (or many people) will lose their job. Following the blank sheet approach, strategic leaders can make these tough decisions based on what the new company needs rather than what some employees want.

The blank sheet approach is not always appropriate for every situation. It works great when you are starting with nothing, but if you already have an existing organization, you need to take a different approach: *conversion*.

CONVERTING TO THE DPM

CONVERSION APPROACH

Old/Merged/Acquired Organization

- Record Model Elements from current Org. to determine "AS IS"
- Develop a model of the Org. as if new—"TO BE" (Use Blank Sheet Approach)
- Compare/Adjust/Modify as needed to gain efficiencies, especially in support/overhead areas

If you are in the middle of a merger and you've used the blank sheet DPM approach to define your ultimate company, you may run into problems when you try to decide which of the old company's resources to use for your new organization. This is especially true if the previous companies do not have processes and resources organized in a DPM-friendly format.

This is also the situation we most commonly deal with on the consulting side of our business, since most leaders call upon us to help fix what is already there. When we arrive, we start teaching the Diamond

Process Model and usually win leaders over pretty quickly when they realize something is missing in their organization. But before we can truly identify the many corrective actions we need to fix the company, we must first convert what they do to the DPM format.

The first step in conversion is to accurately *mirror* the current state of your company. We emphasize the word mirror because as leaders, we are naturally inclined to fix things when we see problems. But before we try to fix anything, we must capture an accurate reflection of *exactly* what it is your company is doing.

Mirroring is a general course of action that is similar to a doctor's office performing lab work when you go in for your annual physical. Your physician needs the results of your lab work to help understand your current condition, provide you a diagnosis, and consequently decide treatment. Once you perform mirroring, you have an accurate reflection of your company's current operations, whether they are right, wrong, or indifferent.

Whether performing a blank sheet or conversion approach, the Diamond Process Model always works the same. You start at the top of the organization with your key drivers, accurately capture the MVGOs in your strategic plan, and record them. If you do not have vision or objectives, simply record that you do not have them.

When moving down to the process component, there is usually much work to do because people generally do not lead processes. You must record your current lines of business (or what you think are your current LOBs) and accurately capture your existing processes. Record all of the groups and individuals and their assigned tasks and roles. If you do not have process maps and flowcharts, do not create them, as you will be tempted to create or fix processes rather than accurately recording what you have.

Moving on through the resource component, accurately identify the people, equipment, and capital you currently use to accomplish the work. With organizations that have no processes, you can mirror resources based on which resources are applied to a particular group. Organizing by group or function under the work process component, you can convert somewhat to the DPM as some processes can be understood.

Once you have mirrored your current organization into a Diamond Process Model format, you can now perform the analysis and see exactly where you stand in terms of balance and what is out of balance. In many cases, we have had organizations quite befuddled at what they find after performing the mirroring process.

We usually find gaping holes in how companies operate. We discover primary processes with insufficient people and capital resources applied to achieving goals. We find no processes applied to achieving a vision. We find funding all over the place in terms of balancing people and equipment. We find groups who are assigned to perform the same task, yet the task never seems to get performed. But most important of all, we find areas for improvement.

It can be a very humbling experience to review the results of your mirror analysis, but it is a good remedy for knowing where you stand with running a balanced and focused organization. Many find they have been focusing on less important things and are improperly resourced to meet what they thought were their key drivers.

A GENERAL'S REFLECTION

When I was a Captain back in the mid '80s, I had transferred from active duty Army to a traditional reservist. I landed a civilian job as a first-line supervisor for a valve manufacturing company. This was one of my first supervisory positions outside the military, and I was quite overwhelmed when I arrived on the job. The previous supervisor had been terminated for mismanaging the unit, and it was my job to get everyone back on track.

My new job was to lead a shop of ten people that were responsible for storing, shipping, and handling a warehouse full of supplies and raw materials used for making valves. Although I did not have the Diamond Process Model formulated back then, I can still think back and remember some of the things I did right and how it helped me realize just how messed up this company was.

I was not a strategic leader so I had nothing to do with the key drivers, and I frankly cannot remember if the company even had a mission or vision statement. I was at the work level, though, and remember how messed up their operations were. My boss told me our biggest problem was keeping the inventory management system updated to keep track of what materials we had in the warehouse.

I wanted to organize the work we needed to perform so I remember capturing what we did on paper through a mirroring-type process. I quickly realized there was no process, which meant people were the process. From a unit perspective, I had three disparate islands of people and they were separated in cliques.

There was one worker who was a raw materials manager, and he was the "one-man show" for all the raw materials processes. Another worker was in charge of pipe parts and sub-assemblies. The third island was the warehouse, which did receiving for the entire company. None of these entities felt the need to communicate anything to anyone else.

It was then I realized my supervisor was not in tune with the real problems. He was correct in that the inventory management system was not getting updated; but this was only a symptom of a much larger issue. The biggest problem was lack of communication and process to accomplish work.

Before we delve into the troubleshooting portion of the book, we wanted to convey that you don't have to be a General Officer in charge of 20,000 people to use the Diamond Process Model. Through the DPM perspective, we can see what is wrong with our organizations and have an idea of what and how to change.

Even if you are not a positional leader, when others in your office realize something is not right, you can offer a different perspective on how to fix it. The Diamond Process Model can help you recognize when things are out of balance, and that vision can enable you to be a better follower and leader.

DIAGNOSTIC RECAPITULATION

Most of us are already in business and are dealing with day-to-day leadership issues. In fact, many of you probably picked up this book to gain some insights on how to fix your organization or how to be a better leader. The first step to becoming a better leader is to convert what you currently do to the DPM format through mirroring; the next step is to troubleshoot.

Up to this point, we've spent a lot of time preparing the battlefield by explaining background information on the model so you can begin to see things from a DPM perspective. Now you are ready to embrace and understand what is at the core of most dysfunction in companies.

Diagnostic recapitulation is at the heart of what we do as leaders and consultants: We identify problems, innovate solutions, and execute. Effectively troubleshooting an organization is so vitally important to complete leadership, we are dedicating the rest of the book to help you!

In the next three chapters, we will provide you with examples of common problems that we've seen as leaders and consultants at the executive/strategic level of leadership, the operational/middle manager level of leadership, and the tactical/first-line level of leadership.

In each chapter, we will also provide fixes for each of these problems from the perspective of the Diamond Process Model perspective.

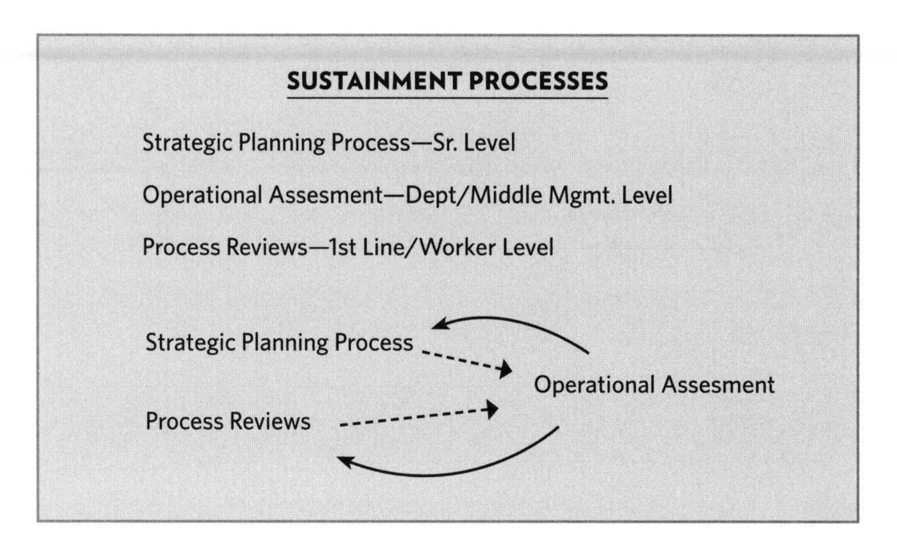

CHAPTER 9

THE IVORY TOWER

EXECUTIVE-LEVEL STRATEGIC ASSESSMENTS

In the rest of this book, we will be enlightening you with all the ways companies can go adrift by failing to maintain balance. The following chapters will arm you with tools we've developed through years of experience and will show you how to use those tools to become a complete leader.

Our goal in this exercise is to provide you a new way of thinking to begin problem solving in your organization. As consultants, we try to identify specific problems by asking questions, as the answers are usually telling. This technique may not solve all of your unique problems here, but it will provide you with a new way to look at your organization.

Throughout each section, we will ask questions that you and other leaders should be asking yourselves. The answers to these questions are the first steps in identifying the problem and will give you food for thought in developing your own DPM experience and strategic inputs. Each section will address these questions with common problems, and present the relevant fixes for each situation.

With this format, it should be possible for you to develop an action plan to use to improve or correct situations that exist in your own organization. We have used this action plan format in training classes so as to equip students with this valuable tool that they can immediately put to work.

We have included our version of the personal action plan (PAP) on our website at DiamondStrategyGroup.com as a free download. Don't hesitate to contact us if you have questions about applying the PAP to your specific situation.

You are now familiar with the Diamond Process so it's time to put this information to good use. Remember that our goal as we perform diagnostic recapitulation is to help you achieve balance in your organization. The Diamond Process Model, and balance, start at the top with key drivers; so we begin by troubleshooting problems with the mission, vision, goals, and objectives. If the key drivers are not right, they will throw the rest of your company out of balance.

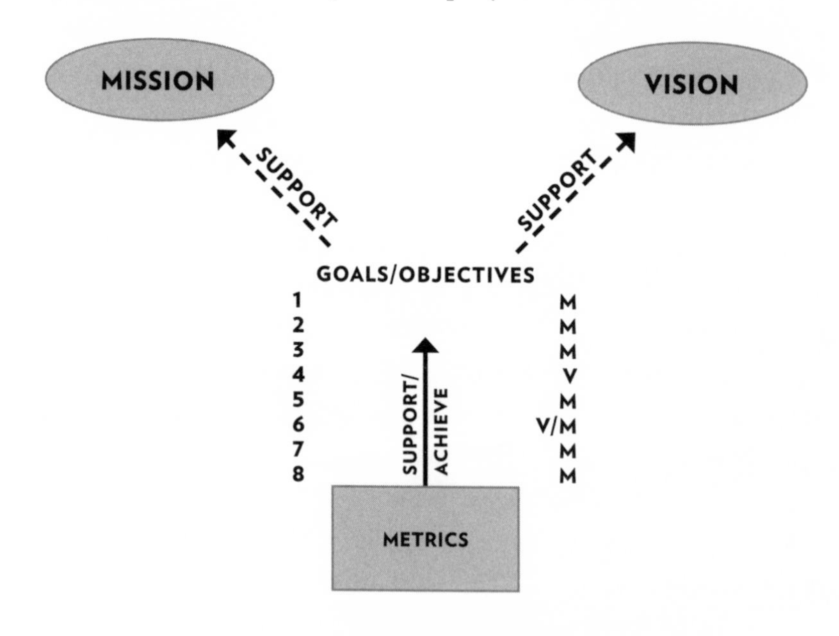

MISSION

"Do we have a mission statement?"

Although this is an obvious question, realistically many organizations simply do not have a mission statement. If you remember from chapter two, the mission statement communicates why you show up to work each day. Not having one is like telling your employees they should just stay home.

Some leaders argue their business is too small to have a mission statement. To this we offer that the mission statement is a key element in the strategic drivers because it tells the employee why the company *needs* them to show up every day. An organization is never too small to remind their employees why they are needed.

If you do not have a mission statement, make one in your next strategic planning session. Don't go crazy trying to make some fancy statement, as playing with words is really not the point. Simply capture your key thoughts that reflect what you truly get up each morning to do through your work and what you want to accomplish.

"Is our mission statement unique?"

A common problem we find with large organizations is that they are a part of a larger unit with which they share the same mission statement. If you share a mission statement with a parent or subordinate organization, it means you are effectively doing the same thing.

Different levels of organizations (like national chains) should be focused on different factors such as support, geographic area, product lines, customers, etc. Later, the work process component will capture how the organization is to deliver on these factors. There should be some particular focus on a single unit that delineates them from the other organizations and allows their processes to be unique in each organization's LOB.

"Is our mission statement current, and does it reflect changes in our external environment?"

Sometimes missions change but the mission statement does not. In military organizations some units are "assigned" a new mission. In the civilian sector, external conditions sometimes force a company to alter its path.

When these situations occur, it is essential to update the mission statement to reflect what you are actually doing. Remember, we are trying to achieve balance; everything you do should be tied to the key drivers in the strategic plan. If you change the mission statement, it needs to be recorded and analyzed because it can have cascading effects on the other DPM elements.

In chapter two we discussed conducting strategic planning sessions and reviewing external factors to ensure your mission is current with laws, markets, and technology. Occasionally external environments change and strategic leaders do not update the mission statement to stay in tune with the changes.

This oversight can cause a company to lose focus on strategic direction because everyone is marching to an old tune. It is important to keep your mission statement updated to ensure balance and unity of effort.

Mike was advising a Colonel who was a newly assigned business development coordinator for the US Army. The Colonel was representing an Army logistics organization and was responsible for soliciting transportation services to other government agencies. The Colonel felt like his boss was not recognizing what he needed to do in order to be successful in his current position, so he asked Mike for help.

When Mike asked him what his mission statement was, the statement did not include the work that the Colonel was doing. After deep diving, Mike realized that the Colonel was assigned to perform new work for this organization because the external environment had recently changed.

Congress had passed new laws that allowed the Army to solicit this type of business. But the organization slated to perform this function did not update their strategic plan in response to the change in the external environment.

What resulted was a disconnect between the new mission that the Colonel was trying to perform and the old mission that was supported by the organization. Since the organization was not set up to support this new function, the unit lost numerous opportunities to develop business and reduce transportation costs for the government. The dysfunction also resulted in a talented senior officer becoming underutilized.

The fix for all problems related to mission statements is to conduct periodic strategic planning sessions. These sessions will not only allow you to ensure you have a mission statement that reflects what you want to do, but it will also give you opportunities to update it to keep current with external factors.

As we discussed in "A General's Reflection" in chapter two, Mike was a commander for the 32nd Transportation Group and noticed the unit was focusing on day-to-day activities but had no real purpose to their efforts. He used a strategic planning session to provide focus to the leadership of that organization, and this resonated through the entire unit. This one session set the new strategic plan in motion, which gave the unit's members a stronger sense of purpose, unity of effort, and increased the efficiency, productivity, and morale for the entire organization.

VISION

"Do we have a vision statement?"

Without a doubt, the most common problem with a company's vision is that it does not exist. This is problematic because your vision is something in the future that you want to move your organization toward.

Mike once worked as Vice President of Strategic Planning and Logistics for a software development company. Shortly after he arrived, Mike realized the company had no strategic direction. Nor did they have a vision statement.

Mike sat down and wrote a key driver set of his own. When he presented what he had drafted to the owner, Mike was told to forget about it. The owner said, "We don't want to box ourselves in with that stuff. We just want to drum up more business."

For the next two years at the company, Mike had the feeling everyone was just walking around aimlessly. The lack of direction weighed on everyone, which was part of the reason their turnover was so high.

How you intend to grow the business will also impact your vision. You may not have the current resources to achieve that vision, but if it doesn't exist then you aren't headed anywhere. Without a vision your organization will become stagnant and growth will be absent. The best you can hope for is to survive.

If you do not have a vision, create one. As we discussed in chapter 2, the vision is the sole responsibility of the senior leader in the organization. Once the key leader has put his or her vision out there for everyone to see, it is wise to allow other subordinate leaders to tweak or make recommendations to improve it. But again, a vision is the key leader's responsibility and something that should not be delegated.

"Have we communicated our vision?"

There is no point to having a vision if nobody knows what it is. As we discussed in chapter 2, a good vision statement can build loyalty with subordinates if it appeals to a shared set of ideals.

A good litmus test is to talk to random workers in your organization and ask them if they understand your vision. You don't necessarily have to put them on the spot, but a quick conversation will let you know if they get it. Another thing we like to do is ask employees of large organizations what their CEO's vision is. You'd be surprised at how many don't know.

If your people do not know your vision, you can resolve that by communicating it. Company events make great opportunities to get the word out. Some companies use posters and flyers. We have found that word of mouth works best, so make sure your immediate subordinates know the vision and urge them to communicate it downward.

A GENERAL'S REFLECTION

In the late '70s I finished my active-duty tour and entered the US Army Reserve. I landed my first job in the private sector and was working as a district operations manager for a building supply company called Moore Handley Homecrafters (MHH). We sold everything there was to sell to building contractors including lumber, nails, tin, roofing—the whole nine yards. I had the responsibility for work processes, deliveries, and inventory management for thirteen stores in the Birmingham, Nashville, and Jacksonville areas.

Continued

At that particular point in time, the building materials markets were all based around building contractors. If you were a do-it-yourself (DIY) type person, everyone would consider you an outsider if you came into one of our warehouses, and you'd probably get some funny looks. This was because DIY was not recognized as a consumer market back then.

Another trait of our business was that all of the markets were small and localized, because that's just the way it was. Back in the '70s, everyone went to their local hardware store, there were few chains, and our customer area was based in small cities around the Southeast US.

I remember when we got a new CEO named Bruce Jacobs. I remember meeting him in some business meetings and my impression was that he was very intelligent and arrogant. He was also hard to communicate with because he seemed to be introverted. Bruce seemed like a duck out of water because he had a background in soft-line merchandising and came to us from Montgomery Ward department store. Fittingly, some of us referred to him as the "bras and panties guy."

Mr. Jacobs had this big idea to revolutionize the building materials business by instituting large warehouse retail stores to serve large metro markets. His intent was to capture the emerging DIY market opportunities. But this business model included expanding our product lines as well as the size of our stores focusing on the DIY market. It included putting stores in major cities like Atlanta, GA, and Memphis, TN, where we had no name or brand recognition. Store size would increase anywhere from 500% to 1000%, which presented quite a challenge for leaders who had been managing stores with 7,000 square feet of floor space.

Many people thought Mr. Jacobs was completely out of line with his vision for MHH building supply. What he wanted to do was so dramatically different from what we did that employees did not buy in. We workers also had the perception that he was trying to force his merchandise background on the building supply market without understanding the impacts it could have.

At the same time all this was going on, the economy declined. Our business did not do well and we began to divest. MHH began selling assets and downsizing, and many of our buildings and products went to this little-known regional company out of North Carolina called Lowe's.

What we did not realize was that Bruce Jacobs had developed the recipe that would eventually become the one Home Depot and Lowe's used in the next decade with monumental success. Moore Handley Homecrafters did not achieve the vision set forth by Mr. Jacobs, partially because of timing and markets, but also because that vision had not been communicated effectively, and he did not get the buy in needed from the subordinate leaders in the company.

"When do we plan to achieve our vision?"

Since a vision communicates the desired future state of a company, it is wise to consider how much time you will need for your organization to accomplish this vision. One problem we see often is a vision that is too near-sighted.

If a vision statement is too oriented to the near-term, then it does not constitute a vision and ends up looking more like a goal. Some leaders even disguise their "vision" as a goal because they do not understand the difference. If this happens, you will suffer the same problems as if you did not have a vision.

On the other hand, some leaders set a vision that is too future-oriented. If the key leader sets a vision that is too far out there, he or she can create a situation that causes the organization to lose sight of the mission. This can also create a tug-of-war for resources between current operations and the desired future state of the company.

Richard Branson is a world-renowned entrepreneur and is the founder of *Virgin Group*, which includes *Virgin Airlines* and now *Virgin Galactic,* soon to offer tourist rides to space for the price of $200,000 per ticket. Although this feat seems feasible today, Mr. Branson had ideas of commercial space travel much earlier. In 2012, he was quoted as saying, "In my lifetime, I'm determined to being a part of starting a population on Mars" (Kaiser, 2012).

At times, we see a key leader who has a vision that outpaces the organization, which can create a chasm between the key leader and the organization as a whole. Some corporate leaders are such visionaries that their thoughts are in the distant future and seem almost to be dreams.

If these leaders fail to communicate this vision and to get buy-in from subordinates, then the key leader is leading with no one following. If this happens, the desired future state turns from a vision to a dream because without support, it will not happen.

The fix for timing problems is to analyze the vision statement at your strategic planning sessions and consider the size of your company in relation to the desired future state. You simply need to understand the size of your organization and depict a vision that fits.

An extremely large organization should have a vision that is seven to ten years out, while a smaller organization should focus on the three- to five-year mark. This is because vision statements are tied to growth or change; it takes less time for smaller companies to change while it takes longer for large ones.

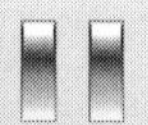

CAPTAIN'S CORNER

I once worked for a military organization whose senior leader seemed genuinely concerned about the well-being of the unit and its members. This particular leader was quite possibly the smartest person I've ever met. I really liked his leadership style and, as a result, I worked very hard to contribute to his organizational goals.

Since he was so intelligent, I really wanted to learn from him and gain insight by asking him leadership questions. However, he was so busy, I didn't get to see him very much and I also didn't get the opportunity to ask him about his leadership philosophy.

He was real big on feedback, so he had us complete anonymous surveys pretty frequently. At the end of a particular survey there was a section for "additional comments," and I decided to take the opportunity to probe him about his leadership philosophy. I simply stated, "I do not know what your vision is for this organization."

At our next "all-call," which is a unit gathering where the senior leader has the chance to address the members of an organization, he decided to go over the results of the anonymous survey. I was only half paying attention until he said, "Someone wrote that they don't know what our mission is!"

What followed was a twenty-minute presentation on our weapon system and why it is needed to win wars. I appreciated the effort, but I think everyone knew our mission. However, he had misunderstood the question: I asked him what his *vision* was for the organization; and he answered what the *mission* was.

A very common mistake is that strategic leaders confuse the mission with vision and vice versa. They are completely separate and represent very different things. Also, if the smartest man I ever met can make this mistake, so can you!

GOALS AND OBJECTIVES

"Have we established goals and objectives for our company?"

Mission is what you do every day, vision is what you want to be tomorrow, and goals and objectives are the path that connect the two. If you simply don't have goals or objectives, no one in your organization will know what you are doing and where you are going.

"Do our goals and objectives support the mission and vision in our strategic plan?"

Goals and objectives should be tied closely to your mission and vision. During strategic planning sessions, once you determine what your mission and vision are, determine what your organization needs to do in order to achieve them. When your organization starts to accomplish these goals, you will know that you have achieved unity of effort in your company.

Mike led the Coalition Coordination Center (CCC) at US Central Command, which had a mission to provide support services for the coalition of sixty-two nations that served with the US in Iraq and Afghanistan. Although there was no vision when he arrived, Mike quickly created a vision: "To see that supported coalition countries succeed in Iraq and Afghanistan."

Mike also realized the organization did not have goals and objectives that supported the mission and vision. The majority of the coalition members were in Europe, yet there was little coordination with the US European Command (EUCOM), which was located amidst these European countries.

Mike set goals and objectives that helped open critical lines of communication with EUCOM staff members thus enabling the CCC staff to provide enormously improved support to these coalition countries by working with US military staff near their geographic locations.

By creating a vision statement, and supporting it with goals and objectives, Mike was able to achieve balance in the CCC organization and provide a level of support that was unseen to date. As a result, coalition nations were being equipped and trained much better to achieve their individual missions in combat operations.

"Do we use goals and objectives to measure performance?"

Goals and objectives are performance targets and you can easily use them as the basis for performance measures. Metrics can communicate your company's ability to meet goals and objectives to achieve your mission today and move toward your vision.

Just as your goals and objectives should be tied to your mission and vision, your metrics should be tied to your goals and objectives. Everything in the Diamond Process Model is designed to balance your company and tie everything to the key drivers in the strategic plan. Without process and results measures that are linked to your key drivers, you have no way to determine whether your company is successful and/or effective.

"Do we have goals and objectives that are time sensitive?"

One key attribute of goals and objectives is that they need to be time sensitive. There are short-term, intermediate, and long-term goals that you should have in any organization. The time sensitivity needs to parallel the size of your organization, such as with the vision statement.

The common mistake with long-term goals is they are not integrated into the vision of the key leader. Long-term goals allow organizational leaders to determine if the company is moving toward the desired future state. Similarly, short-term goals are often not tied to the mission of the organization so leaders cannot measure performance of the current state of the company.

To remedy inadequate long- and short-term goals, analyze them during periodic strategic planning sessions. If you do not have goals and objectives integrated into the strategic plan, do so. If you do have them integrated, then use the strategic planning session to discuss performance of the organization and modify goals for the future.

"Do we have goals that are attainable?"

It is the leader's responsibility to set up workers for success. This means having processes established and providing adequate resources to achieve the goals and objectives outlined in the strategic plan.

Inadequate resources applied to goals and objectives can cause sub-optimized performance, increase worker frustration, and can be detrimental to productivity and profits. If goals and objectives are not supported with the proper processes and resources, they become incomplete; even though they are stated, they are impossible to achieve.

The solution for unattainable goals is to prioritize them in strategic planning sessions. If goals are given a priority, then the processes should have priority for the resources. If resources are simply not available, strategic leaders can use the planning session to determine what is more vital for the company.

"Do we have realistic goals?"

One common problem is that companies become too goal-oriented and have a plethora of goals and objectives. These situations breed chaos and also indicate that the goals and objectives are not aligned with the company's resources.

Too many goals can also give workers the perception that they are not meeting expectations, and thus lead to increased turnover. This is the classic case of doing too much with too little. When "more with less" becomes "everything with nothing," it is time to act strategically.

The solution is to prioritize which goals and objectives are most important to achieve the mission and vision in the strategic plan. Sometimes you can combine goals and objectives or prioritize out some of the extras.

As with the other strategic-level executive assessments, the key remedy is to conduct periodic strategic planning sessions; this is where strategic leaders converge and decide the direction of the organization.

But make sure you capture the content of these sessions by assigning someone as the *keeper* of the strategic plan. Having a single individual trained to record the outcome of these sessions and capture them accurately in the strategic plan ensures quality of the plan. It also designates someone to focus on all these key questions to guide key leaders in accomplishing the critical work at the strategic level.

Strategic leaders should work with the recorder to ensure a proper agenda is set prior to the meeting so other leaders can come to the table with ideas on how to improve the organization. A meeting agenda or list of topics distributed prior to the meeting is also a great idea as it solicits feedback from the participants.

☆☆

A GENERAL'S REFLECTION

In my thirty-five-year military career, I have experienced numerous high-level organizations that have functional sub-units called future operations (FUOPS). These units are responsible for planning future military contingency plans, which should be a part of any strategic planning function.

The obvious choice for someone to take charge of keeping track of the strategic plan would be someone in the FUOPS section. But I've found that contingency planning is only a small subset of the overall focus of the entire organization's strategic plan.

These FUOPS planning units are not in tune with current operations. Lack of focus on current operations is a shortfall for an entity that is supposed to be in charge of maintaining the entire strategic plan. I also realized that in some places, people have a false sense of security, as they believe the strategic planning function is covered because they have FUOPS.

Continued

In my experience, I've found that strategic plans have much higher quality when the responsibility to keep and maintain the plan falls on one individual. This single person directs all efforts related to the strategic plan to include reviews, updates, and impacts. A single person can maintain the strategic plan with a focus between current operations and future planning. In my past, I've dedicated this responsibility to one individual and have had them report directly to me in the chain of command. My "keeper of the plan" approach has paid huge dividends throughout my career and has allowed my organizations to achieve balance.

When using the Diamond Process Model, it is crucial for senior leaders to establish key drivers so they can be *linked* down the organization. Linking occurs when a leader, who has been designated as the champion of a specific goal or objective, establishes connections with all the necessary subordinate leaders, processes, and resources needed to ensure the success of that key driver. Aside from CEOs and small-business owners, most of us do not participate in strategic discussions for our organizations. But understanding these common problems and fixes can provide some insights about what you, as a leader, should be up to on a regular basis.

Next we move toward common problems associated with lines of business. Most people should be able to identify with these issues as this is where the work takes place.

CHAPTER 10

AT THE HEART OF THE MATTER

OPERATIONAL/MIDDLE MANAGER LEVEL ASSESSMENTS

When Mike was a General, he looked at Colonels and Lieutenant Colonels as the ones who made stuff happen. They were the ones who had the ability to absorb the strategic message and transform it into operational and tactical terms so it could be executed. As operational/mid-level managers, you have the power to get things done. You control the processes, resources, and people to change your organization!

If strategic leaders have done their part in setting key drivers in the strategic plan, operational leaders can balance an organization. We discussed *linking* in the last chapter; this is where a leader is designated as a champion of a key driver and must link all the organizational assets down the organization to ensure the key driver is met. This concept is key for operational leaders because they are usually the champions responsible for specific key drivers.

LINK/ SINK/ INTEGRATION

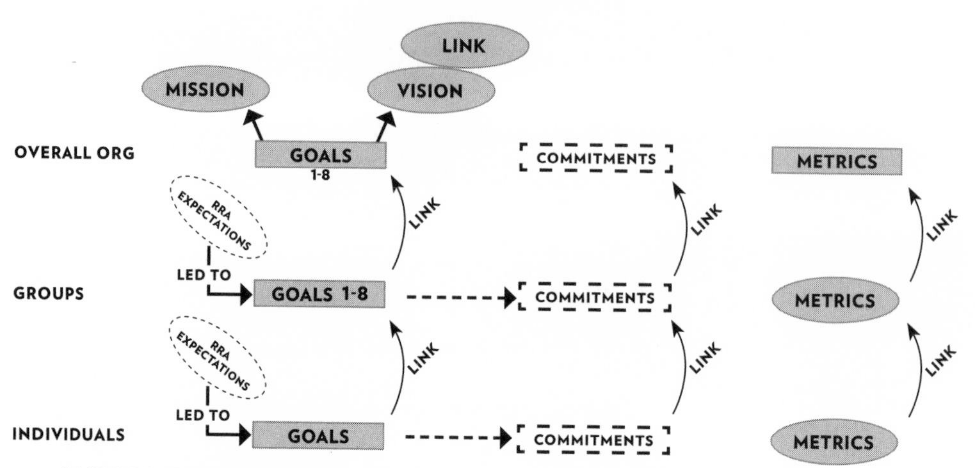

EACH INDIVIDUAL SHOULD KNOW WHAT OVERALL GOAL(S) THEY ARE CONTRIBUTING TO

SYNC

CHAMPION/ PROCESS LEADER	GROUP(S) X 2	INDIVIDUAL(S)	GOAL METRIC
1			
2			
3			
4			
5			
6			
7			
8			

EACH CHAMPION AND PROCESS LEADER SHOULD KNOW WHAT GROUP(S) AND INDIVIDUAL(S) ARE RESPONSIBLE, ACCOUNTABLE, COMMITTED TO CONTRIBUTE TO THAT GOAL/PROCESS

Aside from *linking*, operational leaders must also *synchronize* the organization. *Syncing* occurs when a leader, designated as a key driver champion, communicates with other champions as well as senior leaders to ensure all efforts are achieving the overall intent of the strategic plan. If done properly, operational leaders can achieve greatness by *linking and syncing* an organization.

But in order to realize this potential, operational/mid-level leaders must focus their efforts on making sure they understand the key strategic drivers, and then organize and sustain the work to make it happen.

LINES OF BUSINESS

The Diamond Process Model reflects the strategic-to-operational leadership crossover by visually depicting a handoff from key drivers to lines of business (LOB). Executives in an organization rely on department heads to conduct operational assessments of the company's LOBs to ensure that the work performed in a company supports the strategic plan.

OPERATIONAL ASSESSMENT

L.O.B.s
- **PROCESSES**
  - **PRIMARY**
  - **SECONDARY**
    - **TASK/FUNCTION**

PROCESS REVIEWS
STRATEGIC PLAN (AS UPDATED FROM SR.LEVEL)
EXTERNAL ENVIRONMENT IMPACTS
- **REGULATORY**
- **MARKETS**
- **TECHNOLOGY**

GAP ANALYSIS
PROCESS IMPROVEMENTS
RESOURCES
METRICS

It is during these operational assessment meetings where department heads should ask themselves our next set of questions. Answers generated from asking these questions can be communicated back up to strategic leaders to provide them critical information on whether or not the organization is set up to achieve strategic drivers. Answers should also be communicated down to subordinates to keep them informed on their role in performing the processes that achieve the organization's key drivers.

A GENERAL'S REFLECTION

After I created a vision with the accompanying goals and objectives at my Director's job with CCC at CENTCOM, I challenged my operational/mid-level leaders to conduct an operational assessment to support the new key drivers. My objective for this group of leaders was to examine their lines of business (and supporting processes) to ensure the organization was balanced with the strategic plan and met the requirements of our customers, the coalition nations.

Once I gave them my objective, I empowered the group by delegating the authority they needed to make the necessary changes in the way the organization conducted business. Taking newfound ownership and responsibility for their work, my operational leaders came back with a much-improved construct that enabled the organization to function more productively and efficiently.

Under my direction, the operational leaders made process maps and flowcharts, organized the work, and realized they had to make drastic changes. Instead of organizing themselves in teams like they had in the past, they realized they needed to accept roles and responsibilities, specialize in one area of expertise, and trade services with each of the other staff sections.

These changes, initiated by the operational leaders, resulted in a complete organizational re-alignment. They organized themselves in departments, created a new org chart, assigned themselves roles and responsibilities, outlined expectations to each other, and allocated the necessary resources to each group to ensure the organization was successful.

This exercise resulted in the unit better performing its mission, increased efficiency and effectiveness, and improved morale in the entire organization. The changes we instituted saved time and money, decreased redundancies, consolidated work, and gave everyone a sense of purpose. But the real winners in this scenario were our customers.

The coalition countries we supported realized we were getting them training and equipment much quicker than we had in the past. We were preparing them to help us at war and were holding up our end of the bargain. This built trust among all the coalition nations, as well as the diplomats at many levels whose responsibility it was to cut through the red tape and coordinate this level of support.

This goes to show you the power of operational/mid-level leaders. In less than ninety days, they were able to completely revamp an organization according to my strategic direction. I gave them guidance, the tools that they needed to succeed, got the hell out of the way, and let them astound me with a winning product.

"Do we have clearly defined LOBs with processes that support them?"

A line of business is nothing more than the highest-level primary process that requires other processes to support it. LOBs are containers that hold all of the primary, secondary, and tertiary processes needed to achieve work. If the lines of business are ambiguous, the container is flawed as well as all of the sub-processes contained within.

If lines of business are not clear, it is the operational leader's responsibility to communicate to strategic leaders the need for a clearly defined LOB. Without clear definition of a line of business, some primary process may go unsupported, other processes will duplicate the same work and create waste, while resources will be under- or over-utilized.

The same is true for key drivers: If operational leaders do not understand the mission, vision, goals, or objectives in an organization, they should communicate with strategic leaders to gain clarity. The key drivers establish the foundation for processes through which work is accomplished. If exceptional operational leaders do not understand key drivers, you can rest assured that first-line supervisors and workers do not understand them either.

Operational assessments should take place periodically so that department heads can conduct critical reviews of LOBs and the processes within them. Oftentimes, first-line supervisors get accustomed to the way things are because that is their job: survive and overcome. Operational leaders should always keep a vision of how things *should* and *could* be as part of process improvement.

The responsibility for performing critical LOB reviews is primarily on department-level operational leaders to ensure processes are designed properly and operating at peak efficiency to support the overall line of business. The results from these reviews should be conveyed to senior leadership so they can consider these inputs in their strategic planning sessions.

Without process maps, flowcharts, and metrics, these assessments become ambiguous and subjective. If you do not map out and measure performance on the work, you have no idea what to review. Without clear process definition, you also have no idea what your people are doing—which is a common complaint from workers toward middle managers.

"Do our LOBs support the strategic plan?"

Regardless of why your company is in business, to be successful, everything you do must support the strategic plan. The military refers to this concept as *unity of command*. The mission is what you do today: Are your processes set up to accomplish the work that is required for you to succeed? The vision is what you want to do tomorrow: Do you have goals and objectives which, if achieved, will lead you down the correct path to realize the strategic vision for the organization?

One flaw in some organizational leaders is that they are not strategically focused. They have not developed the skill set to think strategically. Often, operational leaders are promoted because they are the senior technical or tactical experts in their functional area. But when filling the operational role, there is a need to think strategically in order to understand and enable key drivers and transform the mission, vision, goals, and objectives into actionable processes.

Some operational leaders do have a strategic focus and have homed in on key drivers. But sometimes during strategic planning sessions the plan changes. This is especially true for businesses operating in an environment with significant external forces that can modify the business plan. Often changes in technology, environmental regulations, or the external legal environment require strategic leaders to modify key drivers. The growth of an organization can alter the support required of the operational leaders as well.

Whatever the case may be, if the strategic plan changes, then so should the rest of the organizational supporting plans. It is the operational/mid-level leader's responsibility to analyze the changes in the strategic plan and adjust operational processes (LOBs) accordingly.

On the other hand, operational leaders should stay homed in on the external environment in which they operate and be aware of any changes that could drive a modification to the strategic plan. Strategic leaders will conduct SWOT analysis during strategic planning sessions, but they may not be aware of potential changes to the external environment. Operational leaders need to communicate any threats or opportunities to the keeper of the strategic plan so as to have that item as a topic of discussion during the next strategic planning session.

If you recall in November 2008 the federal government bailed out General Motors, Chrysler, and Ford. Since this was the first time in history that US citizens became stakeholders in a private company via federal tax dollars invested, there was much debate and scrutiny over the deal.

Congressional reports that came out of this bailout stated that the automakers were simply not in tune with the auto market, and no one wanted to buy American-made cars. Foreign automakers were dominating the market because they were answering consumer demands for fuel-efficient cars.

As a result of rising gas prices, the consumer market changed from big utility and sport vehicles to fuel-efficient ones. The Big Three failed to recognize changes in the external environment and adjust their strategic plan and lines of business to reflect the changes.

"Do we have a process for recognizing LOB changes?"

Do you, the operational manager, conduct critical operational assessments? Just as senior leaders should be involved in strategic planning sessions, operational leaders should perform assessments that are basically strategic sessions at the department-head level.

Meetings held with other operational leaders and department heads can be quite productive if each understands his or her own department-level processes. Operational assessments are also a great forum through which to analyze LOBs and establish operational-level processes to recognize LOB changes.

In many cases, due to external factors such as markets, technology, or legal, strategic leaders are forced to modify the strategic plan. A common mistake many operational leaders make is they do not change the work inside the LOB to reflect the changes in the strategic plan.

It is important when conducting operational assessments for operational leaders to review work processes and include any changes required to support the strategic plan. This includes conducting analysis on what external factors drove strategic leaders to update key drivers.

Considering LOBs are simply the highest-level process in one area of the business, we must take into account that they sometimes change based on growth/contraction of business or the economy. Sometimes primary processes turn into LOBs and vice versa.

This was the case for Hewlett-Packard when they realized there was a significant market for stand-alone printers. The original primary process to produce printers that supported the LOB of selling computer workstations turned into its own line of business as printer sales became dominant. Had someone not recognized this change, HP may have lost out on millions in revenue.

In a growth strategy, your company may have some primary and secondary processes established under research and development to test prototypes in a new market. If one product line becomes successful and begins providing lucrative gains, the market demand for your primary process may demand it be its own LOB.

If you do not conduct operational assessments and recognize the situation as an opportunity, the new venture could fail. Operational assessments can identify that this primary process needs to be a stand-alone line of business. More importantly, you can communicate successes to strategic leaders who can make decisions to apply more resources to the new LOB and update the strategic plan to reflect the change.

The timing to identify and promote a primary process into a new line of business can be critical for a company. Early action can result in increased market share and profits. Conducting regular operational assessments will ensure you have these opportunities.

If you do not have a process for recognizing change, it could cause a line of business to become inadequately supported. Ultimately, this creates an out-of-balance situation where resources will be allocated improperly. New LOBs will not be established; this will result in a missed opportunity. It can also create waste if you are throwing "good money after bad" or not properly resourcing a growing LOB or process.

If you have a line of business to produce goods to satisfy demand in a market and the market diminishes, then you are wasting resources if you keep resourcing the LOB as if it is producing at its previous levels. If your returns are diminishing, it is essential to downgrade the

LOB into a primary (or secondary) process to save resources. Otherwise, your company is wasting too many resources to support a line of business that is not producing returns.

"Do we have successful measures established to gauge performance?"

One effective way for operational leaders to track progress for specific functional areas in the organization is to align goals and objectives outlined in the key drivers to your specific department through performance measures. This practice will not only help you keep track of progress, but it will ensure unity of effort.

For example, if you have a growth strategy, a goal could be to increase sales by x% in ninety days. If the progress toward achieving this goal is tied to an accompanying performance metric, progress can be reviewed during operational assessments. If sales are increasing slower than anticipated, operational leaders can deep dive to the root cause of the problem and align resources to accomplish the goal.

During an operational assessment of an LOB, operational managers could realize there are an inadequate amount of sales personnel to increase sales. Another finding may be a lack of capital resources needed to increase the travel required for existing sales personnel to sell more products. Once these key limitations are identified, operational leaders can adjust resources accordingly in order to meet goals that are enablers for the strategic plan.

Once you align processes and resources to accomplish a strategically oriented goal, you need to establish process and/or result metrics and review them periodically. It is a good idea to invite first-line supervisors to the reviews so you can communicate to them whether they are meeting expectations.

First-line supervisor reviews will also help discern working-level effectiveness of strategy implementation and to garner feedback as to whether changes need to be made to processes or the attendant resources allocated so as to increase performance. If you do not have measures of performance established, there is no way to tell how you are progressing toward goals and objectives.

A GENERAL'S REFLECTION

In one of my first assignments as a junior operational leader, I was a unit commander for a combat-heavy engineering company (about 150 to 180 personnel). We were responsible for providing engineering support for road building. We ran a rock quarry to provide raw materials, we paved roads once the foundation was built, and even maintained the roads and the heavy equipment used to build them.

When I was conducting an operational assessment of my organization, I asked myself, "What is my single point of failure?" I determined that it was one particular first-line supervisor who was responsible for my most critical primary process. He led a group of people who performed direct support maintenance for all the engineering equipment in the entire battalion.

This individual was our best mechanic but did not understand the importance of supporting the organization's strategic goals. Our organization had a strategic objective to provide timely maintenance for other units so they could keep on schedule with their projects. Since this was a key driver, I had results metrics that calculated the turn-around times (TATs) so I could monitor how long it took us to perform our service and return equipment for use.

Our TATs were not improving or keeping up with our objectives, so I communicated several times to this particular supervisor that he needed to manage his people and processes in order to increase performance. I also told him to let me know if he needed more people or equipment in order to be successful.

Continued

The real problem was that he was more interested in performing maintenance than leading his section. Although he was a good maintenance technician, he did not understand how to lead the processes necessary to accomplish and organize work at the level we needed him to in order to achieve our goals and objectives.

To correct this deficiency, I ultimately had to remove this individual from his role as the first-line supervisor, and I replaced him with one of his subordinates. This was an unthinkable move in military terms because I was firing a guy with over thirty years of experience and replacing him with someone who was two ranks below him.

I changed the role of the former supervisor and had him serve as a mentor to the younger mechanics. Since he was an exceptional mechanic, I knew we could utilize his experience to teach maintenance discipline to the younger soldiers.

I personally mentored the replacement supervisor and taught him how to align processes and resources to achieve strategic goals. I also connected what he was doing to our strategic objectives and explained the importance of that unit's role in the larger organization. He hit the ground running and immediately started leading his people and processes.

The results from my changes were prolific in that the organization began, for the first time, to meet and exceed our senior leaders' expectations for maintenance of the battalion's equipment. Even better, the quality of the work the mechanics were doing was improving, and it was also apparent that the success was helping everyone enjoy their work.

Our new system worked so well that our unit morale went through the roof. We became known as *the* reserve unit to be in for this type of work. As a result, people started showing up wanting to be a part of it, and we were able to grow the overall organization. By the time I left, the organization had attracted eighty more people than when I showed up.

"Do we have LOBs that are mutually exclusive?"

If lines of business are not mutually exclusive or do not pass the LOB litmus test outlined in chapter three, an organization will likely suffer duplications of effort and misuse resources. Although it is the ultimate responsibility of strategic leaders to determine LOBs properly, operational leaders can recognize errors in their respective lines of business and communicate those shortfalls to strategic leaders for consideration.

When Chris was a new officer in the Air Force, he was in charge of managing people and equipment in an aircraft maintenance unit. This particular aircraft squadron was responsible for two primary missions: one for humanitarian relief and another for war.

The squadron managed people and equipment packages for each mission as two separate lines of business. Chris realized that regardless of the mission, the people and equipment only changed in quantities needed to perform each mission.

Chris notified his operational leadership who agreed to combine the LOBs and their processes so the people and equipment were managed the same for both missions. This merging of LOBs reduced redundancies in the unit, saved hundreds of man-hours, and reduced the administrative burden of managing separate deployment packages with similar equipment.

"Where do our processes cross LOBs?"

Some processes, such as financing, contracting, personnel administration, etc., are shared across multiple LOBs. It is important to know which of these processes are shared because if these processes are flawed, they can damage a large portion of the company in one fell swoop.

Often leaders do not necessarily view shared processes as critical; but we ask, "What happens if nobody in your company gets a paycheck next week because of an administration error?" To put it mildly, your workforce will likely get distracted and lose productivity.

Shared processes are critical because they affect large parts of the organization. It is critical to manage these processes with the utmost attention to detail so you can lower the risk of something negative happening to your business or your people. If you are the organization being supported by a shared process, it is important to provide feedback to the owner of the process.

Chris used to work in an aircraft program office and was responsible for modifying aircraft with improved technology for war-fighting. Although each aircraft type had its own program office, multiple program offices shared the same contracting officers. This is because contracting officers are highly skilled and require numerous certifications.

In the contracting office there were two special computers that allowed the contracting officers to access a certain system they needed to certify contracts. One computer was accessible to everyone, and the back-up computer was in a locked room for safekeeping.

One day the accessible computer crashed, which meant none of the contracting officers could certify contracts. The back-up computer that was in a locked room was also inaccessible, because the one guy who had the key was on vacation for two weeks.

This single-process oversight brought the entire contracting office to a stand-still. What was worse, the five aircraft program offices that relied on this one contracting office for service were also brought to a screeching halt because of one guy on vacation with a key. And no contracting actions could be accomplished until the one computer was repaired.

To mitigate risks, the operational leader who controls the processes of departments that execute support roles, such as finance, needs to educate other department heads on their processes and solicit feedback from the supported departments. For example, the operational leader for the payroll department needs to communicate with all other department heads to ensure members of the other units submit payroll data in the format that is needed to support the payroll process.

"How are groups/individuals integrated with our other organizational elements?"

All work processes need groups (and individuals) assigned to them along with clearly defined roles, responsibilities, and accompanying accountability. Even more so, all processes need a leader. Regardless of common practices we've seen and common misconceptions about process leadership, the simple fact is that processes do not lead themselves.

You'd be surprised at how many operational leaders we've consulted who don't claim responsibility for the processes that reside under their leadership purview. They quickly tell us that they lead the *people* but not the *processes* people accomplish. Successful operational leaders start with processes, assign groups and individuals to those processes, and ultimately satisfy the key drivers for an organization.

When operational leaders lack an understanding of process, those processes are not "led." When processes are not aggressively managed, leaders lose control over operations. This colossal mismanagement usually includes a failure to integrate resources, including human resources such as groups and individuals.

Another common mistake made by operational leadership is the fact that they assign business functions or responsibilities to a particular group of people, even though that group lacks process detail. This leads to lack of integration of particular individuals inside the group. Although quite common, this approach leaves too much to chance and creates an ambiguous situation where operational leaders lack positive control of the work inside LOBs.

The fix for these shortfalls is to first understand the work inside an

LOB down to the process level. Next, assign both groups *and* individuals to drive these processes so you will have positive control of all the work performed in your organization. Only by performing this work will you be able to achieve balance between people and process.

Once this work is accomplished, operational leaders will usually find shortfalls or excess personnel in their functional units. Make sure you communicate to strategic leadership existing shortfalls and prioritize which positions need to be filled first.

For excess personnel who have been identified as performing redundant work, communicate with other operational leaders as well as the affected employees so you can find opportunities to cross-train or swap personnel between functional departments.

THE BRIDGE: FROM OPERATIONAL TO FIRST-LINE

Never underestimate how important operational leaders can be to the success of any organization. In the Diamond Process Model, these are the leaders who provide the critical link between the key drivers and the work that is performed in a company. Operational leaders have the ability to take all of the work in an LOB and align it to the key drivers in the strategic plan.

But in order to achieve success, operational leaders must think strategically and always be aware of key strategic drivers and the strategic plan. These leaders must also maintain awareness and communicate any deficiencies up the chain of command to strategic leaders and down the chain to first-line supervisors. If operational leaders do these things well, they can ensure balance and unity of effort in an organization and move it closer to operating at a championship level.

Few of us are leaders at the operational level, but understanding how middle managers should be focused on their duties allows us insight as to how we can better communicate with them to focus their attention on relevant matters. Operational leaders have control of processes and resources and have the positional power to change organizations. But they cannot do it alone.

Middle managers rely on technical and tactical experts to ensure the work gets done right and that they have the correct information from the technical/tactical level to make good decisions at their own level of leadership. Just as operational managers are the glue that binds the key drivers and work process components, tactical managers are the gel that connects processes with people and other resources.

The next step on our journey to complete leadership is to understand how tactical, or first-line, supervisors relate to the Diamond Process Model. In the next chapter, we will examine common problems with leadership at the tactical level and provide some insights on how you can be a better supervisor or employee.

CHAPTER 11

WHERE THE RUBBER MEETS THE ROAD

FIRST-LINE SUPERVISOR CHALLENGES

First-line supervisors are at the battlefront of all work that gets performed in an organization. Not only are supervisors required to become tactical experts in their functional area, but they are also responsible for managing the workers and the "people issues" that arise. At this level of leadership, it is easy to get sucked in to dealing with management issues (paperwork, discipline, appraisals) and lose sight of the processes needed to accomplish the work.

Through our experiences, we've found that the most challenging part of getting first-line supervisors to lead processes is convincing them to take time away from management issues and stop "firefighting" long enough to perform the necessary process work. We've also seen that those who make this initial investment not only find that many "people issues" dissolve, but also begin to achieve balance and unity in the workplace. It is important to note that ISO certification standards require first-line supervisors to assume ownership of the processes they are responsible for and develop flowchart-based process control documents.

KNOW YOUR WORK

If you remember back in chapter four, we asked two important questions: "What are my single points of failure?" and "Why?" The answers to those questions should help you identify critical and primary processes from which you can prioritize and define work. Asking yourself these questions at this point in the chapter will get you in the right mindset to absorb what follows. This mindset will also help to address the follow-on questions of what the steps are and how they are accomplished.

A GENERAL'S REFLECTION

In 2004, while serving as Commander of the Theater Support Command in Iraq for OIF, we conducted the sizable OIF force rotation of 125,000 people and 250,000 pieces of equipment. After a few weeks of moving people and equipment in and out of theater, it became real obvious what our single point of failure was.

We had a requirement from US Customs to clean the returning equipment before we loaded it on the ships that would return to the unit's home base back in the States. We knew about this requirement and we had a couple wash racks we felt were capable of washing enough equipment to satisfy the operation.

What we did not realize is the cleanliness standards of the customs inspectors. They didn't just have white gloves but "white silk gloves." We weren't allowed to have one single speck of dust, or as they called it, "foreign soil," anywhere on our equipment. Imagine taking your family to the beach and having to make sure not one speck of sand was on any of the kids before they got back in your car to go home. Now imagine your kids are armored tanks and you have thousands of them. We were simply not prepared, considering the time it took to clean one piece of equipment to these standards.

We had to seek out someone who could replicate the KSAs needed to design and supervise this extensive cleaning activity. After exhaustive screening, we found a gold mine in one of our soldiers who ran a car wash back Stateside. I cannot remember the Captain's name, but we deemed him the "Wash Rack Czar," and at that point in my life he had the most important job on the planet.

Captain Czar designed the facility we needed along with the equipment required to accommodate it to adequately clean the massive amounts of Army-issue metal we were shipping out. Mind you, we're not just talking about setting up a washing station. Since we were in the desert where water is the most valuable natural resource, each cleaning station had to be designed as a 100% closed-loop system that caught the run-off water, cleaned it, and recycled it for use again. We felt like we had finally overcome our single point of failure, and the "attaboys" were in great supply.

Our celebration was short-lived, as we found that we could only get a small number of equipment units through the wash process and onto the ships each day. Although we were meeting the cleanliness requirements, it was still taking a significant amount of time per piece of equipment to get items through, and we were limited to running the wash racks during daylight hours due to low visibility.

As a result, we maintained a bottleneck that was getting us behind schedule, as our process and results measures were pointing out. In all my years having visions of serving as a Brigadier General, I never thought the biggest pain in my ass would be a wash rack.

Fast-forward a couple months to one afternoon when Captain Czar and I were briefing my boss, Major General Steve Speakes, during one of our metrics meetings. At this point I felt like we had

Continued

done all that we could do. With assistance from the great Captain Czar, we had built two separate wash facilities with a total of more than thirty separate washing stations to try to keep up with our schedule, but we were still lagging.

MG Speakes, who was clearly thinking outside the box that day, asked the Czar what would keep us from doing 24-hour operations. The Czar's reply was the need to see what we were cleaning and ensure that they met Customs cleanliness requirements. The other piece was that the US Customs inspectors only inspected during the day so they could see what they were inspecting.

The boss's answer was to acquire about fifty thousand dollars' worth of light sets that enabled us to wash around the clock. MG Speakes's influence was also helpful when he leveraged his high-ranking position to negotiate with the chief customs inspector to have his folks inspect around the clock.

We had identified and overcome that single point of failure (knowing what our work process needed to be) and succeeded at one of the most critical events that had to be done successfully to support combat operations in Iraq. When in a pinch, we leaders are pressed to come up with a solution; but we should be vigilant about our processes constantly so that we can make critical decisions more effectively and efficiently.

"Have we defined our work processes, sub-processes, tasks, and functions and organized them into flowcharts and process maps?"

Very few companies develop processes, so they don't know what they don't know. By not having a handle on process, you open yourself up to a myriad of problems. If something is broken, you cannot determine *what* is broken, *why* it is broken, or *how* broken it is.

For example, if you have a leak of water that manifests itself on the bottom unit of a sixteen-floor apartment building, you don't know whether the leak is coming from the first floor or one of the other fifteen floors. The same thing can happen with your processes if you have not drafted flowcharts and process maps for the work that gets accomplished in your organization.

Another problem is that without process development, everyone will have his or her own interpretation of what the process entails. In our consulting exercises, we often ask clients to tell us the steps in one of their particular processes. As we go around the room, we hear almost as many versions of the process as there are people in the room.

This ambiguity can create the prison mentality of "He who is loudest is right." Some first-line supervisors will direct their people to perform a process one way while other supervisors will direct their personnel to do it another way. This creates conflict between work sections and supervisors, results in worker unhappiness, and prevents balance and unity of effort.

THE GENERAL'S SYMPTOMS OF WORK PROCESS PROBLEMS

Aside from perceived "people issues," lack of process can cause other problems in an organization. Throughout this book, we provided a diagram called the Diamond Process Matrix, where we compiled a list of common symptoms that we've seen in troubled organizations. Using our past experiences, we highlighted the DPM areas that can cause these symptoms.

Through our analysis, we found that twenty-four out of twenty-seven total symptoms listed in the matrix can be tied back to process in some way. The diagram shown is a modified version of the Diamond Process Matrix, which shows only the eight leading symptoms primarily caused by lack of process.

To fix a process, you must first be able to understand it. For this

ORGANIZATIONAL & GROUP LEVEL					INDIVIDUAL			
SYMPTOMS	MVGO	LOBs	PROCESS	KSA	ROLE/ RESPONSIBILITY	EXPECTATION/ STDS	HUMAN RESOURCES	EQUIPMENT RESOURCES
A. WORK								
Duplication of work		X	X		X	X		X
Incomplete work		X	X	X	X	X	X	X
Poor work quality/ irregular or inconsistent product			X	X	X	X	X	X
Lower priority tasks performed before higher priority tasks	X		X		X	X		
Lack of process ownership			X	X	X	X		
B. PEOPLE								
High Turnover		X	X	X	X	X	X	
Individual Under-performer			X	X	X	X	X	X
People overworked	X		X	X	X	X	X	X
Confused workers / customers	X	X	X	X	X	X	X	
Numerous individual disciplinary issues			X	X	X	X	X	
Underperformance by supervisors/ subordinates	X		X	X	X	X	X	
Worker & Supervisor motivation / inspiration/ frustration	X		X	X	X	X		frustration only
Boredom	X	X	X	X	X	X	X	
C. ORGANIZATION								
Dysfunctional organization	X	X	X	X	X	X	X	X
Lack of growth	X	X		X	X	X	X	
Inability to accomplish primary mission	X	X		X	X	X	X	X
Lack of unified effort	X	X		X	X	X	X	
Not able to determine success or failure	X		X	X	X	X		
Lack of org effectiveness	X	X	X	X	X	X	X	X
Excessive outsourcing		X	X	X				X
D. RESOURCES-EQUIPMENT/PEOPLE/MONEY								
Idle equipment inventory			X					X
Premature depreciation/failure			X	X	X			X
Obsolescence			X					X
Excessive Overhead			X					
Misallocation of funding			X					
Lack of investment	X		X	X				
Lack of resources	X		X	X			X	X

Dark Grey shows the most important cause for the symptom

Medium Grey shows second most important causal factor for the symptom

Light Grey shows that this is a minor/possible cause

reason, you must do the work to build flowcharts and process maps if you want to understand how to optimize the work that is performed in your organization or work section.

With flowcharts and process maps you will be able to visualize and understand process problems and take the appropriate actions to correct process flaws. By planning and designing your work, you can preempt problems that may occur and react to symptoms before they arise.

Process maps and flowcharts also serve as great tools to train new employees as part of their orientation so they can see what gets accomplished in the organization and how. This can also improve the quality of the flowcharts and process maps, as the new workers have no previous understanding of the work and can bring a fresh set of eyes to it. They may see things more clearly and recommend changes to make the flowcharts and process maps better.

Since we have already stressed the importance of process maps and flowcharts, we will not repeat ourselves over these next three process questions. For the sake of this discussion, we will assume that you have at least recorded some basic processes via flowcharts and process maps.

THE PROCESS IMPROVEMENT PROCESS

"Do we have a process for process improvement?"

Process improvement does not happen by accident. Great organizations are keen on developing a process to handle process improvements. Process improvement exercises should be conducted at the tactical/first-line levels of leadership and overseen by mid-level/operational leaders because this is where the work happens.

If you do not have a process for process improvement, start scheduling periodic process reviews. Set goals in these reviews to establish process or improvement targets in your work section. If your business is growing rapidly, or if you have a process-intensive LOB like hard manufacturing, you will want to have process reviews more frequently.

Keep two things in mind when conducting process reviews: First, make sure the processes you lead are still being accomplished just as you have them recorded in your flowcharts and process maps. This approach stays true to our *mirroring* method for using the Diamond Process Model and ensures what's on paper matches reality.

Second, look for ways to improve the process. Analyze any process problems from feedback you have related to any process. These sources of feedback can be metrics, workers, other functional areas, quality assurance, or even customers. Look for ways to reduce the amount of resources needed to complete a process, decrease the time needed to complete it, or whatever the key drivers in your strategic plan require you to do.

Before presenting the following example by Mike, we need to define a couple of terms to explain a concept the military uses but that civilian organizations rarely understand. Some organizations are *supported*, whereas others are *supporting*. The supported unit is the one who is performing the main operational objective. All other units, for purposes of completing the objective, are supporting units.

For example, if a Navy SEAL team were to go out on a mission to rescue a downed pilot, they would be the supported unit. All other units such as intelligence, airlift, communications, fire support, and close air support would be the supporting units. We will use this reference in the following example, as well as the rest of the chapter, as it is helpful when understanding the roles of different departments or organizations in establishing support for processes.

In 2005 Mike returned from his one-year OIF deployment and was serving in his position as the Deputy Director of Logistics for US Central Command in Tampa, FL. The first item on his agenda when he returned to work was to fix the sea-land container debacle, which we used as "A General's Reflection" in chapter 1. But before he could tackle specific challenges, he needed to establish a process for process improvement.

Mike found two talented US Navy staff officers and gave them an additional role as members of his process improvement team. The first thing he had to do was train them on how to establish process maps and flowcharts so they could examine specific processes for bad handoffs and dead ends, and could establish process and results metrics to analyze the effectiveness of each process area.

Once Mike trained his staffers, they began applying the techniques to other supporting organizations, including US Army Transportation Command (TRANSCOM). They began analyzing ship times for parts leaving the US for the theater because there is arguably nothing more important in war than resupply. What they found was a target-rich environment for process improvement.

When the staffers brought Mike the details during their scheduled biweekly process improvement meetings, he started to get involved with the TRANSCOM leadership. Mike presented the process analysis information and began working with the supporting organization on getting parts to the shipping dock faster. As a result, supplies were now getting to the soldiers down-range up to 30% faster.

As results started piling up, this process improvement exercise started getting lots of attention and became quite contagious. The two-star Director of Logistics at TRANSCOM was so impressed that he created his own process improvement team and deployed the same techniques Mike was using with his team.

The TRANSCOM team continued work on their end, along with the two Navy staff officers from Mike's team, and produced even greater results. TRANSCOM logistics pulled the Defense Logistics Agency (DLA) into their process improvement effort, since DLA was a supporting organization to TRANSCOM. They devised a plan to outsource some of the shipping services for parts once the parts arrived in the theater of operations.

Ultimately the expanded process improvement team between DLA, CENTCOM, and TRANSCOM negotiated with the National Logistics Corporation (NLC) in Pakistan and reached an agreement for Pakistani contractors to ship parts once they arrived in the theater. This resulted in faster ship times, reduced costs, and ultimately saved lives of US soldiers who now didn't have to worry about running convoys through hostile territory. And to think all of this started with just a simple process improvement process initiated by Mike and two US Navy staff officers who were looking to fix a container problem.

THE WASTEFULNESS OF WASTE

"Do we have unnecessary redundancies?"

When Mike was a Captain he started working for a new organization as a first-line supervisor, and this was right about the time computers started making their way into the common office environment. He noticed the unit was producing dozens of handwritten reports at different frequencies; some were daily, others biweekly and monthly.

When he began mapping processes, Mike identified a dead end with one of the reports. He decided to investigate all of these reports and realized that two thirds of them were no longer needed. For the remaining third, he streamlined and digitized the process for reporting, which ended up providing a lot of time back to the workforce.

Redundancies are a huge problem for any business. If any process ever gets accomplished twice when the need is for it to happen only once, then you have 100% waste. If you ever go to any "Lean Six Sigma" or process improvement class, the first thing they will tell you is to eliminate waste, or *muda* as they call it, which is the Japanese word for "useless."

One redundant-rich environment is created when organizations reorganize, move departments around, acquire other companies, or merge with other sections. This is because most people don't take the time to look for inefficiencies or process improvement areas; they just pile it on and keep doing what they were doing before.

So when workers finally stop the merry-go-round and really do flowcharting and process mapping, it becomes the blinding flash of the obvious. People say, "Why haven't we done this before?"

SUPPORTING REDUNDANCIES

When translating the military concept of *supporting* versus *supported* units to the civilian sector, it is important to remember that the units or departments in your organization that are completing your strategic objectives are the supported units. Supported units can be sales, service operations, and manufacturing, just to name a few. The supporting units are contracting, human resources, payroll, or any other branch of your organization that helps another to achieve the main objective.

In business, process improvement is vitally important in supporting organizations because these organizations are usually seen as overhead. So if by improving processes you can also reduce overhead, it bodes well for your company.

Redundancies tend to be prevalent in supporting organizations because they are not mission oriented and usually do not understand the work that is performed by the supported organizations. Oftentimes this lack of understanding can be mitigated with good communication, but it is easy for units to get sucked into day-to-day activities without having the broader understanding of who you support and why.

Redundancies are also relevant in supported organizations. One reason is that leadership fails to conduct process reviews to eliminate waste and increase efficiency. Another is because the situation changes and the processes are not updated to reflect the changes. This can be anything from a change in operations, a change in people, or a change in equipment.

During process reviews, if a redundancy is discovered, it is essential to coordinate resolution with all parties who have a part in the process. It is important to achieve immediate resolution to eliminate the redundancy so it can no longer create waste in your company.

"Do our processes have bad handoffs?"

Bad handoffs can be discovered by examining process maps and flowcharts where a process transfers from one sub-unit to another. You can also get feedback on poor handoffs by reviewing process metrics that calculate handoff times. Bad handoffs usually present one of two problems: Either there is an unnecessary time lag or the process stops or turns into a *dead end.*

Bad handoffs usually occur because the handling group and the receiving group aren't communicating. Often the receiving unit has no idea the process is being transferred to them. Handoffs can be subtle and don't always shout, "Hey, it's your turn!" If the handling person sends an email to a receiving person, and the receiving person has 1500 emails in his or her inbox, there will likely be a time lag. In this case, clicking "send" does *not* constitute communication!

Dead-end processes constitute another common problem with handoffs. Many supporting units create reports for supported units. Sometimes the situation changes and the supported units no longer need these reports. The problem is that no one tells the supporting organization, so the reports keep coming. Dead ends are wasteful and are easily detected in process reviews. If a process suddenly stops, all a first-line supervisor has to do is ask, "Why?"

Process reviews are vitally important to any organization because they can capture many process problems and improve the efficiency of your company. We suggest you update process maps and flowcharts during process reviews and have all of the relevant supervisors in the room to agree on the changes. Another good idea is to sign and date the process maps to avoid any changes before the next meeting.

Mike learned early on in his career, while managing inventory warehouses, the importance of process maps and flowcharts. As a young Lieutenant he managed obsolete parts for obsolete vessels that the US Army was still using in some operations. Since nearly all of the parts in his warehouse were obsolete, he had to figure out which ones were still being used and which were of no use to anyone.

Only by mapping out processes was he able to identify the truly obsolete inventory. It was a good thing, too, because carrying inventory that is no longer needed is not only a dead-end process but is also wasteful. Inventory is the polar opposite of wine; it does not get better with age.

Carrying inventory is one of the greatest costs for a company, as it requires space to store, money to buy and maintain, and man hours counting and accounting for all of the stock on hand. If this inventory is no longer needed, then all of the resources to acquire and maintain it are a complete waste.

But without process maps and flowcharts, any attempt to remove obsolete inventory may do more damage than good. If Mike had unknowingly thrown away usable parts in an effort to reduce waste, he could have put the US Army, and himself, in quite a predicament. Mapping out processes helped him prevent these problems.

SAY WHAT YOU MEAN; MEAN WHAT YOU SAY

"Do we hold people accountable?"

As we discussed in chapter five, accountability is only possible once groups and individuals have been assigned roles, responsibilities, and expectations. As a tactical/first-line supervisor, you cannot hold people accountable for what they don't know.

People are not only a resource assigned to enable a process, but they also drive the process. Some individual or group should be assigned ultimate responsibility over each process in your work section. If they are not, you will have processes that are driving themselves; this becomes dangerous because you will not have positive control of the work performed in your section.

You should also make sure each individual or group in your section understands which person is assigned as the process leader. If everyone knows the single point of contact (POC) for each process, you can ensure you receive all the feedback for process problems. Having a single POC also helps when you need a representative to attend process reviews.

Another reason processes go uncontrolled is because there are so many people in the process. If several work sections are involved in completing a single process, you can easily have a situation where everyone is in charge, but no one is in charge. Although these situations need to be resolved at the middle-manager/operational level of leadership, first-line supervisors have a responsibility to communicate these challenges up the chain of command.

Once individuals and groups have been assigned processes for them to lead, you can hold them accountable. Flowcharts and process maps become the basis for assigning responsibility and accountability for steps in a process or the process as a whole.

Process responsibility can be easily captured in the individual employee's commitments to communicate roles and expectations. Likewise, process performance feedback makes great inputs for individual performance reviews. Tying an individual's performance rating directly to group and process success aligns the worker's goals with the organization's goals. Metrics in the form of process and results measures can also be used as inputs toward people's appraisals and can provide a firm basis for employee recognition.

Ultimately having groups and individuals accountable for processes in an organization ensures success. It also makes sure that people are doing their part in sharing the workload of the unit. Sometimes you may find that some of your good people are failing not because of bad processes or poor performance, but simply because they are trying to do the work of five people.

WHODUNIT?

"Do our employees have a balanced workload?"

Perhaps there's no better murder mystery in the business realm than the mystery of why some first-line supervisors murder the careers of their best employees by overloading them with too much work. Work overload can cause some of your best employees to feel (and look) like failures because they have so much to do, they can only hope to survive and are prevented from thriving.

We talked about the 80/20 rule in chapter 7, where first-line supervisors allow 80% of the work to be accomplished by 20% of the people. The only reason 80/20 is present in any organization is because supervisors allow it to exist. Although this approach may be effective at accomplishing the entire workload, it is unfair to those who bear the burden. It is also self-defeating as it denies growth and development for the 80% category of people.

Aside from your great employees being perceived as mediocre or under-performing, living by the 80/20 rule can create worker unhappiness in the unit. Your workhorses can get burned out from the workload and perturbed at other workers who are not pulling their weight. Also, the other 80% can get ticked off if you suddenly decide to make them start working for a change. Additionally, those with a strong work ethic can get perturbed if they are underutilized or feel as though they are not trusted with higher levels of responsibility.

The best fix to avoid this type of a mess is to fairly and systematically assign roles, responsibilities, expectations, and accountability through process leadership. Distribute the workload in your functional sub-unit based on the knowledge, skills, and abilities of your workers. Measure success via process and results-based metrics and communicate this success (or failure) in frequent feedback sessions with employees.

Invite groups and individuals assigned to drive processes to your process reviews so they can get feedback from others. This helps to avoid a situation where workers think you are unfairly targeting them or trying to single them out. During your feedback sessions, simply reflect what others have said regarding process.

When Mike was assigned as an Operations Officer for an engineering group, he wanted to become familiar with the type of work his employees were doing on a day-to-day basis. He had each worker create a *smart book*, which outlined some basic flowcharts and process maps for the work they performed.

Mike reviewed the smart books with the other leaders of the organization and realized the workload was unbalanced. He resolved the situation by redistributing the workload equally among employees based on the individual's knowledge, skills, and ability level.

He then communicated the new roles and responsibilities to each member of the organization in an expectations brief. He also let them know they would be held accountable for ensuring the success of each of their newly assigned processes. For Mike, the smart books turned out to be such tremendous resources at that point in his career, he has used them ever since.

WORK WITH WHAT YOU HAVE, TRY TO GET WHAT YOU NEED

"Are we communicating resource shortfalls?"

Everyone in business is used to doing more with less, but you can't do everything with nothing. First-line/tactical supervisors understand this more than anyone in the organization because they are the ones who organize the work and have to deal with shortfalls. But there are things you can do to help the situation.

First, you need to take the *KSA approach* when dealing with resources such as people, equipment, and capital; that is, plan for the optimal situation. In a perfect world, first-line supervisors should be looking for ways to optimize their units into champion work sections. Design the ultimate work unit based on no resource limitations, then compare those requirements to what you have today.

The gap left between what you ultimately desire and what you already have denotes your resource shortfalls. Next, prioritize your *needs* from your *wants* and determine where you need to place your limited resources to survive. Also, prioritize where you would place additional resources if they were to become available, all the while considering the goals and objectives outlined in the strategic plan.

Once you have organized work and resources in this fashion, it is easier to communicate shortfalls to operational leaders. Keeping the boss apprised of these wants/needs on a constant basis is good communication and accomplishes a few good things.

First, it shows your supervisor you are actively engaged with the problems of your section. Second, it provides operational leaders an opportunity to provide feedback and recommendations of which you may not be aware. Third, it builds good working relationships between the middle and lower levels of leadership. Finally, it gives your operational/middle managers ammunition they can use to fight for resources if or when they become available.

The bottom line is that tactical/first-line supervisors understand what they have, what they want, and what they need. Any good tactical leader will fight to get their people the resources they need to succeed and overcome shortfalls.

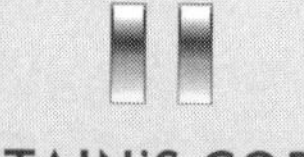

CAPTAIN'S CORNER

My first assignment in the Air Force was as a maintenance officer at Creech AFB, NV. As a brand-new Second Lieutenant, I was responsible for a Maintenance Flight of seventy-five people who performed maintenance and servicing for aircraft support equipment.

One of our flight's responsibilities was to maintain the equipment needed to support aircraft deployments. This equipment included numerous items the flight-line maintainers needed to work on aircraft in a deployed location such as generators, air compressors, bench grinders, tool cribs, engine hoists, aircraft jacks, etc.

My first day on the job I met my senior enlisted Flight Chief, Master Sergeant Chesnutt. He was a seasoned veteran and had over twenty years of experience taking care of Aerospace Ground Equipment (AGE). MSgt Chesnutt was a jolly fellow who liked to tell stories, and it was apparent he had a good handle on running the flight.

During one of his stories, he was telling me how he had been trying for two years to get a storage unit so our maintenance folks could store some deployment equipment, and how his previous Officers-in-Charge (OICs) had failed to deliver. I immediately saw this as an opportunity because, as his leader, I knew I had to do something to win his trust and let him know that I was going to look out for the needs of our unit.

I scoured Creech AFB for two days until I finally found a storage unit for MSgt Chesnutt. I found the owner of the units, did the required paperwork, and got it transferred to our flight's equipment account. I will never forget calling MSgt Chesnutt on the phone and asking him, "Hey, do you have a forklift?" Of course I knew he had one but it was a great set-up. He said, "Yes, why?" I responded, "You wanted a storage unit, right? It's waiting for you to pick it up."

I felt great as a first-line supervisor because I had delivered where others had failed. I prioritized the needs of the Airmen who were performing great work and I won over the Flight Chief immediately. MSgt Chesnutt, being the storyteller he is, told everyone he came in contact with the story of how I got him a storage unit and how I was an awesome leader.

This single event helped me build trust with my team, and they knew they could depend on me as a leader. They also realized that if I was capable of overcoming that one hurdle, I could probably be of use with other issues. For the remainder of my time in the unit, countless Airmen approached me and MSgt Chesnutt with other shortfalls that we worked through together. I could tell our subordinates were inspired to have leadership willing to fight for what they needed to succeed.

"Do our people have the right knowledge, skills, and abilities?"

Not all of your resource shortfalls are related to equipment or money. Sometimes you have the quantity of people you need to perform work, but not the quality. All processes need a leader and sometimes, as a first-line supervisor, you have a process that is not piloted by the right person.

Make sure you record this shortfall as a KSA gap and get the person some training if funds are available. If not, make a contingency plan to help that person until they get the needed training. If money is the issue, communicate to your operational leadership the importance of the needed training and explain it from a process perspective. Another way to get training is on-the-job training (OJT) or mentoring, so there are ways to mitigate KSA gaps even when funds are short.

Leaders must understand that the ultimate responsibility for training their people resides with them and them alone. Once a first-line supervisor discovers a training discrepancy, he or she must fight for the resources to fill that need. Otherwise, the supervisor will just be playing "catch" and have a bag full of problems at the end of each day.

Since the most common KSA shortfall is lack of experience, not all shortfalls can be resolved with training. It is incumbent on the first-line supervisor to work with each respective employee to develop an action plan to mitigate any lack of experience.

Some solutions may include working with other sections within the organization to cross-train employees or conduct on-the-job training with more experienced personnel. It is left up to the creativity of the first-line supervisor to correct this situation.

★★

A GENERAL'S REFLECTION

When I was deployed to Iraq in 2003/04, my duty day normally went into the wee hours of the night and ended with what my attorney and I dubbed "Night Court." All of my legal issues were handled at the end of my day, normally after midnight. One of the more prominent issues that we handled was *negligent discharges,* which is what the US Army calls a firearm that goes off when its owner didn't mean it to.

Those of you not familiar with the military legal system should know that each military member is held to the Uniform Code of Military Justice (UCMJ). The UCMJ allows military "Commanders" the authority to award Non-Judicial Punishment (NJP) for UCMJ infractions. NJP can be anything from reduction in rank, reduction in pay, forfeiture of pay, restriction, or probation in any combination; and the Commander is judge and jury.

I preferred to handle the Night Court visits as training experiences for the guilty because handling a weapon is one of those processes that US Army soldiers just ought to know how to do well. Instead of simply having the person that discharged the firearm come pay me a visit in the late hours, I had them bring their first-line supervisor and their unit commander.

When they were all in the room in front of me I always had the perpetrator go through the incident with excruciating detail. They usually tried to roll through it fast, so I would ask them questions such as "How many people were present there?" and "What was the lighting like?" until they got the point to go slow and not exclude anything they could remember. This process usually gave me a chance to size up the situation, the accused, the supervisor, and commander all in one fell swoop.

When the soldier who discharged the weapon finally stopped talking, I would turn and look at the first-line supervisor and ask him or her about the training they provided to the individual. I would then ask the Commander what actions they took to ensure the training did in fact occur.

These sessions would last thirty to forty-five minutes each and proved to be quite painful for the participants. But I wanted each and every participant to feel the weight of responsibility for training and the impending repercussions of not training properly. From the feedback I received, the soldiers who reported to night court once did NOT want to come back for another visit with me.

In the military, training is everybody's business and is something I'd like to see civilian organizations adopt. We win wars due to our training, as that's one of the most essential factors in building the ultimate employee. If training deficiencies exist, they should be identified at the lowest levels of leadership and should be passed up the chain of command. Then, as leaders, we all take responsibility and fight until we have the resources to make it happen.

First-line supervisors are critical to an organization because they are where the rubber meets the road and are the *first responders* in an organization. Supervisors at this level understand the work that needs to be accomplished in a specific area of an organization and are the experts for that work. Leaders at this level should be able to identify shortfalls in processes as well as the resources applied to them; it is essential they effectively communicate these discrepancies up the chain of command and fight for remedies.

Up to this point, we have discussed unique problems at the top, middle, and lower tiers of leadership. This is exactly what we do when we go to an organization and coach/train/consult its leadership. But if this were a normal coaching or training session, you would not have had the added benefit of "listening in" on the other conversations.

You should now have keener insight because you have been involved in the troubleshooting process at each leadership level. You should begin to see how leaders at the different levels of an organization are linked, both in life and with the Diamond Process method. This linkage is a good thing because once everyone starts walking down the same path, you will have unity of effort and will begin realizing returns on your process investment and moving your organization forward.

It is now time to continue our troubleshooting, not from a specific level of leadership perspective, but for all leaders at every level. Regardless of your current position, there are some challenges that we all share. In chapter 12 we will give you some *process enablers* that are crucial to understand in order to lead processes (and people) the right way.

CHAPTER 12

THE HELPING HANDS

Regardless of where you work or at what level of leadership, the Diamond Process Model helps you organize work through process development. Whether your job requires you to formulate a strategic plan, make process maps and flowcharts, or discover training shortfalls with your personnel, it all leads to the same general result, which is identifying organizational requirements.

Once you establish requirements you must turn them into capabilities by applying resources, whether they be human, equipment, or capital. This is where we've seen companies fail time and time again by applying (or failing to apply) resources of the wrong kind, at the wrong quality or quantity, and at the wrong place.

When using the DPM to integrate resources, we must start with people first because they are the most important resource within your organization. People lead processes, enable processes with manpower, improve processes by reporting deficiencies, and enable each other's processes through effective communication.

In the next chapter, we will show you how to apply resources to processes using the Diamond Process Model; including people, equipment, and capital. But people are much more than a simple static resource. For this reason, it is necessary for us to discuss in this chapter what it is that makes people different, and how we should address these differences.

USING PROCESS ENABLERS TO EMPOWER PEOPLE

Unlike equipment and money, when we acquire people for our organization they are all unique. New employees arrive with different backgrounds and experiences, and they have the ability to learn and improve. And although people are a resource to our business, they often control the other two resources, which makes them much more important.

Since people are so important, we've identified some concepts called *Process Enablers* that will help you empower people to help your organization succeed. By going through this next set of questions you will see how to get the most out of your people so they can, in turn, get the most out of your processes (and other resources).

Good help is hard to find: Getting the right people

Since all processes need a leader, the ultimate process enabler is people. The problem is that businesses use inadequate hiring practices, so you often get the wrong person for the job from the very start. This is why we advocate using the KSA method to hire the "optimal employee" for a position that supports your mission, vision, goals, and objectives in the strategic plan of the organization.

According to Forbes.com, four out of the top nine "hottest trends in corporate recruiting" are software related. This software does everything from applicant screening and potential employee tracking to metadata analysis on how to get the "best" employee. But if everything is measured against an oversimplified job description, you are not likely to find the type of worker you are seeking (Bersin, 2013).

By using the KSA method to hire people, the method itself

becomes a process enabler because it forces you to do a thorough job of identifying all of the salient requirements for the job. If you have the right people, you can integrate them to processes that will drive your company to meet or exceed the key drivers in the strategic plan. There are several questions we ask to gauge whether a company is using the correct approach for new hires.

"What is our process for capturing the KSAs needed for people to drive work processes?"

The overall responsibility and process for hiring new employees reside with the Human Resources (HR) department. HR should lead the process used to hire new people and also lead the process to track the KSAs needed for each position.

Although the Human Resources department owns the hiring process, they are a supporting role for the overall organization. The hiring process should be designed with this support function in mind, which means HR will cooperate with the other operational departments to identify the right knowledge, skills, and abilities for the person that you are hiring to be your future process leader.

The largest mistake companies make when hiring new employees is what Mike refers to as "job description syndrome." This is where the hiring supervisor describes a position on a piece of paper or email and sends it to HR, who then screens an applicant's resume and schedules an interview.

It should not be surprising that putting in this little analysis yields a new employee that is not suitable for the job. Especially when there is growing evidence that the resume/interview process is a weak hiring method in and of itself (Bateson, Wirtz, Burke, and Vaughan, 2013).

Correct job analysis should include evaluating the processes that need a leader. Once this work is done you should have a good idea of the background experience and any associated skills the new hire may need to be an ideal candidate and have the potential to evolve into a champion employee. Any KSA shortfalls should be coordinated from the HR department to the owning organization so the leadership who is to receive the new employee can discuss tradeoffs for the position.

The same goes for hiring workers that will fill leadership positions. To capture the true experiences, knowledge, and abilities needed to meet a supervisory role requires time, insight, and dedication. Some people subscribe to the philosophy that a supervisor is a supervisor is a supervisor; this is dangerous because these individuals will be leading your people who drive your processes; and this hiring method can lead to mediocrity.

"Are we hiring and training people to help us achieve our vision?"

Achieving unity of effort in an organization means that everything you do is tied to the key drivers in the strategic plan. The reason you hire employees in the first place is so you can turn resource requirements into organizational capabilities. Processes need people to lead and execute them. Companies need processes to meet today's mission and to achieve goals and objectives that move the organization toward the company's vision tomorrow.

One fundamental flaw in some organizations is that they do not hire workers with the company's vision in mind. They have a *live for today* mentality and are merely in survival mode. Hiring new employees with the company's vision in mind is essential, as it increases the capability of the work force and also increases flexibility so your team can react to change while striving toward the vision of the company.

In order to meet the desired future state of your company (vision), it is important to keep in mind what the employee of the future looks like. There are many ways to characterize what this employee needs to look like on paper. The easiest is to use the benchmarking technique copied from a best practice pioneered by a similar organization. You can also develop your own way by recording the KSAs you want for your ultimate employee. The important thing is to know where you want your organization to go and what kind of employee you need to get you there.

Once you have established the ultimate, world-class employee of the future, it is possible to compare that to what you have today in an existing worker or new hire. Then you can decide how to mitigate the KSA gaps to get to where you need to be to meet the vision of your strategic leadership. Sometimes the person driving a process needs to be replaced or swapped with a different person. Other times the worker/process match is fine to meet the mission, but the employee simply needs to train or develop to meet the desired future state of the company.

"Do we have adequate training programs?"

Common training programs include new-employee training (NET), professional development, and continuing education programs. Training programs can be process enablers because they mitigate KSA gaps and prepare the people in your company to meet future challenges.

Within large organizations, in order for employee training to be adequate, the programs need to be managed by the HR department to ensure standardization, consistency, and quality. Similar to KSA management for new hires, other operational departments should give continuous feedback to Human Resources to ensure new workers are getting sufficient high-quality training when they first arrive.

Let us caution: We are not talking about your grandma's orientation training. Yes, we need to make sure new workers understand where the bathrooms and emergency exits are located and how to fill out a time sheet. But more importantly, HR should be keeper of all the training materials for each department's specific training requirements as well as provide oversight to ensure new employees are trained correctly.

What we've seen is that some departments train new employees well while others sit the new guy in the corner, throw information at him, and just hope that something will stick. This is no way to treat or develop your future champion employee who has the potential to thrust your organization forward to meet the vision of your company.

As a certified trainer, Mike tends to pay attention to training scenarios more than most people. One of his hobbies is to evaluate the training of staff members at fast-food restaurants while he waits for his food.

Once he was standing in line at a local ice cream parlor near his home in Birmingham, AL, when he witnessed a brand-new employee arrive for his first day on the job. He witnessed the manager give the new employee a hat, apron, and headset, as well as assign him as the drive-through window cashier.

Mike stared in wonder as the new employee struggled to figure out the audio equipment and cash register—with no assistance. Later, when Mike got his food, he asked the kid what kind of training he'd received to help him on his first day. The young man said, "Sir, I don't have a clue. I guess I'll just do what they tell me."

New-employee training should enable new hires to be oriented on what tasks they should be performing up to the 80% task level. The quality of this program depends on the quality of input from other operational departments on how the tasks are performed. Much if not all of the inputs should come from process maps and flowcharts provided by the operational departments.

HR can keep the training materials for all departments in the NET master training plan. They can also oversee the new-employee training and ensure it gets accomplished the right way. The different departments can actually conduct the training sessions from either corporate trainers, supervisors, or peers via on-the-job training, but the HR department should oversee the process.

Continuing education programs are those training activities an employee receives that provide additional training beyond the introductory level to continue to help them be more effective workers in their current job. These programs should be designed to mitigate KSA gaps that have been identified between the employee and the requirements of their current position.

Continuing education activities should also keep pace with technological and other environmental changes to stay relevant. Again, much input is needed from other operational departments to ensure the training is adequate for the projected needs of the company.

Professional development programs are those educational activities aimed at mitigating KSA gaps for employees who will drive critical processes or fill needs of the organization at some point in the future. Many successful organizations have supervisor development programs so they can grow leaders within their organizations. These programs should be in line with the goals and objectives in the strategic plan so they can help the company move forward.

Training standards for all training programs should be at a champion level so employees are prepared to perform the work processes to which they are assigned. The point of employee training is not to simply fill a space with a person; it should optimize an organization based on a role that an individual fills or is preparing for in their assigned group.

Mike recently visited a training conference where a pharmaceutical company won a *Training Magazine* award for an outstanding new-employee training program. What stood out to Mike was that the new-employee training activities were tied to goals and objectives in their strategic plan. He knows from experience that employees feel an elevated sense of self-worth when they are shown how to contribute to the company's key drivers. Representatives from *Training*

Magazine note that high-quality training programs can provide significant returns to a company (Business Wire, 2015).

Any type of training program is only as good as the critical planning that went into designing it. But if you design the programs right, they can provide helping hands. This is why it is critical to identify KSA gaps for each position in the organization so they can be tailored to the company's needs.

"Do we use benchmarking?"

Sometimes there is no point in reinventing the wheel. Some organizations have KSA design figured out and do not mind sharing the lessons they've learned to become successful. It is a great idea for HR specialists to use benchmarking as a process in raising the standards for developing KSAs for their organization as well as developing and monitoring training programs.

We discussed benchmarking in chapter 5 as it applies to assessing skills needed from groups and individuals. We see this assessment process as a partnership between Human Resources and the operational departments to improve the quality of workers, potential candidates for the organization, and the overall quality of training programs. Using the benchmarking method improves the KSA posture of an organization and is underutilized as a planning tool.

When using a benchmarking method, make sure you allow for cultural differences between your company and the one you are comparing yourself to. When we discussed the KSA hiring method we mentioned that you are also looking for employees who are a good fit for your organizational culture. By keeping this in mind, you can improve the hiring/training cycle, which can impact the three Ps: performance, productivity, and profits.

ROLES, RESPONSIBILITIES, AND ACCOUNTABILITY . . .

You will see that our Diamond Process Matrix (p. 194) illustrates that RRA problems are the primary driver for eleven out of the twenty-seven symptoms associated with failing organizations. Mismanagement of roles and responsibilities, and assigning accountability, are secondary and tertiary drivers for ten additional symptoms. This is indicative of the fact that roles, responsibilities, and accountability management issues are at the root of what many supervisors deem "people" issues.

The good news is when you get your RRA problems sorted out, you have taken a big step in solving a bunch of your "people issues." This is also why we deemed RRA management as a process enabler—because it affects so much stuff. It behooves you to get a grip on the roles and responsibilities for each group in the organization. People want, and deserve, to be treated fairly and to understand what part they play in the daily work grind and in the future of the organization as well as the bigger picture.

"Does everyone in our organization understand his or her role and responsibility?"

Most companies we've seen assign roles and responsibilities to only a few people instead of *all* their workers. And those who have been assigned roles may or may not know exactly what those roles and responsibilities include.

Mike was consulting with one company and put this very question to a boss in a private meeting. The boss's response was, "Of course he knows what his responsibilities are!" When Mike took the boss to talk to the employee, he quickly realized the worker had been assigned a new responsibility more than two months earlier, yet he had no idea what he was supposed to do.

Roles and responsibilities are important to establish in an organization because they lay the foundation for accountability and ensure success of work processes. Leaders must ensure that employees clearly understand what is expected of them, and not just assume they know—as the boss did in the previous example.

If workers know what role they play, and which responsibilities they have in the organization, then they can become dedicated to achieving their processes. If those processes fail, then the leaders of the organization know whom to talk with to find out what went wrong.

All groups and individuals in an organization should be linked to at least one work task or process. This is a fundamental principle for good process leadership and helps to maintain organizational balance.

The key point here is to follow up and get feedback from employees so you have no misunderstandings. Ensuring people understand roles and responsibilities is at the heart of RRA management. Once you successfully communicate roles, responsibilities, and accountability to employees, you have enabled the critical processes that those workers lead in your organization.

"Do our individuals and groups understand each other's roles when working together to achieve a process?"

Think back to the story mentioned earlier about the NASA janitor who, when asked about his job, said, "I am helping to put a man on the moon!"

Only when dealing with classified government information do you want a scenario where the right hand does not know what the left is doing; so unless you are building a combat space vehicle, make sure the people and groups you have working together know what the other folks need to accomplish a process. It does not pay to keep team members in the dark on what part or role the other plays in the big picture.

If your workers understand the roles of process leaders in the organization, it becomes a powerful process enabler because the employees can enable each other's processes. Understanding which person is the leader of a process will help when workers have information they need to communicate about that particular process. This understanding also improves the quality of process relationships, especially if those two processes are connected with a handoff.

Another benefit of having everyone understand a process is that it can increase productivity because workers are better prepared to fill each other's roles when needed. If one employee has a more critical part of the process, leaders can identify the critical role and cross-train other members to fill the role on a temporary basis.

This is, once again, another value in having flowcharts and process maps depicted so workers have an illustration of what they do as part of the bigger team. The more the individual worker knows about what others around them accomplish, the more they can help improve the overall process.

"Does every work process have someone assigned to be responsible and accountable?"

Each work process should be covered by both groups and individuals with the right KSAs to produce the quality of work that is needed for the organization. The process should have the right people with the right skills to produce champion work. It is not enough that a process has a warm body; the role of process leader should be filled to meet expectations of that champion organization you are building.

Remember, each process needs a leader to oversee and maintain it. This person will fill the role of subject-matter expert for that particular process, serve as the point of contact to that process, and have responsibility and accountability to the process. Ultimately, this process leader will enable the process. Take caution when assigning process leaders so as not to build in conflicts with process leaders and positional leaders. Your organizational chart should support the achievement of the work processes.

Once you verify that a process has the right person or people assigned with the appropriate knowledge, skills, and abilities, you should also double-check to make sure each person or group has the right responsibility. If someone is assigned to a process but has no responsibility for the process, then the individual won't take ownership of the process. Allowing workers to have ownership in the work they perform helps not only with the quality of the work but also improving the process itself.

As a process leader, one should know what groups/individuals are responsible and accountable for performing that process. This becomes a way of syncing processes back to individuals. And it enables an easier way of syncing key drivers back to processes and then down to groups and individuals.

This linking and syncing ensures that the organization is not only well balanced but wired for optimization. Every process has groups and individuals identified that will accomplish the tasks necessary to perform that process, and each group and individual are given the tasks/processes for which they are responsible.

"Do we hold people accountable to their process responsibilities?"

Accountability is the ultimate process enabler because it forces the process leader to account for the successes and failures of the process. All groups and individuals should be held accountable for their roles and responsibilities to ensure work quality. Just because you assign someone responsibility for a process role does not mean you are covered; you have to follow up to ensure accountability for people and processes.

A complete leader will ask an individual or team leader to illustrate how they are accomplishing the process, or their role in the process. An informal process review is a great way to ensure workers know and understand their role, their responsibility, and the process itself.

This exercise also helps a supervisor provide feedback to their superior process leader. You can ensure quality of process by reviewing process or results metrics. You can also use process reviews to ensure adherence to organizational guidance or policies, and verify that the process owner understands the big picture of the larger organization and parent process.

Process reviews are also a great way to find out if a role or responsibility has changed without it being properly recorded or needs to be changed because of a recent event in the internal/external business environment. Organizations and the environments in which many of them function are dynamic and change constantly; process reviews can make sure your processes accurately reflect what is happening in your company.

As a senior leader, a good way to ensure that other leaders are holding their people accountable for processes is to review the feedback those leaders have provided to their subordinates in their annual appraisal. If process leadership is present, it should be apparent in the feedback contained in the appraisal.

Another good link and sync exercise is to ensure processes are tied to and from an individual's performance appraisal. This practice ensures complete accountability between individuals and processes and, when supported with metrics, becomes a powerful management tool.

ASK NOT, WANT NOT

Once workers are assigned roles, responsibilities, and accountability, they should be given a realistic set of expectations from supervision. When referring to the Diamond Process Matrix (p. 194), you will see that the lack of realistic expectations is the primary force behind nearly half of the twenty-seven total symptoms of failing organizations.

Lack of clear expectations is one of the most common problems we see when consulting with businesses. This is surprising to us because of the problems it causes. If you fail to provide clear expectations for employees, expect to encounter a plethora of "people issues" including chaos, high turnover, and lack of motivation; some organizational problems, such as lack of growth; and some resource problems, such as extensive overhead.

It is also important to communicate expectations properly. Many times a leader will attempt to communicate expectations. But if the expectations are not clear, there is no telling what you will end up with. This is represented in the following US Army joke presented by Mike.

☆☆

A GENERAL'S REFLECTION

One of my favorite jokes is "The Colonel's Order." It goes like this:

The Colonel issues the following directive to his executive officer: "Tomorrow evening at 2000 hours, Halley's Comet will appear in this area; this phenomenon occurs only once every seventy-five years. Have the soldiers report to the battalion area in fatigues, and I will explain this rare event to them. In case it rains, we will not be able to see anything, so assemble the men in the theater and I will show them films of the event."

The executive officer issues the following directive to the company commander: "By order of the Colonel, tomorrow at 2000 hours Halley's Comet will appear above the battalion area. If it rains, fall the soldiers out in fatigues, then march to the theater where this rare phenomenon will take place, something that occurs only once each seventy-five years."

The company commander issues the following directive to the Lieutenant: "By order of the Colonel, be in fatigues at 2000 hours tomorrow evening. The phenomenal Halley's Comet will appear in the theater. In case of rain in the battalion area, the Colonel will give another order, something that occurs only once every seventy-five years."

The Lieutenant issues the following directive to the Sergeant: "Tomorrow at 2000 hours, the Colonel will appear in the theater with Halley's Comet, something that happens every seventy-five years. If it rains, the Colonel will order the comet into the battalion area."

The Sergeant issues the following directive to the squad: "When it rains tomorrow at 2000 hours, the phenomenal seventy-five-year-old General Halley, accompanied by the Colonel, will drive his comet through the battalion area theater in fatigues."

"Do we have a process to communicate expectations?"

Supervisors should give a set of clearly defined and specific performance expectations for the process tasks and functions assigned to each worker. Similar to roles and responsibilities, we encounter situations where either the boss thinks he or she has communicated expectations but in reality has not; or the employee thinks he or she understands the boss's expectations but really has no idea what they are.

Whichever the reason may be, if your workers do not understand the right expectations, you will run into the same problems as if you had no expectations—or roles and responsibilities, for that matter. Appraisal reviews are inopportune times for an employee to find out they are not meeting the boss's expectations. To avoid these situations and to ensure quality of process work, good organizations develop a process to communicate group and individual expectations.

Setting expectations is not rocket surgery. Our recommendation to make sure you communicate expectations to workers is to schedule expectation meetings with them. These meetings can be married up with feedback sessions, which are normally required with appraisals. They are also stronger if tied to commitments, agreed to between boss and subordinate, and backed up with process or results metrics to avoid perceptions of subjectivity.

If expectations are not tied to commitments, we recommend an initial expectations brief for new employees to set performance expectations. We also recommend a follow-up feedback session within six months to communicate whether the worker is meeting, exceeding, or failing to meet those expectations. We recommend face-to-face meetings as well as some form of private written record of the communication.

"Do we provide accurate and honest feedback?"

Feedback is the key to improving employee performance, as feedback sessions give the leader an opportunity to communicate expectations to an employee. Therefore, feedback is a process enabler because it helps to either correct the behavior of process leaders or reinforce the fact that the leader is on track.

Feedback sessions also give subordinates a chance to communicate with supervision, which can sometimes allow for an adjustment to be made depending on input from the worker. Sometimes processes fail to meet performance or process targets because of a change in the organization or a problem with other dependent processes. These feedback sessions can capture some needed changes before they cause serious problems to the productivity of the organization.

Employees should also understand how their performance is measured. It is not enough to simply communicate expectations; you need to also explain how the worker's performance will be measured against those expectations. Once again, process and results metrics make great measurements to help gauge worker success.

This communication also gives workers a chance to voice their opinions on which performance and process metrics are most appropriate to grade them against. Good communications help build a proper employee-supervisor relationship; they empower the organization with optimized individual and group performance.

"Do we have a process for updating expectations?"

There are several situations that cause expectations to change, including a new process, modification to an existing process, new supervisor and/or employee, or changes to the internal or external business environment. Technological advances or changes occur much more frequently these days than in times past, and this can change the needs of a business. Also, laws or markets change from time to time, which may modify your processes.

Processes should be established before setting expectations for employees; this creates a good basis for recording a process to update expectations. But as their career responsibilities evolve, and when the environment changes, you need to update expectations because workers need to know their process priorities.

Expectation management can be accomplished as a separate review process or part of a current process but should ensure that each group and individual has a current, written set of expectations. Strategic planning sessions with senior executives and operational reviews with middle managers and first-line supervisors provide great opportunities to establish expectation management processes.

To be effective, processes to capture expectations should assess work processes, roles, responsibilities, accountability (RRA), the impact of external environment factors, and process improvement opportunities or focus areas. As leaders, we must strive to balance the entire process component in an organization to achieve overall balance. Doing so will allow us to establish metrics that cover all process-related activities.

When Mike was deployed as a general officer in Iraq, he not only gave initial expectations to all of the commanders in his organization, but he periodically updated the expectations when he performed KSA assessments. One particular commander in Mike's unit had worked on his staff a few years earlier and was familiar with Mike's process for developing knowledge, skills, and abilities in his organizations.

This commander had also personally experienced the positive impacts KSA management had on Mike's previous organization as he was part of the team and had witnessed individuals in the unit who improved personal and team performance. Having personally witnessed these results, the commander recognized the value of Mike's process for developing KSAs, but he suspected there was more to it than Mike had shared. For that reason, the commander sought Mike's mentorship so he could learn how to impact his own organization in a similar way.

Over the next several months, Mike mentored him by showing the commander how to extend KSA management to include roles and responsibilities for each member of the organization. Once these were established, Mike explained that the workers must be held accountable to these roles and responsibilities, and he stressed the importance of establishing performance metrics to gauge worker performance. Through their deployment in Iraq, Mike continued to develop the commander's leadership skills. He asked the commander to record knowledge, skills, and abilities; mitigate KSA gaps; assign roles and responsibilities; establish performance metrics; and communicate expectations so he could develop the skills to be an effective leader to his own people.

Following the commander's deployment in OIF, he went back to his civilian job and put these practices to good use. The commander, now the boss, began to see the same results with the workers in his civilian organization. Mike kept in touch with him throughout the years, and it was obvious he'd had a successful career, given that he retired as a high executive in a major defense-contracting firm. The commander attributed much of his success to using the expectations-management techniques Mike had taught him.

"Have we established and communicated standards of behavior to our workers?

Standards of behavior embody the values in an organizational culture. These standards may seem like common sense to leaders, but you will be doing a disservice to your business if you do not establish behavioral standards and communicate them to employees. You should not leave to chance something so simple that can be easily remedied by a brief memo or new-employee training (NET) topic.

Standards of behavior are those minimum actions that are deemed acceptable for your workforce in carrying out their activities for the organization. Behavioral standards should be set in your organization's culture so employees know what to expect from other workers.

In some cases, these standards of behavior carry over from the professional to the personal environment. A good example of well communicated behavior standards are professional athletes who sign contracts and agree to standards of behavior that represent a favorable impression of the employer both on and off the field. Such agreements are common for organizations whose members provide a reflection of the company.

"Have we established and communicated standards of performance to our workers?"

Supervisors should translate expectations for workers into standards of performance, which are specific performance targets that can be measured. Performance standards must be specific and quantitative enough so metrics can be established to measure success or failure. Performance targets must then be communicated to employees in order to be effective. If workers do not know what you want, you cannot expect them to deliver.

Like anything else with the DPM, standards of employee performance must reflect the goals and objectives of the organization. Everything we do as leaders should advance the strategic vision of the organization, and performance standards are no exception. If by meeting a performance target a worker has helped the organization achieve a goal or objective, you know that performance standard is spot on. For this reason, we encourage the use of flowcharts and process maps to help establish performance standards. Throughout the Diamond Process, charts and maps are established to record critical processes for an organization. Setting individual performance targets that enable effective processes makes sense.

What is most important with process maps and flowcharts is that they accurately capture the work in an organization and record the critical processes. As long as these process enablers accomplish this objective, they are correct. As such, the creation of process maps is only limited by the creativity of the leader making them.

When Mike was a deployed commander in Iraq, he used the previously mentioned *smart books* to train new members of his HQ staff. These smart books were Mike's idea for recording process maps that depicted how each position on his staff functioned and how the processes should be performed to fill the roles of that position. This idea was quite creative, as the smart books served different purposes.

First, the books were a hands-on reference guide to help workers perform their duties. Each smart book contained not only process maps and flowcharts, but also helpful forms, reports, and reference sheets needed for that particular position. The smart books served to help each leader with his or her daily functions. Since each staff member always had the books on hand, process maps were continuously being updated—which improved their accuracy.

Second, these smart books served as training guides and provided the 85% solution to new-employee training. After studying the books, new staff members required less on-the-job training before they started producing as members of the unit. This was especially beneficial in a war zone, where events occur nearly four times as fast as at the home station.

Third, the smart books provided continuity when primary process leaders were away. If Mike needed to cross-train someone to backfill another position, it was much easier, as the back-up person was already familiar with using the books and simply had to learn how to read the new one.

Another added benefit of using process maps in this way is that Mike stayed true to the culture of the US Army. The Army has been using field manuals since its inception, and these smart books were right in line with what soldiers are accustomed to. When making process maps and flowcharts for your organization, you can get creative, but be mindful of your organizational culture.

Along with goals and objectives in the strategic plan, organizational values provide fertile ground for selecting performance targets. For example, if your company values superior customer service, a good standard of performance for a sales representative would be to maintain a minimum customer-satisfaction rating. The sales supervisor can review the ratings as one of the measurable performance targets during feedback sessions.

Once standards of performance have been established for workers, they must then be communicated clearly. There is no substitute for face-to-face meetings when communicating expectations to workers. A private setting will allow intimate communication and provide employees ample opportunity to ask questions without worrying about eavesdroppers.

Along with face-to-face meetings, we strongly suggest documenting the feedback sessions so there is little chance for workers to dispute the expectations at a later point. If an employee does not meet expectations and is negatively impacted, they may resort to claiming they did not know of the performance standards. Written documentation signed by the worker removes doubt and protects the supervisor from such claims.

"We're doing our job; are you doing yours?"

Since people are your organization's most valuable resource, we've spent a lot of time in this chapter showing you how to empower them through not only managing their knowledge, skills, and abilities, but also by managing roles and responsibilities and by setting accountability and expectations.

Focusing on individual people and the processes they lead is a necessary first step. This is because we must ensure our people and processes are normalized, which means we all have a common set of expectations as to how things should be in our organization. Once we have this shared understanding, it is time to move forward.

Now that we know how to get the most out of our people, we can next look at how to apply people along with the other resources to fuel processes. With the Diamond Process Model, everything we do as an organization should lead us from our mission today to our vision tomorrow. The way we apply resources is key to that application.

CHAPTER 13

THREE INVALUABLE RESOURCES: PEOPLE, MONEY, AND EQUIPMENT

When it comes to integrating resources, we've found that most companies have it backward. Usually an organization will start with an org chart and put *this* person in charge over here and *that* person in charge over there. Once the organization is structured, the leaders are left to figure out how to make it work in their own department, not knowing what the other leaders are doing in theirs.

The Diamond method takes a much sounder approach. We start at the top with a strategic plan that is comprehensive in that it sets your mission, vision, goals, and objectives that have been agreed upon by all the senior leaders of the organization. Ultimately these key drivers in the strategic plan generate a list of requirements for *what* your company needs to accomplish.

Next, through the Diamond Process Model we organize the work processes that describe *how* the work needs to occur within an organization in order to support each line of business. The first half of managing your line of business is to make sure each process supports the requirements in the strategic plan. The second half of LOB management is to identify yet another set of resource requirements needed to make the processes work effectively.

Finally, it is time to allocate resources to the process requirements we've identified. Once we do so, we add fuel to the fire and turn all of the requirements in your organization into capabilities. But we must take great caution when applying resources; we must keep track of what goes where so we can make future adjustments to get the most out of what we have.

We have devised a set of questions related to resource integration that we use when consulting businesses. By carefully answering these questions for your company, you will be prepared to make the appropriate decisions when integrating scarce resources. This is the final and most crucial part of learning to use the Diamond Process Model.

GETTING IN THE WEEDS

Having the proper resources is imperative to being able to deliver high-level processes to meet your key drivers and be successful. Leaders must make critical resource decisions to balance the other two components (work processes and key drivers) sufficiently.

☆☆

A GENERAL'S REFLECTION

On the eve of OPERATION: Iraqi Freedom, we had staged all of our war assets in Kuwait and were conducting the final planning phase of the mission prior to execution. During our reviews, many of the Generals at my level and above noticed there was a severe lack of US Army vehicles to haul local assets like supplies, materials, and equipment.

I could not understand the shortage of vehicles since it is the bread and butter for the US Army to be able to move stuff. I did notice a trend, however, that the shortage was a role usually filled by a US Army Company that provided medium trucks.

I wanted to gather some *lessons learned* through my experience with planning the war effort, so when I returned to the States I started investigating the shortage of medium trucks. I quickly discovered that the shortage was due to a miscommunication.

The Secretary of Defense at that time was Donald Rumsfeld, and he had a reputation as a hands-on leader. I learned that while preparing for the war effort, he personally reviewed the deployment lists that outlined each and every unit scheduled to deploy as part of the initial forces. The reason he was so involved is that he was attempting to minimize the sheer number of ground forces that were to be deployed.

During his review, when Secretary Rumsfeld came to the line that showed "MED TRK CO," he assumed that meant it was a Medical Truck Company and decided the US Army did not need that many medical trucks. He consequently lined through most assets that had that particular designation, and in doing so severely limited the US Army's ability to haul materiel because "MED" did not stand for "medical," it stood for "medium."

This decision impacted leaders immensely in theater until an emergency request for forces was processed to send the proper units. The shortage also contributed to delaying the capability of the US Army to wage war at that time and resulted in a two-week delay to the start of the operation.

The resource component in the Diamond Process Model can be a game changer for organizations. Resourcing can often be the difference between success and mediocrity, between growth and stagnation. Champion organizations identify, develop, and sustain top-level human, capital, and equipment resources.

As leaders, we strive to have the right people with the right equipment funded at the correct level to perform our processes at a champion level to meet or exceed our key drivers. Since we have already addressed using process enablers to empower people in chapter 12, in this chapter we will focus more on the other resource components and how they can be integrated successfully to support your organization.

PEOPLE POWER

"Have we assigned the right personnel to lead and fuel our processes?"

The reason we use process enablers like KSA and RRA management is to understand our people just like we understand our processes. Thoroughly developing processes helps you to understand all of the work that needs to be accomplished in the organization in great detail. Developing KSAs and RRAs help to understand your people in the same detailed way.

Now it is time to match people to processes. During process definition, you identified how the process needs to get accomplished. In other words, you identified a process requirement. Matching the right people to fill that process requirement is the first step in integrating resources effectively.

For each process there must be a process leader to not only manage the process but to be accountable for the process. This process leader should also serve as your subject-matter expert for what resources he or she feels are needed to optimize the process for success.

Human resource allocation is very important. At this point in the Diamond Process Model, every process in the organization is tied directly to the key drivers in the strategic plan. If you have the right process leader and resources in place, the process will be successful and so will your business strategy. If the process is successful, you will meet the organization's mission today, goals and objectives tomorrow, and thrust the company toward your future vision.

Once process leaders are in place, it is time to allocate other human resources to further processes. We understand that people are limited, so leaders must be smart on how to integrate scarce human resources. However, the Diamond Process Model has already given you the right tools to make the correct decision of who goes where.

When we began to formulate our lines of business (LOBs), we made a priority listing of processes so we know which are critical. Since critical processes are obviously more important, you should put the higher-skilled, more experienced workers, or a greater number of them, to enhance those processes. Allocating people in this way will protect your critical processes and ensure that if you are going to "take a hit," it will be in a place that will least affect your organization.

Since you have a known weakness, you can use metrics reviews to confirm whether reality is following your plan. For example, if your critical process is succeeding at the same time your secondary process is struggling, you know exactly why. Because that is the way you planned it.

In chapter 11, through "A General's Reflection," Mike presented a story of a talented captain he deemed the "Wash Rack Czar." If you recall, Mike's strategic plan changed because he did not realize how stringent the US Customs requirements were for equipment returning back to the States. He found the Wash Rack Czar and reassigned him to lead an area that was the single point of failure preventing Mike from meeting his strategic objective to rapidly return heavy equipment back from theater. It was only through using the Diamond methodology that he was able to solve this problem.

First, the only reason Mike knew of the Wash Rack Czar's abilities was because he forced his staff to perform KSA analysis on every member in the unit. It was during one of these KSA reviews that the Czar's commanding officer documented his excess knowledge, skills, and abilities that, unbeknownst to them at the time, would be so critical in the future.

Second was the fact that the Czar had been assigned as an assistant operations officer to implement the critical processes of continuing logistical operations during the military operation. He was identified as the #1 replacement for the process leader for those operations.

When the wash rack crisis took place, the leaders under Mike's command quickly surveyed their process leaders to identify possible human resources to shift to the new wash rack facility. In these process reviews, potential candidates were submitted along with their KSA assessment data.

Mike's leaders quickly identified the Wash Rack Czar, appointed him as the subject-matter expert and process leader, and used his excess KSAs to resolve the single point of failure. As the strategic objectives of the organization changed, so did the process priorities that support the strategic plan. Using these priorities and the Diamond Process Method, the unit was able to react quickly to an external threat on the organization.

"Do we have enough of the right people?"

A shortage of people will negatively impact your ability to perform work processes at a sufficient level to meet the key drivers in your strategic plan. Manpower shortages can be discussed during process reviews, either at the operational or first-line supervisor level of leadership. It is important to record whether you have a process with nobody to run it or a process that is not optimized with enough people.

Several organizations pride themselves on doing more with less, while others are faced with "mission creep" where additional work is heaped on without any additional resources. Both of these situations are certainly not the intent of the Diamond Process Model, as they will put an unnecessary strain and imbalance on the overall organization.

Departmental leaders should get involved with the Human Resources department to attempt to fill the manpower shortage. Process maps and metrics provide great justification for getting a position filled, justifying an authorization, or establishing a new position. HR should already be looking ahead based on the key drivers of the organization, anticipating any future shortfalls, and implementing risk mitigation strategies to reduce the impact of those shortfalls.

The better HR can manage these risks, the better the organization will be postured for future success. But they can't mitigate what they don't know, so communicating with the folks who hire new workers is key.

While you wait, it is a good idea to check with other operational leaders in case someone happens to have an overage. Although it is highly unlikely to find a leader who will admit having too many people, it never hurts to ask. It is, however, the right thing to do for the good of the overall organization and is expected behavior of complete leaders.

If the person you need will drive a critical process, it is prudent to find someone already in the organization that has the right KSAs for the job, especially if that person is not currently leading a critical process. It is easier to hire someone from outside the company for a less skilled or less important position. There are great advantages, when reassigning someone to spearhead a critical task, to choosing a person who's already familiar with the company and its strategic goals.

If you are completely unable to fill the shortage, then you should record it on a decrement list (covered later in this chapter).

☆☆

A GENERAL'S REFLECTION

While I was a young Captain in the US Army Reserves, I was finally given an opportunity to command a unit. My first assignment as a company commander was for an Engineer Support Company whose mission

Continued

was to build and repair roads in a theater of war. I was very excited about this job because I'd always wanted to command a unit and finally had the opportunity. I was also excited because I knew the Battalion commander I would be reporting to was an outstanding officer.

During my first day on the job, all that excitement came to a screeching halt. It was obvious this unit went without good leadership for a long, long time. Right off the bat, I noticed morale and attitude were lacking. The equipment situation was dismal; we had millions upon millions of dollars worth of heavy equipment and it looked like crap. Some of it was broken and a large majority hadn't been maintained properly. None of the soldiers in the unit had pride in their work and everyone shared the "show up and go home" mentality.

I started looking at the books and the bad news kept coming. The manning roster showed that I was supposed to have 150 people, of which I had less than 120. Of those 30 vacant positions, many were skilled positions that, if left vacant, meant the unit could not perform its mission. The equipment accounts were also messed up because there was major equipment we were supposed to have but did not; and our supply folks were not accounting for individual items either.

After a couple of days, I realized that I was going to be busier than a one-armed paper-hanger. The US Army does not mess around with units that cannot perform their mission. If it is discovered that a unit is non-mission capable, the Army will completely dissolve the unit and disperse its members and equipment to other units that have proven they can perform. Also, the leader of a dissolved unit, regardless of how long they have been in command, gets a bad reputation that follows them throughout their career.

I asked myself the key question, "What is my single point of failure?" I looked at the basics of what type of work the unit was supposed to do and found my answer. This unit was supposed to build and repair roads. To do so, we needed to operate a rock-crusher quarry, paving machines, bulldozers, and bucket loaders. The single point of failure is that I did not have anyone qualified to operate the rock crusher or paving machines.

I put out an All-Points Bulletin/Be on the Lookout (APB/BOLO) for operators that could run these machines. I found some soldiers who could operate these on the inactive reserve roster who were looking to get back into the mix. The good news was that these personnel worked civilian construction jobs full time, so they could immediately get to work and bring their road-building experience. I was able to not only fill my manpower shortages, but do so with personnel who had the right KSAs for the job.

Armed with fresh personnel to fill key positions, I revamped the organizational structure and made some sweeping personnel changes. I replaced many of the positional leaders in the organization with younger, more motivated personnel. I set milestones for the unit via strategic goals and objectives and challenged them to answer the mail.

We conducted frequent inspections and operational exercises, and I found that once the unit started scoring some wins, the whole attitude changed. People began taking pride in their work, the equipment started looking better, and most of all, we recaptured the ability to successfully perform our mission. But none of this would have been possible had we not filled our key manpower shortages.

TOOLS FOR SUCCESS

"Do we have the right equipment for our people to succeed?"

If you hire the champion employee and communicate high expectations for worker performance, then it behooves you to equip your folks to do their jobs properly. If you cut corners on the quality and quantity of equipment for the workforce, you will see the negative impact in your finished product, whether it is products or services.

This may sound matter-of-fact, but it is not always intentional.

Many organizations mean well but fail to integrate and manage resources properly. It is easy enough to spend capital resources on hiring and training a future champion employee but then run out of money before purchasing equipment.

For this reason, it is important to manage the entire integration process so it is funded at the correct level to get everything you need. If you have good workers with bad equipment, you risk increasing worker frustration and experiencing high turnover as a result.

Equipment shortages are not always obvious. Good workers tend to make do with what they have and get the job done. This is why it pays to have process measures that can help provide indicators that you are having equipment problems. Root-cause analysis on an underperforming area of a process can certainly lead you to the conclusion that you need more (or better) equipment.

For example, a manufacturing company that produces baseball bats may be producing their target of 100 bats a week. If you look at a result metric, which is a lagging indicator, you will realize that 100 bats were produced and your goal was met for the week. This results measure alone will not indicate that there is a need for equipment.

On the other hand, if you had a process measure that times the production of a baseball bat between workstations, you may realize that one particular station is slower than the rest of the process. This is a leading indicator and can signal to management that intervention may be necessary. Once examining the reason for this workstation's delay, you may realize that it is old and has a lot of downtime for repair.

When it comes to equipment, process and task knowledge are essential. This means you should include your experts, including your process leader, when making decisions about equipment resources. If you discover an equipment problem or shortage, you will need to involve the appropriate department in your organization to acquire the right equipment. Once again, process and results measures can make the argument for you.

When allocating equipment, you can use the same priority system we use for allocating people. Use all the tools that the Diamond Process Model has provided you including process leaders, metrics, and the priority of the process. All these components combined will help you make the right decision.

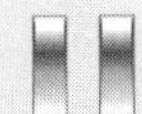

CAPTAIN'S CORNER

I remember my first deployment experience as an enlisted member of the Air National Guard. This was shortly after 9/11, and my unit was tasked to go out to California to backfill some positions that were vacated by active-duty personnel deploying overseas.

One standard requirement of any armed forces member is to out-process from one unit before in-processing to a gaining unit. In the scenario of a mass deployment for war, units usually set up some sort of "mobility line" to process everyone at once.

We had numerous administrative requirements to make sure all the paperwork for departing members was good to go. One of those requirements was to have a set of dog tags in case you were selected to be retasked out of the country. In mobility preparation, the higher-ups decided that everyone would have a good set of dog tags before we left.

I remember being in a processing line of around seventy people, and it seemed like all seventy came to a complete halt when we got to the location to get our dog tags. Everyone in the military understands these administrative exercises are usually "hurry up and wait," but this one was definitely more "wait" than "hurry."

The poor girl behind the counter was obviously stressed-out that her machine was slow and breaking. She was using a large cast-metal machine that appeared to have come straight out of the Smithsonian Museum. I waited impatiently as I watched her hammer out a single

Continued

set of dog tags in twenty minutes. After three sets, the machine broke completely, and the other sixty-seven people in line had to reschedule.

This is a prime example of not having the right equipment for the job. The wastefulness of using old, antiquated equipment in this case meant that nearly seventy people preparing for a deployment had to reschedule a time to get a stamped piece of tin. The mobility office had to take on the administrative burden of scheduling each of us, and the entire out-processing line was broken over a small piece of faulty equipment.

DEAD PRESIDENTS

"Have we funded the right people and the right equipment for them to succeed?"

Under-capitalization is a huge threat to the Diamond Process Model because a lack of funding jeopardizes the entire work process component. Lack of funds can cause a severe out-of-balance situation and makes it challenging to meet the mission, vision, goals, and objectives set by strategic leaders.

Aside from poor planning, under-capitalization is the top reason most new businesses fail within the first six months (Pendrith, 2014). In your existing business, sometimes you need to change your business model and update your strategic plan with new goals and objectives. When this happens, it is just like starting a new business. If you do not fund the new business model sufficiently, it is also likely to fail.

The main cause of under-capitalization is leaders who do not understand where to put the money. If you have equipment problems and you hire more people, the problem only gets bigger. Regardless of the scenario, if you apply scarce capital resources inappropriately, you can continuously chase problems with bad fixes. This death spiral spells the end for some companies.

The key to successful capitalization is knowledge; you must know where to place the money and how much. This is why the Diamond Process Model is so beneficial for companies—it tells you exactly where to place scarce resources. Funding should be applied in an organization to balance all of the DPM components. Many times this means funding the right areas to overcome shortages that you've identified throughout your Diamond Process Model planning.

Maintaining processes will allow you to know exactly how much money is needed to fuel your key drivers. Even more, you can estimate how much more capital will be needed to accomplish one or more additional strategic goals or objectives. Strategic leaders in an organization need to have this type of information at their fingertips during strategic planning sessions so they can make crucial, informed decisions.

Although the Diamond Process Model was not designed specifically for capitalization, it can provide information that can affect the critical decision-making process of leaders looking to invest capital resources in the organization. But the DPM does not replace the budgeting activity of an organization, as that is a highly specialized function for which the model was not designed.

Resource allocation is a tremendous part of leading an organization. Many companies fail miserably because they do not have a process to satisfy work requirements with the proper people, equipment, or funding to achieve success. We recommend using the Diamond Method to provide information and balance when performing operational and strategic reviews so leaders can make informed decisions.

"How much more money do I need? And where do I need it?"

Strategic leaders should be asking this during strategic planning sessions not only to ensure the company is meeting its mission but also to plan for contingencies. Once your company is stable and producing, you should be constantly playing the "what if" game when planning for resource integration.

A great tool to use in this mental exercise is a *decrement list*, which is a document that contains all the identified needs of your organization. We mentioned this list earlier in the chapter when discussing human resources to identify when a position needs to be filled, but decrement lists can also extend to capital and equipment shortfalls.

Middle managers should be keeping their own decrement lists that can be updated during operational reviews. Organizations that have a process for managing decrement listings will be better prepared for successful resource integration.

Senior leaders should strive for balance in funding the right people and work processes at a champion level. Proper budgeting can enable an organization to maintain this balance by enabling people to drive critical and primary work processes.

Resources must be tied to the strategic plan and should be focused on the short-, medium-, and long-term goals and objectives of the organization. Be mindful that a focus on a term that's too near or too long term will create an out-of-balance situation.

Once you have a process for updating and handling the decrement list, leaders should establish a plan and priority for how *new* resources will be allocated if they are made available. Guidance from strategic leaders is critical at this stage of contingency planning so the company can stay prioritized with the key drivers in the strategic plan.

All in all, decrement planning is a team effort. First-line supervisors identify shortfalls to middle managers during operational reviews; middle-managers update the decrement list and provide inputs to strategic leaders; and the top executives of the company capture where the company is and what resources they need to move forward.

MATERIAL WORLDS

"Do we have the right material for our processes?"

Although not large enough to be a separate resource component, raw materials can be very important in carrying out processes and should be managed accordingly. Similar to equipment and other resources, materials need to be applied to processes. Metrics or other symptoms could highlight that materials used in your processes could be flawed or inadequate for the products or services you are trying to provide.

To identify these flaws, it is best to utilize the people who perform the various steps in processes that use materials. These subject-matter experts can also be great sources of information if you need to acquire different materials to fuel a process. If a material vulnerability is discovered, it needs to be remedied immediately.

We have found that many manufacturing and production organizations rely heavily on materials as one of their primary resources. If you are in such a company, you need to have a quality-assurance (QA) process for not only the materials but also the products and services so you are providing the highest quality to customers. The quality of the final product is a direct reflection of the people, materials, and resources used to produce it.

Lumber Liquidators, a flooring supply company, has suffered recent challenges after *60 Minutes* reported that one of their product lines contained toxic levels of formaldehyde. According to BusinessInsider.com, the company's sales fell 7.5% in a little more than a week after the episode aired, and the company's stock fell 40% in two weeks since the report (Oyedele, 2015).

Although this particular product line was reportedly sourced from China, Lumber Liquidators would have been served well by a proper quality-assurance process. Had the company instilled safeguards, they could have avoided the damage caused by this event.

Some organizations realize the importance of QA safeguards, as demonstrated by the Blue Bell Ice Cream company. In April 2015, the company issued a voluntary recall of all its products due to a possible contamination by listeria, which is a virus that could cause harm to some people including children, the elderly, and pregnant women.

The contamination was detected in house by Blue Bell employees as part of their self-initiated quality-assurance program called "enhanced sampling" (Blue Bell, 2015). The situation was unfortunate, but the company was able to detect it through quality-assurance process measures and take action to prevent further damage to the company. Although the recall will undoubtedly cause temporary financial losses, the negative effects of this event will be much more muted than if an outside organization had made the discovery.

We also caution companies that are materials-dependent to be cognizant of external threats. Some materials are hazardous in nature and can be banned by the federal government. Some past examples include toxins found in DDT pest-control substances, incandescent light bulbs, and R-22 from Freon™ gas. Aside from toxins, these companies are also at risk of obsolescence from technological advances as well as market changes.

Once again, when using the Diamond Process Model we strive for balance. The number-one enabler of balance is good information on which to make decisions. It is helpful to have a process to collect information on material quality and provide that data to leaders of the organization along with the impacts material has on processes. This process should enable leaders to be poised to take the appropriate actions to remedy any problems that may arise.

Diamond Process Model planning is more than a one-time exercise; it is a way of thinking and managing your company. You must be aware that everything changes constantly, and so should your model. When allocating resources, whether they are people, equipment, or capital, those resources will be wasted if they do not support the key drivers in your strategic plan.

The way to stay on top of the DPM is to conduct regular strategic planning sessions, operational assessments, and process reviews to understand the internal and external environments of the company. As the direction of your strategic leadership changes, so should everything else in the business. This is the only way to guarantee unity of effort in an organization while responding to frequent environmental changes.

THE MISSING PIECE

At this point in the book, you are more of a Diamond Process Model expert than most, which should give you lots of confidence. You are ahead of the competition because you have a solid strategic plan, you've outlined all the work processes to support your business, and you've applied resources to fuel those processes to propel your organization toward your desired future goals. There is only one question remaining: "How do I know if it is working?"

The answer is easy; we have to check our work. In the next chapter we will show you how the Diamond Process Model uses metrics to tell us whether our company is moving in the right direction. Metrics is the missing piece to the puzzle. When this piece is added, you will have a complete picture of the health of your organization. When you understand how to use metrics with the DPM, you will be unstoppable.

CHAPTER 14

MEASURING UP TO CHECK YOUR WORK

Metrics is the gauge that tells us how our organization is performing as a whole. If we measure the right things, the metrics will tell whether we are accomplishing our goals and objectives and achieving our mission and vision in the strategic plan.

If we are executing our Diamond Process Model and keeping our company in balance, then metrics should reflect just that; they will indicate we are meeting and exceeding the performance and process targets we set for the company. On the other hand, if something is wrong with the organization, metrics can give you an indication that it is time for leader intervention. But this only works if the metrics themselves are appropriate for your specific organization.

Establishing the right metrics for an organization can be tricky business. There is no cookie-cutter solution that we can apply to everyone. So to help you on your journey to complete leadership, we've compiled a list of questions that we've found to be very helpful when consulting with companies looking to decide if their approach to metrics is solid.

☆☆

A GENERAL'S REFLECTION

When I was serving as Commander of the Theater Support Command during OIF in 2004, I conducted monthly materiel metric reviews to assess supplies that were being delivered to units in Iraq and Afghanistan to support the war effort.

During one of my routine walkthroughs of the local warehouse, I noticed a lot of incoming shipments piled up everywhere looking rather small. I made a comment to one of the workers, "I thought you guys were a regional distribution warehouse here." He said, "Yes sir, we are." I got the feeling that something wasn't quite right.

I went to our next materiel review and couldn't wait to ask about order quantities. But I noticed that the Order Ship Time (OST) was thirty to forty-five days for goods to arrive via ship. This meant when we placed an order it took four to six weeks to arrive, which seemed an exorbitant amount of time; it was also puzzling, because we seemed to have shipments piled up on top of each other.

I asked my staff if they felt like thirty to forty-five days was an acceptable OST. They replied with the obvious answer that it takes time for ships to sail across the oceans. I told them that I did not think this timeframe was acceptable, so I asked a member of my staff to meet with the supporting organization and set some process measures to gauge the ships' transport time from port to port.

I then asked about reorder quantities and my staff told me that they used an algorithm that automatically triggered at a certain reorder point, made an order of the quantity of goods needed, and maintained an overall level of stock on hand in the warehouse. I directed them to investigate the algorithm and report back to me at our next meeting.

My next materiel review was quite revealing. My team told me the algorithm that was programmed in the stock system was one used in the continental US and was not geared toward deployed operations. They took the initiative to adjust the numbers so we got a few large shipments rather than a plethora of small ones to maintain our stock levels.

The process measures we established to record ship transport times from port to port revealed that thirty to forty-five days for shipping times was overwhelmingly generous. Under the current system, the time lag was not the ships themselves getting across the ocean but rather commercial vehicles getting the goods to the port.

I took the information from our process measures and delivered the numbers to the supporting organization that was responsible for shipping goods to my unit. Their commander agreed to launch a process improvement event to help us lower the ship times. Ultimately, the improvement event resulted in goods getting in-country more quickly—in fifteen to twenty days.

"Do we have metrics in our organization?"

One of the most common mistakes we encounter is when organizations do not measure anything. Complete absence of metrics is unacceptable because it robs you of critical information on which you can make leadership decisions.

When this happens, it is an indicator that there are deep-seated process problems in an organization. If a company does not have a process to develop, report, and utilize metrics, it is indicative of an organization that lacks process altogether.

Successful metric management goes much deeper than the mission, vision, goals, and objectives in the strategic plan. If you are managing metrics correctly, you will be measuring performance all the way down to the task/function level of the organization, which means you have established effective process measures.

"Are we measuring the right things?"

Another dangerous situation arises when companies have something that resembles metrics, but those "metrics" are not based on the numbers needed to make sound decisions. If measures are misleading and don't tell the leader what he or she really needs to know about a process or result, then the leader may make decisions based on false information.

Most organizations we've seen do not develop metrics by going through their processes. Instead, they pick results they want to measure, which are usually short-term results measures such as quarterly profits. It is dangerous to base strategic decisions on short-term results measures because businesses will always encounter ups and downs due to the normal business cycle.

We understand the temptation to evaluate results measures frequently, especially in the United States, since we are a short-term driven society, as evidenced by the stock market and other economic indicators such as quarterly financial reports required by publicly traded companies. But we caution that you should have measures established to gauge the long-term goals of your business as well, and include the vision of your organization.

To be most effective, leaders should study trends over a long period of time, like twelve months. Once you have six months of data, you can tell whether you are increasing or decreasing performance because you can see whether you are trending up or down; this is important because you can also ask "why?" Ultimately, measuring the right things is crucial to bringing about the balance that leaders strive to achieve.

Mike was once consulting for a warehousing firm that sold building materials. While evaluating their results metrics, he noticed a discrepancy: Even though sales quantities for 2x4 pine boards were through the roof, the company was losing money in that area.

Mike went to visit the warehouse manager and when he went to look at the pine boards, there were none. The manager stated the contractors liked to buy their boards at his warehouse because they felt like they were getting a good deal. When Mike informed the manager he was losing 15% per board sale, the manager replied, "That's okay, I'll just make it up in volume!"

"Who is providing our metrics?"

The organization or person responsible for recording a metric should be the entity in the process chain that has the best position to record the metric. For example, a good place for process measures is in the handoff portion of the process. Therefore, someone or some mechanism in the immediate area of the handoff should be there to record it.

Another option used by larger organizations is to have an outside person, office, or some mechanized process responsible for recording all measures. If your company has a quality-assurance or analysis section, those individuals should suffice.

What is most important is that the person, organization, or mechanism recording the measure does so accurately. Otherwise, leaders will be presented with misleading information on which to make decisions. Such was the case in recent news of the Veterans Administration when it was found to have misleading results; the outcome was senior leaders had no idea veteran patients were waiting exorbitant time periods before having an opportunity to see a physician.

It is also important to ensure only one person/organization is responsible for reporting the process or results measure. If more than one source is providing metrics on the same process, misinformation could be presented to the leader. It can also create confusion if the same process is measured twice and the measurements differ from one another.

If at the end of a process something is delivered to a customer, we recommend you get feedback from the customer regarding your results measure. Although external customer feedback may be delayed longer than you wish, it can be the most useful type of feedback you can receive.

"How and when do we report metrics?"

Many leaders utilize some sort of visual metrics tool (such as a presentation) to help them lead and manage their organizations. In recent years, these tools have been commonly referred to as *dashboards*. Effective dashboards provide timely and accurate information that enables leaders to react and make decisions to produce the results their customers and employees need.

Effective dashboards focus on presenting to the leader the most relevant information. The strategic leader should be presented metrics that reveal information related to the key drivers in the strategic plan. This ensures the highest leader can make strategic adjustments to the company to ensure the mission and vision are accomplished.

When to report metrics depends greatly on what you are measuring and who is viewing the information. First-line supervisors should have frequent process metrics so they can identify problems early. It is not a bad idea for these types of leaders to review metrics on a daily or weekly basis.

Metrics should always be reported to the person who has the role, responsibility, and accountability for the process or result that is being measured. We often find that measures are reported at a way higher level than they need to be. Metrics should be reported (initially) to the leader closest to the work so he or she can make changes and redirect resources to correct deficiencies.

Also, process measures should be reported more frequently than results measures because they are *leading* indicators that tell you that there is a problem now which could impact your results. Results measures are *lagging* indicators and tell you what already happened. Since they cannot provide information to prevent immediate problems, they need not be reviewed as frequently.

Leaders at higher levels of management do not need to review metrics on a daily or weekly basis. Monthly reviews for operational leaders and quarterly reviews for executive leaders typically suffice. Higher-level leaders need to know whether the company is trending in a positive or negative direction. This information cannot be derived from daily metrics.

Our own version of a dashboard—the Balometer, as mentioned earlier—enables leaders to keep all elements of their organization in balance with respect to the three components of the Diamond Process Model: key drivers, work processes, and resources. Metric inputs can be tailored to each company and presented in the preferred output and frequency to the appropriate positional leader in the organization.

"Do we have process metrics?"

Process metrics provide leading indicators which give leaders a chance to proactively remedy situations before really bad things happen. If you don't have process metrics, your leaders are deprived of this invaluable opportunity to do their job.

Many metrics are results measures that cause leaders to spend much time and effort chasing down what went wrong after the problem occurred. This fire drill would be completely avoided had they used the Diamond Process Model and built-in process measures that provide time for corrective actions.

A valuable goal of any leader is to take as many preventive measures as he or she can to avoid problems down the road. Having effective process metrics that provide preventative information can empower leaders to provide positive results for the organization.

When Mike was deployed as the theater logistics commander in OIF, he was responsible for a sizable force rotation. From past experience, he understood that this type of effort should take sixty to ninety days, so he set that figure as his standard for process metrics.

Within three weeks, his established process metrics began providing critical information that indicated the movement of war assets was failing to meet the standard at various geographic locations throughout the Middle East.

Having been provided this information, Mike was able to make a critical leadership change in the unit that was responsible to his organization for the movement of these war assets. Due to the quick leadership change, Mike ensured the timely relief of combat forces at a moment when lives were at stake. The only reason he was able to make effective, informed decisions was because of the leading indicators provided by the process measures he had previously established.

"Do our metrics reflect the goals and objectives in the strategic plan?"

In order to be effective, metrics should be designed just like the Diamond Process Model. Start with your lines of business (LOBs), which are your top-level primary processes, and make sure they are linked with the mission, vision, goals, and objectives in the strategic plan. Once you are confident that your processes support the key drivers in the strategic plan, you are ready to measure success.

Once your highest-level processes are validated, move through the Diamond Process Model and embed process and results measures throughout the LOB, all the way down to the lowest-level processes, which are tasks and functions. As you analyze work through process maps and flowcharts, make sure you have results measures recorded at the end of all processes and process metrics at each handoff within the organization.

A good quality control exercise is to check how well you are measuring all of your goals and objectives, as well as your mission and vision. If you do not have all of these key drivers measured, there is no way to check for balance within the organization. Supporting the strategic plan with processes is why you exist as an organization, and measuring those processes with appropriate metrics is how you will assure your continued existence in a dynamic business environment.

As mentioned in chapter 12, linking and syncing individuals, processes, and key drivers with and between each other ensures optimum performance of the organization. Metrics of all of these should be linked and synced as well.

SHOW ME THE MONEY

With a solid approach to metrics, your company is unstoppable. The leaders in your organization will be equipped with all the knowledge they need to make correct decisions for the company. Metrics will indicate whether or not you are performing and moving to achieve the goals and objectives in the strategic plan.

At this point in your Diamond Process Model planning, you have completed all the necessary process work for your organization. If metrics indicate you are underperforming in certain areas, it's not that big of a deal. There can only be a few reasons why you are not succeeding, and those areas are now being highlighted using the DPM.

The first reason you may not be succeeding is that a process could be broken. However this is unlikely, since we've recently spent all the time and effort to develop processes and we continually critique them in weekly process reviews.

The second reason you may not be meeting metric targets is that the goal for the metric was unattainable. This is a simple correction in an operational review to make sure your goals are reasonable. But since we've recently revamped our metrics, this is also somewhat unlikely.

The third, and most likely, reason your company may be underperforming is because you have not allocated the proper resources to include people, equipment, and capital. Time and time again we've seen companies fail because they do not integrate resources properly. But that is okay, because you are not most leaders.

OUT OF THE WEEDS

Operational reviews (or any meetings for that matter) in which you review metrics will often identify resource shortages. Like a mother bird returning to the nest of hungry chicks with a mealworm, it is difficult to tell where to apply scarce resources. One thing is for sure: If mother bird was to feed only one or two chicks each time, the others would die from starvation.

But if mother bird were a CEO and that nest of chicks were the employees in your company, you'd hope mother bird had a plan. The Diamond Process Model is that plan, and it can enable strategic leaders to maintain balance in an organization, especially when it comes to applying resources to fuel work processes and checking those decisions with metrics.

Up to this point in section two of our book, it was necessary to drag you through the weeds to help you understand how the DPM can resolve problems at any level of leadership. We have gone through our diagnostic recapitulation to show you how you can always ask yourself a specific question regarding "what is wrong," and somehow use the Diamond Process Model to find the answer.

Like mother bird returning to the nest, it is now time for us to get out of the weeds a little and take a bird's-eye view of other situations where the DPM can be effective. It is also time to depart from the bird metaphors. Next, we introduce you to major section three, which shows you how to optimize the Diamond Process Model so it can be the best tool to help you make decisions.

MAJOR SECTION THREE:

GETTING THE MOST OUT OF THE DIAMOND PROCESS MODEL

CHAPTER 15

USING THE DIAMOND PROCESS MODEL TO MAKE BETTER DECISIONS

Up to this point in the book we've defined the Diamond Process Model and how it can help with starting up your company or troubleshooting an existing one. Now let's talk about how it can help you when you don't even know you need help.

If you had to sum up what leaders really do in just two words, what would those two words be? We argue that the answer is "make decisions." Leaders are in positions of authority to decide the strategic direction of the company: who to hire, how to make a competitive advantage, where to place resources, the list goes on forever.

If you agree that a leader's job is to ultimately make decisions, then you should also agree that resources to help leaders make effective decisions are priceless. This is why the Diamond Process Model is so valuable to leaders: It is the ultimate decision-support system.

A decision-support system (DSS) is any process that enables a leader to make informed and effective decisions. In this day and age, a good DSS is a necessity, because in a competitive global economy there is little tolerance for quick and inaccurate decisions. CEOs and other leaders are hired with expectations of immediate success, and there is little room for error.

The Diamond Process Model is the ultimate support system for decision making because it is an all-encompassing DSS. We refer to the DPM as a closed-loop system because it captures everything leaders need to think about when making decisions affecting their companies.

The Diamond Process Model resembles a zero-sum game where changes to one area must be countered with changes to another area to maintain the balance an organization needs to be successful. For example, if you change a process to support a line of business, then you must also look at applying resources to that process. Those added resources must either be new resources (which require capital adjustments) or they need to be shifted from another area of the organization.

The DPM forces you, the leader, to answer all of these questions and simultaneously commits you to a decision-making process. Having a sound process for making good decisions is an absolute necessity for any leader wanting to successfully lead an organization.

Many companies do not have a support system or a decision-making process and they simply try to "wing it." This is a dangerous practice as the absence of a DSS forces organizations to be in reactive mode, which many refer to as "firefighting." Leaders in these types of organizations simply react to the latest crisis, usually caused by a lack of proper planning and earlier poor decisions.

Let's look at a hypothetical scenario that involves a simple leadership decision to illustrate the difference between using the Diamond Process and the "wing it" method. Bob is a financial manager at a manufacturing company. Bob's spouse became sick, so he had to retire with little notice. Since the finance office cannot go without a manager, the company needs a temporary replacement for Bob in order to give HR time to hire a replacement supervisor. Since the supervisor position will be temporary, the company decides to fill the position from outside Bob's office to prevent inter-office personnel conflicts.

Company A does not use the Diamond Process Model. During one of their weekly supervisory staff meetings, it is brought to their attention that Bob has left the company and they need a replacement. Someone in the room mentioned that they have a worker named John who used to do Bob's job a long time ago. This sounds like a great fix to the problem, so company A decides to replace Bob with John.

What company A did not realize is that since John moved from Bob's old position to his new position, he developed relationships with several suppliers to procure materials for the manufacturing line. There are several different suppliers, and each one has their own process for ordering, which can be tricky. Also, the suppliers know to call John and discuss long lead times for material shortages when necessary, enabling John to make the decision to place an early order if needed.

During the next weekly staff meeting it is presented that the manufacturing lines are slowing down. The leaders in the meeting decide to assign more people to the production line to help speed it up. Also, someone mentions that supplies are running low so the company orders an emergency shipment, which costs more money. Since the suppliers are also running low with long lead times, the production line will stay under capacity for several weeks, even though company A has already ordered emergency shipments.

Now let's look at company B, which uses the Diamond Process Model as a decision-support system. During an operational assessment, someone mentions that Bob needs a replacement. Another person suggests John is a fit since he used to do Bob's job. But after conducting a KSA assessment, John's boss realizes he supports a critical process in the organization. So instead, the supervisor offers up Pete because the KSA assessment revealed that not only does Pete have the right KSAs to be a financial manager, but he also just completed his supervisor development course and would benefit greatly from the leadership experience.

In this scenario, company B made a basic leadership decision to temporarily replace a supervisor that retired. While doing so, they avoided a myriad of problems by using the Diamond Process Model as a decision-support system. This is just one example of how the DPM can not only prevent problems before they occur, but also fix problems you didn't know you had.

Another critical flaw in failing organizations when it comes to making decisions is that they deem some person the "decision maker." These companies usually have some autocratic leader that makes all the decisions for the company and expects his or her subordinates to feed them information on which to base those decisions.

While in a US Army Reserve training unit in the late '80s, Mike worked for a boss who wanted all decisions to be his and his alone. He refused to delegate decisions of any type or quality to the other leaders in his organization. This particular leader went to the extreme by demanding he be the only person to speak for the organization in briefings and meetings, whether the target audience was a higher military leader or a customer.

Although the leader was trying to maintain positive control of the unit, his tactics caused severe damage to the organization for several reasons. First, since everyone in the unit was trained to defer decisions to the boss, the organization became paralyzed whenever the boss was away. Unfortunately this happened often, as senior military leaders are required to travel a great deal. If the leader was unavailable by phone or email, decisions simply did not get made and production came to a halt.

Second, when the boss was in town, he became inundated with every decision in the unit. This meant decisions were not made at the appropriate level to resolve issues quickly. Every new decision that needed to be made went at the end of a long list and waited for the boss. By the time he got around to making a decision, the situation had changed, as had the information needed to make that decision.

Third, the boss had no person that was trained as a second-in-command, and this hurt customer relations. One time the boss was out of town and another leader in the unit had to attend a briefing with a customer. Since the fill-in did not know the details of the situation, he was unable to communicate important information to the customer. He also could not answer questions the customer asked, which damaged the relationship between the two units.

Finally, the leaders in this training unit were not allowed to develop. Up-and-coming leaders need to have their own responsibilities and be held accountable for their decisions. If you do not give them room to make mistakes, they cannot learn from those mistakes. More senior officers should be allowed the opportunity to fill in for the top leader as well. It is only through this experience that they will learn to become effective senior leaders themselves.

★★

A GENERAL'S REFLECTION

When I was commander of the Theater Support Command in Iraq during OIF, I continually used the Diamond Process Model to increase my organization's effectiveness. One of the unique challenges of leading a military organization with 27,000 members is dealing with the many levels of command. Since the organization was so large, it was broken up into many subordinate organizations.

I served on the theater support command level of leadership at the top. Below me were the brigade, battalion, and company levels of leadership. I was in charge of several brigade commanders, who each had several battalion commanders, who each had several company

Continued

commanders and all associated personnel. This created a decision-making problem as many decisions had to be elevated through the many levels of leadership. And like my previous training unit, many of the commanders wanted to be the single decision maker.

Further exacerbating the problem was the fact that we were performing logistical operations in a war zone, which means things happen very quickly. As the battlefront changes, so do logistical requirements. When soldiers are on the front lines in contact with enemy combatants, the last thing they want to hear is you can't get them food and ammo because you are waiting for a memo to get signed.

I knew I needed to set a process for quick and accurate decision making to cut through the bureaucracy and get the mission done. So I set up a team called the "fusion cell," which included representatives from each level of command. The team was set up using KSA assessments to ensure the right people were involved. I empowered the cells to make the necessary decisions to support the mission on one condition: The cells would make all the decisions on behalf of their commanders while keeping these commanders fully informed.

By using the DPM to create this decision-making process, we began to make rapid improvements to the way we did business. For the first time since my arrival, all levels of leadership were involved which improved unity of effort throughout the organization.

During these team meetings the company-level operators could present problems to the battalion, such as not being able to make a new shipment that was requested because they didn't have enough trucks. The battalion could take this information and either prioritize the new shipment over an old one, or simply assign another unit to the task. The brigade representative in the room would then bless the plan and issue the operations order (OPORD) to the appropriate level of command to make it happen.

We began realizing the immediate effects of this decision-making process because the right people with the right information were involved, and they were making the right calls at the right level of command. I also solved the problem of everyone wanting to be the autocratic decision-maker—a problem that the commanders didn't know they had, but was fixed anyway with our new decision-making process. This also allowed commanders to devote their time to more critical issues inside their own units.

Using an appropriate DSS like the Diamond Process Model separates the good companies from the great ones. Effective decision-making is a game changer in and of itself for most organizations. We are amazed by the number of companies that rely on the knee-jerk method to make most of their decisions.

Since decision-support systems are so critical to help leaders, we should do everything in our power to make sure our DSS is optimized. This means we have the understanding that the control of information and knowledge is the lifeblood of any decision-support system. How knowledge and information are handled has a direct effect on how effective the DSS can be for leaders.

INFORMATION IN THE INFORMATION AGE

Military organizations thrive on intelligence, which is essentially information. How military leaders use and disseminate this information to enable effective decision-making is often realized in the execution of military power. Without intel, and hence information, military leaders basically become blind to what is going on around them.

The Diamond Process Model is only as good as the information that is in it. External information flowing into our DPM is one of the factors that makes it a decision-support system. As such, it behooves us to make sure the right information gets accounted for; this means we start by setting up a process to manage information. But first we need to understand the three different types of information, which are *important*, *critical,* and *interesting*.

Let's face it: We are living in the information age, so there is much information out there and not all info is created equal. The two types of information leaders should focus on are *important* and *critical*.

Important information is something that is useful in our daily work activities. For example, if you are a technology company and the market introduced a new piece of computer equipment that could make your processes more efficient, you may want to recognize this as important information because leaders could use that information to better the organization.

Critical information is that which, upon learning, creates significant risk to our organization and should make leaders stop immediately and take some sort of action. In the military, commanders view critical information as so important they need to be awakened in the middle of the night in order to hear it.

One example of critical information would be if the state where you operate passes a law that severely regulates the sale of one of your products. Whatever the reason, if you were unaware of the law before it passed, the information of discovering the law becomes critical to your organization. If you do not take immediate action to mitigate risks, you can lose sales, market share, profits, etc.

At a minimum, we as leaders must have some sort of ability to get critical information to the right person at the right time to enable effective decision making. Not having this capability will jeopardize your organization's ability to operate. You may want to have similar mechanisms in place to handle *important* information by getting it to the right work group or individual, but important information is not an emergency like that of critical information.

A third type of information is called *interesting* information; we must discuss this because many leaders unfortunately become derailed by it. Interesting information is that which is noteworthy but should not cause leaders to act the minute they hear it.

This type of information is much of what we hear or read about in news outlets and can be compared to gossip. One of the only benefits of interesting information is that it sometimes enables learning. If we read or hear things related to our business that prompts us to do some research and come up with good ideas for process improvement, then this type of information is useful.

The danger with interesting information is when we as leaders allow it to get in the way of important or critical information. Some organizations get stuck on interesting information and never place the appropriate priority on important or critical information. An example is government agencies, like the US Congress, that get bogged down on minutia (steroids in baseball) and miss more important things (American public education) that need to be addressed.

Identifying, classifying, and disseminating information are all considerations that leaders must take into account in order to pass the right info to the right person at the right time. Remember, the real purpose of gathering, sorting, and passing information is to enable sound decisions. It will not help your boss if you tell him something tomorrow that he needed to know yesterday, as in the following story presented by Mike.

☆☆

A GENERAL'S REFLECTION

In 2003–2004, when I was commanding the Theater Support Command, one of my commanders was on his way out of theater and stopped to address a concern with one of the Kuwaiti ministers.

Continued

The Minister of the Airport Authority wanted to have a meeting to discuss our US Army encampment that was located near his property at the airport.

The minister had been planning an off-ramp for the new eight-lane highway that led to the local airport. The problem was that the current location of my US Army camp was right smack-dab in the middle of where the off-ramp was planned to go.

Unbeknownst to me, my subordinate commander had signed a contract with the Kuwaiti Airport Minister on behalf of the US government which agreed that we would move the camp out of the area within a period of two months.

Fast-forward three weeks, when I get a call from the minister inquiring as to why I have not started moving my camp. I said, "Excuse me, Sir, but I have no idea what you're talking about." He agreed to meet with me later that day, and I cleared my schedule.

When I was in his office, he showed me a copy of the contract that my previous subordinate commander had signed. I had no choice but to agree to the terms, shook his hand, and informed him it wouldn't be a problem. Of course, that was all saving face, because on the inside I was wondering how I was going to move an entire camp in less than thirty days.

As I delved into the contract I realized this was not merely an exercise of picking up people and equipment and moving them from point A to point B. Part of the terms and conditions of the contract was that we had to completely reconstitute the soil of our camp, which meant we had to dig eight feet of soil and purify it of possible contaminants.

To make matters worse, this camp was responsible for in-processing every US military member and all government contractors entering the theater of operations. I had to stop everything that everyone was doing and focus all personnel and operations on the move. I was forced to disseminate information to my commanders that they should have had four weeks prior.

This lack of information put my entire command in jeopardy and greatly impacted our day-to-day operations. Even worse, it created a crisis out of what should have been a routine maneuver for trained soldiers. To this day, I don't think the commander who signed that contract has any idea of the situation he caused upon his departure.

GATHER YOUR INTEL

Information has to come from somewhere, so we need to develop sources. There is no particular best practice for an organization to gather information. But what is important is for leaders to consciously develop a plan for how they want to gain or receive information and how their companies should process it.

Most of this responsibility should be placed on whoever handles Information Technology (IT) functions, such as the Chief Information Officer (CIO) or Chief Technology Officer (CTO) for larger firms.

Sources for gaining information can range anywhere from open source (Internet) to information services to vendors or agency partners. It is prudent for leaders to develop within their plans how to gather certain types of information from specific organizations and how to handle them.

Other processes you want to consider are those for sorting through and processing the information you gather to pass on to leaders in the organization. Remember, the key here is to get the right info to the right leader at the right time.

We also offer that there should be much consideration given to protecting critical information. Just as you wish to gain information and knowledge, so do your competitors. In this day and age of phishing, snooping, and cyber attacks, it is most important to take precautions to safeguard what is important.

No matter who you are or what type of business you are in, poor information management can cause a lot of bad things to happen to your company. Chris was reading a 2014 article the other day on the Huffington Post which had nothing to do with process or information management but was discussing major businesses that were in serious trouble.

In her article "9 Iconic Brands that Could Soon Be Dead," Renee Jacques pointed out that Abercrombie & Fitch was struggling because they make teen clothing that all looks the same, whereas teens nowadays have become more individualistic and don't want to look like each other (Jacques, 2014).

If A&F had developed sources of information with experts such as those who contributed to the aforementioned article, they could have processed this critical information into useful knowledge. This knowledge, in turn, could have enabled leaders to make better decisions about setting goals and objectives in their strategic plan.

Stated in a different way, this company failed to understand critical information that was important to them. The Diamond Process Model and its elements apply to stuff all over the place; in this case, the fashion industry.

LEARN TO LEARN

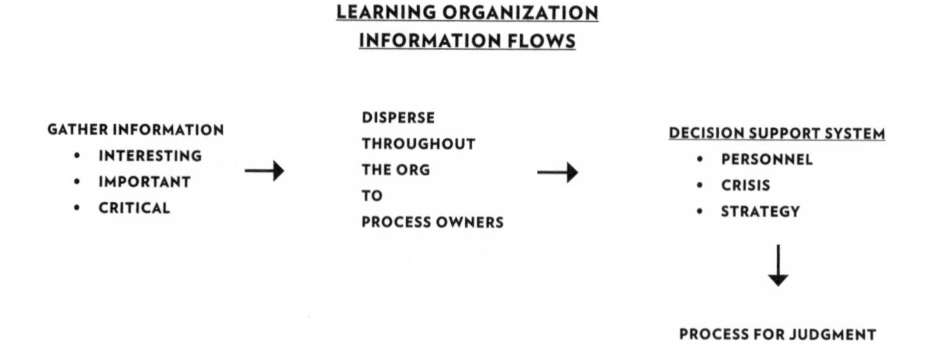

Information that is processed by an organization via a decision-support system can be converted to useful knowledge for the company. *Learning* takes place when your organization uses that knowledge to make the company better. Just as information control fuels a good DSS, learning is what enables leaders to benefit from knowledge and information.

An organization that subscribes to learning will gain new knowledge, whether created within or obtained from an external source, and then use that knowledge to better their business practices. Learning organizations will also retain knowledge and build upon it over time.

Learning is often a cultural item in an organization and is embedded in how your company conducts business. Learning allows you to keep pace, or even lead technological changes. It enables your organization to be a change agent, not only inside your own company but also as a thought leader for an entire industry or sector.

Learning can be as simple as setting an initial process for learning to take place in your organization and then tweaking it as you go. But like other processes, sometimes we just don't take it seriously enough to put it in our strategy and write it into how we do business every day. But some of the most successful companies in the world do. Like Toyota, for instance.

Chris remembers that when he was in college studying business, all the professors taught Toyota business practices to students. It left a lasting impression on Chris that a company's practices could be so renowned they were actually inserted in collegiate academics as the entire basis of the curriculum. It is hard to talk about product quality and best practices without talking about Toyota.

Jeffrey Liker points this out in his book *The Toyota Way*, where he lauds Toyota as the ultimate learning organization (Liker, 2004). The company's practices—which include the five "whys," LEAN, and *kaizen*—are often taught in university business schools. Liker claims that their success is no mistake, as Toyota subscribes to a concept called "hansei," which endorses an organizational culture that includes responsibility, self-reflection, and organizational learning (Liker, 2004).

Learning is also essential for understanding your ultimate employee and is a key component to any organization's training and development programs. When we evaluate our employees and compare them to the "champion" employee, we must understand the difference between what we have now and what we need in the future. Overcoming KSA gaps mandates that we learn and understand what knowledge, skills, and abilities we need, as well as KSA mitigation strategies to overcome those gaps.

SOUND JUDGMENT IS KEY

Everything we've discussed in this chapter up to this point involves getting good information to the right leader. What that leader does with the information is also critical and involves judgment, which is the process of making decisions.

The Diamond Process Model enables sound judgment by providing leaders the right information to make the right decisions and is the ultimate competitive advantage when using the model. But if you have identified any DPM elements that are incorrect, you must make the decision to fix your organization and achieve balance.

We suggest establishing this decision-making process centered around three key domains presented by Bennis and Tichy (2009): people, strategy, and crisis. Since we've already discussed people and strategy, we will focus on analyzing the crisis domain through the Diamond Process perspective.

CRISIS: IT JUST HIT THE FAN

Judgments during crises can either break the back of an organization or bolster how it is perceived in the marketplace. Johnson & Johnson's Tylenol and the Department of Veterans Affairs are recent examples where crisis action either aided or hampered the organizations involved.

Johnson & Johnson had a scare in 1982 when a malicious person poisoned bottles of their Tylenol medication. The company responded by temporarily pulling all their products off the shelf and began informing the public through media channels. The American public quickly forgave the company and respected their crisis strategy, which saved the product line.

Johnson & Johnson's deliberate response to this crisis suggests they had a well thought out plan. If companies do not have any type of contingency plan to deal with various types of crises, it is usually noticeable in the chaos that ensues after an unforeseen event.

It is also apparent that the company put the customers first, because they made a sound decision not only to pull inventory to protect the customers but also to engage very openly with the public. During strategic planning sessions, Johnson & Johnson likely set a strategic objective that if any crisis were to occur, they would put the customers first and be fully transparent.

More recently, the (VA) has been involved in a scandal where they were caught tampering with patient wait times to make them look more favorable. Many critics argue the VA's crisis management strategy has been less than admirable, and public opinion still wanes.

Although you would think a government organization would be professionals when it comes to contingency planning, the opposite rang true with the VA scandal. The organization seemed to have no plan at all for responding to allegations that it was masking the real wait times of patients, and that dozens of service men and women died awaiting care.

The poor decisions during this crisis resulted in the top two VA officials being terminated and the VA being subjected to investigations from the VA Inspector General and the US Department of Justice.

The difference between making good or bad judgments in crises often depends on the level of contingency planning. During strategic planning sessions, leaders should "what if" different scenarios and have a basic plan for emergencies. Contingency plans are effectively macros for future decisions. They provide information in a time of crisis, which is much better than starting from scratch.

Of course you can't plan for every contingency, but some base plans are suitable for many situations. Contingency planning is an area worth learning about from the military's playbook. They do a good job of developing contingencies because many lives depend on the creation and quality of these plans.

☆☆

A GENERAL'S REFLECTION

When I was a Commander in Iraq, I took it upon myself to review the contingency plans (CONPLANs) for both my command and the lead command to which I was assigned. One day when I was "kicking the tires and checking under the hood," I noticed that the port I was in charge of had some assets that would be quite vulnerable and do considerable damage if they were targeted by air strike or a creative terrorist with an Improvised Explosive Device (IED).

I felt a contingency was important for a couple of reasons. First, the port was one of the most important logistical nodes in the theater and was the key to most of the shipments of materials and supplies for the Iraqi theater.

Second, the port was surrounded on one side by massive tanks of chlorine, and on the other side was surrounded by massive oil tanks from the oil fields of the Arabian Peninsula. Any attack on either one of these could destroy a tremendous amount of important real estate. Who knew what could happen if the two were to combine?

I was surprised to discover that there was no CONPLAN for this scenario, so I asserted myself to ensure that those responsible developed a good one to address this potential disastrous event. To this day, that particular CONPLAN is still in the archives, and will undoubtedly help in case of disaster.

During contingency planning sessions, you should analyze the full range of potential situations that surround your business. It pays to be creative, and the military often does this by assigning a "red team" that represents an enemy. In the corporate world, you can follow suit by assigning a team of creative people to think of different scenarios for which you need to plan.

You must decide both what you anticipate for future challenges and also which operational leader should handle the situation. Whichever leader is deemed the appropriate one to manage the situation identified in the contingency should review the plan to ensure you have a winning response if the situation occurs. It is important to insist on high-quality planning because decisions made now can affect you greatly in a crisis down the road.

Operational leaders should take charge of developing these crisis action plans and should be assigned for the planning and execution of such plans if they are needed. It is also a good idea to review these plans periodically to make sure they have been kept up to date and that any new situations are captured. Updating contingency plans are also a good idea in case the would-be operational leader assigned to drive a crisis response is still within the organization.

PREPARING FOR GREATNESS

Now you know *why* to use the Diamond Process Model; it helps leaders make sound decisions by providing the necessary types of information to enable sound judgment. Although leaders should always use the Diamond Process Model to help balance their organizations, there are certain high-risk situations for which the Diamond Process method is well suited to integrate resources and processes. To continue answering the *when*, in the next chapter we will present six game-changing applications for the DPM.

CHAPTER 16

SIX GAME-CHANGING APPLICATIONS

The Diamond Process Model provides a bird's-eye view of an organization in its entirety. Oftentimes during our strategic consulting sessions, we ask leaders to provide a list of everything they need to manage in an organization. Most leaders identify around 60% of the elements contained in the Diamond Process Model, which would be okay if we were playing horseshoes or hand grenades. But in leadership and business we absolutely must have that other 40% because that missing piece is mandatory when it comes to leading.

The Diamond Process Model is like a preflight checklist for a pilot. You should already know a lot of the material, but when it counts it helps to have a friendly reminder so you don't miss anything. The DPM can also provide the 100% view when you are preparing for a big change or important decision. This is yet another way to get the most out of the Diamond Process Model; use it when it counts.

Regardless of what type of business you are in or what function your organization performs, there are some scenarios all leaders will face eventually. This is because businesses are inherently subjected to the business cycle, which means your organization will have normal ups and downs, just like the larger economy.

These ebbs and flows create challenges for leaders because sometimes you have to grow while other times you have to shrink. You also have to make decisions based on the changing external environment, which is also subject to business cycles. The Diamond Process Model can be used in many useful ways by leaders and strategic planners to assist in leading an organization toward adjusted goals they may have.

Some common examples where the Diamond method is extremely useful are process improvement, growth, cost-cutting, downsizing, outsourcing, and reshoring. Leaders who make decisions in these crucial times based on a good decision-support system like the DPM tend to fare better than those who don't. Some leaders will perform analysis when making these decisions, but probably will not include the attention to detail that the Diamond Process Model requires.

As you read the following game-changing scenarios, we'd like you to keep a few things in mind. First, remember that the DPM is a closed-loop system. This means that everything in the model is self-contained and each element of the model has interdependencies with the other elements. For example, if we make a change to our people, it will also affect our processes and other resources and potentially our goals and objectives.

Second, understand that the only way to keep an organization effective is to keep it in balance. If you make a change in one area of the organization, you need to account for all of the other attendant changes that need to take place. An oversimplified example is a company that purchases thirty new cars with no new drivers.

Third, understand that we live in an era that is becoming more short-term oriented. Investors, analysts, board members, and leaders are looking for a magic potion or secret sauce that will deliver instant results. As you will see, this proves to be a costly approach to conducting business. We offer that you should consider a longer term and a steady posture when leading an organization. This is exactly what the Diamond Process Model allows you to do in these six game-changing applications.

GETTING BETTER AT WHAT YOU DO

Whatever you are in business to do, common sense says you'd probably like to get better at doing it. The first step to process improvement is to understand your work and actually have processes that produce the desired outcome. This is why we went through all the trouble of outlining lines of business and identifying critical processes and resources to apply to them. After all, you can't improve a process if you don't have one.

The next step is to have a process for process improvement. With the DPM, we always start at the top; and process improvement is no exception. Senior leaders need to set the expectations for process improvement through strategic planning sessions so they can set goals, objectives, and expectations for other leaders in the company to follow.

Once the strategic plan is updated to capture the expectation for process improvement, these expectations should be discussed during operational assessments at the middle levels of leadership and process reviews at the first-line supervisor level. That way, subordinate leaders can devise detailed plans on how to carry out the new strategic direction of the company.

Once this plan is devised and agreed upon by the leadership of the organization, it is time to assign roles and responsibilities for those workers and leaders responsible for the process improvement.

With process improvement it is also essential to establish feedback channels. Process and results metrics should always be a large part of the feedback loop for process improvement, as the metrics often identify successes or failures within a process. Process reviews and operational assessments are a good venue to review this type of feedback.

Another feedback channel comes from the employees responsible or involved in the actual processes themselves. In these periodic reviews, it would serve us well to ask for and discuss employee suggestions. This exercise will allow us to gauge whether process improvement efforts are meeting expectations of both leaders and workers, as well as capture any suggestions for improving the process.

Process improvement events can yield huge efficiencies for an organization through searching for and identifying duplications of processes, inefficient processes, and dead-end or disjointed processes. But with the DPM we must always remember that the model is only as good as the information it contains. Once process changes are identified and implemented, it is essential to make the attendant changes in our process maps and flowcharts.

Also, those groups and individuals affected by the change need to be informed of the new process streams to be placed into effect. When doing so, we must make sure we recognize which contributions led to the process improvement. This will vary among companies but is important so you can learn how creativity manifests itself in your organization.

We discussed information control in chapter 15 and how some companies consider themselves learning organizations. Corporate learning can have a continuous impact on process improvement since the process of learning results in knowledge that can be used to improve the way you work. Businesses can gain information from different sources, learn from the information, and then use the process improvement process to provide useful returns.

There are many different ways to spark a new process improvement initiative, one of which is customer service. The closer you are aligned with your customers/clients, the more effective your process improvement will be. Customers can bring about feedback in the form of a suggestion or complaint, propose better ways of conducting business, and report deficiencies in an area that needs improvement.

Service representatives can review and analyze customer feedback and determine the need for process improvement, which can be passed up to the appropriate channels during process or operational reviews. In our experiences, we have found that when an outside group brings feedback into an operational review of the organization owning the process, the new perspective can cause drastic improvements.

Another requirement for process improvement can stem from organizations with research and development staffs. If R&D discovers new ways of accomplishing work or new equipment that performs more efficiently, leaders can analyze the discoveries in periodic reviews and determine how to integrate them into processes to improve them.

Similarly, employees who attend training courses from outside the organization can bring new ideas into the company that can spur an opportunity for process improvement. These training courses may also identify organizational needs for newer or other types of training. KSA managers can also update potential skills or abilities by learning of them in external training courses.

Finally, external environment factors can also present requirements for processes to be altered or improved. New laws or regulations can change processes such as they did in the Marketplace Fairness Act of 2013 requiring online businesses to collect state tax. Markets can change the way certain processes are done; for example, the way the recent economic decline forced companies to take cost-cutting measures. Technology can also drastically change processes or bring about the opportunity to do processes differently, especially if initiated by competitors.

GROWING WITH A PURPOSE

Other than the basic need to get better at what we do, there are some situations that leaders will find themselves in where the Diamond Process Model will come in handy. The second application in which the DPM is extremely useful is for a company in the growth stage.

Growth is a common strategic objective for many companies, but it does not happen by accident. Leaders must take deliberate actions in order to make their companies increase in size or market share. In order to pull off an effective growth strategy, companies need to have a well thought out and synchronized plan.

> In 2009, a small software company called Zynga launched one of Chris's favorite Facebook games of all time: FarmVille (you may have heard of it). Within six weeks from launch, the game attracted ten million daily users (Lien, 2012). The popularity of the game attracted venture capitalists and the company moved toward an initial public offering in 2011. Zynga was set to raise billions in capital and move toward growth.

One of the biggest downfalls we see with growing organizations is they do not understand the cascading effects of their decisions. This is why the DPM is so useful for a growing company; it allows organizational leaders to see what attendant changes may be needed in all elements of the model in order to achieve growth targets, such as additional equipment, facilities, processes, etc.

Since we always start at the top with the Diamond Process, let's say the executive leaders in a company conduct a strategic planning session and decide to set a strategic objective to increase market share. In order to complete this objective, they also set an intermediate goal to grow a business by 20% over twelve months to upscale operations.

Once these key drivers in the strategic plan have changed, the organization must also change to ensure unity of effort. Working down through the Diamond Process Model, the work process component must also be updated to increase work capacity by 20%. Groups and individuals need to be assigned to processes while maintaining balance. Operational leaders will work with first-line supervisors to identify process changes and resources needed to meet the goal.

Once requirements are identified, human, equipment, and capital resources need to be allocated to processes to achieve the goal. These resource requirements must be filled from within other areas of the company or be acquired with new capital.

Finally, leaders will monitor progress via metric reviews. Results measures will indicate whether the business is headed toward its goal of 20% growth. Process measures will indicate whether the organization is in balance or whether resources need to be adjusted.

Other than growing market share, another use of the DPM is to help companies who want to grow product lines or divisions. The product line could be the result of an emerging corporate capability from excess KSAs in the organization, from opportunities presented by the research and development arm of your organization, or from emerging market opportunities.

The influx of capital to Zynga was apparent by viewing their new strategic plan. In 2012, during the company's annual *Zynga Unleashed* event, they communicated plans to release a plethora of mobile applications, launch a new gaming website, and partner with other game providers to offer options outside of the Facebook platform (Grant, 2012).

As always, the strategic plan should be updated so the vision, mission, goals, and objectives signal the company's new direction to achieve this type of growth. All associated elements in the model (and your business) should then be linked and synced to enable this goal to become a reality. Once strategic direction is updated, the necessary processes and their attendant resources need to be adjusted, much the same way we did with our 20% growth goal.

Some companies grow by acquiring or merging with other businesses. The Diamond Process Model is extremely useful for this exercise as it is especially geared toward finding those redundant and dead-end processes that will occur when companies are merged or acquired. Through process development, it not only helps you understand the processes of the recently acquired organization, but how the work should be accomplished in the newly combined organization.

If your business is in the growth stage for any of the aforementioned reasons, then you need a plan to grow effectively. Without putting the thought and planning effort that the Diamond Process forces you to do, you could just get bigger and increase costs. Many businesses increase in size without gaining an acceptable return on investment. This is because the act of growing doesn't necessarily mean you understand what you have, how it needs to fit together, or what additional processes and resources will be required to accomplish the anticipated growth.

> When Zynga attracted millions of users in 2010, the company realized a profit. But after they went public, their business started declining. In 2011, Zynga more than doubled its revenue but also tripled its total costs and did not make a profit for investors. That same trend continued in 2012, and the company's stock price went from a high of $13.51 down to a low of $2.21, the price range where the stock is currently trading.
>
> Although the company had a plan to grow, that plan was not well executed. They tried to do too much too fast and lost track of their core competencies along the way. Critics of Zynga have accused the company of losing focus, hiring too many employees, trying too many new ventures, and acquiring too many other businesses.

The Diamond Process Model can help avoid bad growth by making sure each growth initiative is well planned. We have to make sure each activity is tied to the strategic plan and directly relates to one or more strategic goals or objectives. We have to execute that plan by applying resources to processes that will help us achieve those goals. Any imbalance will cause unacceptable results against your plan. We also have to measure our progress through process and results metrics to make sure we stay on track, or to make sure we have an exit ramp so we can bail out of the initiative before we become too invested. You can't just go buy a bunch of stuff and expect to win while you figure out the plan on the way to the store.

A PENNY SAVED

In times of competing or declining resources, leaders are required to look for ways to reduce costs. Requirements for cost-cutting initiatives can appear in times of economic decline, following an overextension of capital expansion, perhaps after launching a new product line that hasn't worked or other circumstances such as when competition causes you to reduce.

We have seen cost-cutting initiatives carried out in some very crude ways, which usually leaves organizations in total disarray. Some organizations simply terminate a predetermined number of junior workers while others close stores or production facilities to save a predetermined amount of expenditures.

Many of these initiatives lack a focus on organizational balance and are carried out by leaders who did not give consideration to anything other than costs. Thoughtless cost-cutting can have detrimental effects that are far-reaching, including employees' families, loss of human resources vital to a company's future, cost deficits due to idle equipment and storage, destroyed momentum, and organizational imbalance. Often after the dust settles, companies realize they cut too much.

We have seen companies slash workforces and reduce costs only to meet a short-term objective. The next year these same companies may try to hire back the same number of people they just cut. The major problem with this yo-yo reaction is that you don't get back the workers you've previously trained, which means you double training costs and lose corporate knowledge.

By using the Diamond Process Model, capital resources can be reduced by a certain percentage or amount, and leaders can see the attendant effects on the other elements of the model, such as people, equipment, and work processes. But, more importantly, the impact of cost-cutting measures must be analyzed to determine the effects on the key drivers in the strategic plan. If you cut costs, you must also modify expectations. This will result in also reducing goals, objectives, and possibly the mission or other key drivers in the strategic plan.

One such ill-conceived cost-savings initiative occurred when Microsoft was designing the Xbox 360 gaming console. They decided to cut production costs for the console by designing their own computer chip instead of simply purchasing a third-party chip that was readily available on the market. The move was projected to save $10M, but backfired when the chips continuously overheated and resulted in $1B worth of product recalls.

If the company had been using the Diamond Process Model, they probably could have been saved from this debacle in a number of different ways. First, they could have saved $10M by streamlining production processes through various process improvement initiatives. Identifying dead-end processes and redundancies alone will save tons of man-hours that can equate to great savings.

But we can assume that this initiative was probably not part of the strategic plan. If, during a strategic planning session, executive leaders decided to pursue a goal of saving $10M, many ideas probably would have surfaced. On the other hand, one wonders if this initiative was probably the result of some leader looking at how much computer chips cost and had the idea of, "Hey, we can make these and save this $10M!"

Second, they could have outlined the primary and secondary processes needed to produce an in-house computer chip. Through this exercise of Diamond Process Model planning, they would have been prompted to assign human, equipment, and capital resources to drive these processes. By assigning resources to processes, leaders would have been prompted to perform KSA analysis and may have concluded that they did not have the hardware expertise for such a specialized part.

Finally, through the sustainment process and risk analysis, the company could have probably determined that the new venture would be too risky to the cost, schedule, or technical performance of the development program. A business case analysis with legitimate data would likely have indicated it would be much too costly to in-source this capability than to simply outsource it with a dependable—and proven—product.

BURSTING AT THE SEAMS

Downsizing is another cost-cutting measure some companies use in an attempt to save money by reducing the number of organizational liabilities. Although companies could theoretically downsize by selling equipment, in this day and age the term "downsize" is usually synonymous with a reduction in workforce. Downsizing usually includes larger cuts that are far greater than what most leaders believe they can accomplish by precision cost-cutting measures.

In our experiences, most companies that are looking to downsize are doing so because external environmental factors forced their hand. Since there is added pressure to take immediate action to solve a financial crisis, we've found that many businesses use drastic measures to downsize without fully considering the ramifications of the decision.

For example, some companies lop off capabilities during downsizing that they, all of a sudden, want to immediately add back when things pick up again. Unfortunately, things don't work this way, as you need to keep the big picture in mind when making these important decisions.

The Diamond Process Model provides that big picture along with a more stable, long-term approach that enables sound decision making. By adjusting goals, objectives, or other key drivers in the strategic plan, leaders can signal that the company needs to change direction to achieve downsizing. After these targets are adjusted, the scope of the company is also adjusted to reflect fewer people needed to produce products and services for the organization.

Since the company is producing less, attendant processes must be updated to reflect the changes. This includes a reduction in human, equipment, and capital resources to fuel those processes. By downsizing in this manner, the organization will remain in balance and ensure the company is still in sync with the strategic leader's direction.

SENDING IT OVERSEAS

A common trend among businesses in the United States has been to move some work processes outside the country to take advantage of lower labor and manufacturing costs. The idea behind this is it's cheaper to spend capital to have an outside company perform a mundane task that would require critical resources within your own business.

One fatal flaw many companies make when outsourcing is basing their decisions solely on financial analysis. Just because it's cheaper doesn't necessarily mean it's a good idea. Like everything else, leaders need to base these decisions on the right information with the entire business in mind.

The Diamond Process Model is especially suited for companies looking to outsource because it makes leaders look at the big picture and analyze all the effects on the organization. If you are thinking about outsourcing, you need to first examine what primary and secondary processes you want to outsource.

Second, you should remove all of the outsourced processes from flowcharts and process maps along with the resources that support them. Once they are removed, your company (and the DPM model) will surely be out of balance. This exercise will allow you to analyze the effects of taking such a drastic measure against company operations.

Third, you can perform analysis and examine the second- and third-order effects of the removal of processes and resources. These effects are not always bad. For example, one common effect of outsourcing is that it makes available resources that were previously taken by processes.

If your strategic leaders developed a contingency plan during a strategic planning session, they may have identified an opportunity for company growth. However, at the time, there may not have been ample resources to put that plan into action. With resources made available by a recent outsource, it may be time to dust off that plan and start a new growth plan.

Other effects aren't so positive. Sometimes your company loses synergy when it loses a particular function. You also may realize that you cannot outsource an entire process chain because other lines of business use primary and/or secondary processes that you will have to keep going even after you outsource. If this is the case, you may decide that outsourcing that particular function does not pass the litmus test for a business case analysis.

Either way, it is wise to do a full-scale analysis of how the suggested outsourcing will affect your entire business plan. You can see how the Diamond Process Model can help in this situation. Without it, companies are either left blind or are making important decisions based on sub-par analysis or a lack of complete critical information.

BRINGING IT BACK HOME

Reshoring is the opposite of outsourcing and occurs when you bring a capability or process chain back in the company. Reshoring often happens because companies fail to identify those second- and third-order effects before they make the move to outsource. Once bad things happen, such as an adverse customer-service impact or some unanticipated cost increase, people try to undo a bad decision by reversing the process.

At this point in our understanding of the Diamond Process Model and the planning that goes into it, we know that planning is the important part of the process, as well as recording the right information on which to make a decision. If you were in this company and followed the Diamond Process, you may have originally decided that outsourcing was never the correct solution to start.

As consultants, we don't have the benefit of coming onboard before a problem has started; we only get there after the bad decisions have been made and something needs to be fixed. Although this presents some challenges for us as consultants, it does help in that it puts us in a good position to explain what to do if you recently arrived at an organization and need to fix it as soon as you get there.

In any event, let's say you recently arrived at an organization whose leadership previously jumped on the outsourcing bandwagon and decided to outsource based on lower labor rates or some other lower cost factor. Now those labor rates or other cost factors have increased because the outside country has risen in economic maturity and the country's markets have become more competitive. You definitely have an advantage in dealing with this type of situation because you are a DPM expert and know how to use it.

The Diamond Process Model serves a purpose in this scenario just like it did in outsourcing. You merely pull in or add the process chain or outsourcing function back to the flowcharts and process maps of the organization. This sounds easy, but reintegrating processes can be tricky business because we have to capture all the intricacies of entire process chains.

All of the process map work is necessary because it will prevent process pitfalls such as dead ends and bad handoffs. Correctly updated process maps and flowcharts will make sure our process streams are sound.

Once the processes are mapped correctly, we now must reassign resources to drive those processes. This includes assigning a process leader to drive the process, applying equipment resources to enable the process, and applying human resources to support the process. If any or all of these resources are absent, we must also decide how we are going to acquire new resources.

The reshoring plan should be discussed in detail at process reviews and operational assessments to make sure every person or department that has a part in the process is allowed to provide input and gain clarity on the new way of performing work. These process reviews should also discuss which process and results metrics should be used to measure success or failure.

Finally, before making the decision to reshore the process chain, we must make sure the process will help us meet goals and objectives in the strategic plan. If we have a process that does not help us achieve our mission or move the company toward our vision, then the process is wasteful.

At this point, don't forget to perform your process analysis so you can capture all the effects of this reversal. You need to not only look at the human resource and cost impacts to the company by pulling this in, but also gauge the effects on all the elements of the Diamond Process Model so you can keep it in balance.

Changing external environmental conditions can also create the need to reshore. If you outsource labor to a foreign country, the political leaders can change laws that increase labor or shipping costs. If US customers demand "made in USA" products, you may need to move everything back in-house to capture the demand. If you have products such as textiles that go in and out of style rapidly, you may need to reshore to have a smaller supply chain that can adapt quickly and deliver faster than your competitors.

In 2012 a company called Intertech Plastics decided to reshore capabilities back to the US. Their president, Noel Ginsburg, cited both increasing shipping and labor costs as the reason for the move. But he also stated that many of his customers desired only to deal exclusively with firms that made products in the States (Antosiewicz, 2012).

Since external conditions serve as a requirement for reshoring, strategic leaders need to talk about external risks during strategic planning sessions. If there are proposed laws or statutory regulations that pose risks to our business, we need to include contingency plans that outline how we will respond if those risks become reality.

We have presented applications that should provide great payback for using the Diamond Process Model as a tool to gain organizational control. The DPM will also help you create balance in the wake of chaos and help you achieve goals for your organization. The Diamond Process Model allows us to keep our organization linked and synced with the ability to expand and contract as we feel necessary or as external conditions dictate.

Although these six scenarios are game changers, they are only examples of how the DPM can help you when you most need it. But the DPM is a useful tool all of the time and will serve you better if you don't have to start with diagnostic recapitulation during a potential crisis.

The Diamond Process Model, and process leadership in general, is a different way of thinking about leadership. Taking the time to go through the Diamond Process will give you a new set of eyes and help you keep the important things in focus. Keeping the DPM up to date in your organization will give you an overall situational awareness and attention to detail; it will give you eagle eyes like a General.

PUTTING IT ALL TOGETHER

Like Dwight Eisenhower once said, "Plans are nothing, planning is everything." What he was talking about is when you sit down and think about how to get something done, you get smarter about it. This is because planning forces you to become more familiar with what you are doing. Even better, if you have a thorough planning process, you can get the most information out of what you are doing and put it to good use.

Armed with the Diamond Process Model, you have the right tools for planning and leading effectively. You know that the first step in creating order out of an organization filled with chaos is to develop a strategic plan containing key drivers that complete your mission today and help you achieve goals that will enable your vision for tomorrow.

You also know that the only way to achieve goals and objectives in the strategic plan is to organize your lines of business in process detail. It is only then that you can know your work and understand how to organize your work processes and assign resources to those processes to create a desired outcome. Even better, you know how to measure those processes and outcomes to have complete information on how your work is getting done.

Never again will you have to wonder what is wrong with your organization or how to fix it. By learning the three Diamond Process Elements—key drivers, work process, and resources—you can now keep the model, and your organization, in balance.

As leaders, we are faced with many choices: who to hire; what strategy to implement; which market to pursue; how much money to invest and where. But now you are uniquely prepared to make those choices. The Diamond Process Model is the ultimate decision-support system and will help you stay focused on what is important.

As leaders, we are also faced with many problems. Some of those problems originate within our own organizations—such as lack of process. Often people have no idea what is expected of them, which means work doesn't get done and the person who doesn't do it may not even know it was his to do. Even better, the boss may think it is actually getting done until one day everyone shows up and there is no more paper for the printers.

In other organizations, people are expected to pull off miracles with janky equipment because some manager thought it was a good idea to save money or because there is no equipment maintenance and accountability program so leaders aren't aware the machinery even exists.

Then there are the oh-so-common understaffed and overworked organizations. These are the ones whose corporate executives only see people as a major expense. They do not realize how important people can be as a resource and are focused only on the bottom line. These are the organizations whose mission statement is "do more with less," and have increasing requirements serviced by a decreasing workforce. One good thing about this type of organization is its employees usually have polished resumes—given the way they apply for other jobs so often.

Some of the problems we face as leaders are the results of bad leadership. We discussed a few of these types in the intro of this book; recall the *Incompetent Mole*, *Selfish Steve*, and *Ticket-Punching Tammy*. But fortunately you are now more prepared to deal with these challenges as they arise.

So the next time the *Incompetent Mole* tells you that you have a new strategic goal or objective, you will be able to produce process maps and flowcharts to show how many additional resources are needed to achieve that goal. When he or she tells you to "do more with less," you will be able to use the same tools to show how that attitude can be detrimental to the organization. The next time *Selfish Steve* wants to personally task your top performer to complete one of his personal projects to make him look good, you can explain that the task should go to the process leader instead. When you present Steve a list of individual roles and responsibilities, he should understand that you have properly distributed the workload in your section to achieve optimum efficiency.

You can also point out that you have clearly communicated expectations to each worker and have tied their performance ratings to process and results measures. Perhaps if *Selfish Steve* did the same to *Ticket-punching Tammy*, you may be able to replace Tammy with another top performer that actually serves as a valuable resource.

Other problems we face as leaders come from outside the organization. But you are also better prepared to deal with those external factors. You now have the awareness that changes in markets, technology, and law can and will have an impact on your organization. Even better, you know how to develop contingency plans to deal with these issues as they arise. You also know how to process information so that your organization can learn and evolve over time.

If you use all these tools, your company will reach the Diamond level, which means your organization will have balance and your people will thrive. You will achieve unity of effort so everyone in your organization is focused on achieving the same goals. Your people will know that you understand them as individuals first but also what they do and how they do it. And you will make the best use of every resource to get the most out of what you are doing.

Not everyone will be able to achieve the Diamond level after reading this book. Sometimes it is in your best interest to call in consultants, especially if there are many changes that need to be orchestrated. Please know that we are dedicated to curing the world of bad leadership, and we are here to help. You can visit our website at www.diamondstrategygroup.com to send us an email if you have a question. There you can also download some free Diamond Process tools, read our blogs, or sign up for our newsletter. We look forward to hearing from you!

Although understanding process and balance is an essential first step to becoming an elite leader, there are many other things involved. In chapter 1, we presented the idea of a *complete leader* because we feel that workers want to be led by complete leaders and that organizations need complete leaders. But we had to start out by communicating the importance of process, since that is the biggest missing piece preventing current leaders from becoming complete leaders. But this is not to say the other tenets of complete leadership are less important.

In our next book we will continue the journey with you to help you become a complete leader. We will present a complete leader model that will provide you the necessary leadership traits and behaviors, and we'll show you how to combine them with process leadership to be successful.

Putting together the ability to design and structure an organization for success—while being a complete leader for your organization and the people who work in it—will certainly set you apart from a large percentage of the population. It places you on a pinnacle of leadership that will undoubtedly make you feel very fulfilled and proud. Your organization and your people will also feel much the same way.

By reading this book, you have a good idea of how to establish your organization for optimum success. Are you ready to make it happen? Are you ready to further work toward becoming the complete leader that most leaders aspire to be?

BIBLIOGRAPHY

Bateson, J., Wirtz, J., Burke, E., & Vaughan, C. "When Hiring, First Test and Then Interview." *Havard Business Review*. Nov. 2013. https://hbr.org/2013/11/when-hiring-first-test-and-then-interview

Bersin, J. "The 9 Hottest Trends in Corporate Recruiting." *Forbes.com*. Jul. 4, 2013. www.forbes.com/sites/joshbersin/2013/07/04/the-9-hottest-trends-in-corporate-recruiting/3/

"Blue Bell Creameries Voluntarily Expands Recall to Include All of Its Products Due to Possible Health Risk." *Bluebell.com*. Apr. 30, 2015. http://www.bluebell.com/the_little_creamery/press_releases/all-product-recall

"PPD Honored for Employee Development Programs that Deliver Results for Biopharmaceutical Clients." *Businesswire.com*. Feb. 10, 2015. www.businesswire.com/news/home/20150210005604/en/PPD-Honored-Employee-Development-Programs-Deliver-Results#.VQnf206ihpt

"From Bangalore to Boston: The Trend of Bringing IT Back in House." *Deliotte.com*. Apr.2013. http://www.deloitte.com/assets/Dcom-UnitedStates/Local%20Content/Articles/IMOs/Service%20Delivery%20Transformation/us_sdt_the%20trend%20of%20bringing%20your%20outsourced%20IT%20deal%20back%20in-house_030113pdf.pdf

French, J. R., & Raven, B. H. "Group Support, Legitimate Power, and Social Influence." *Journal of Personality* 26, no. 3, (1958). 400-409.

"The Bases of Social Power." In *Studies in Social Power*, ed. D Cartwright, 150-167. Ann Arbor: Institute for Social Research, 1959.

Jacques, R. "9 Iconic Brands that Could Soon Be Dead." *Huffington Post.* Jan. 27, 2014. http://www.huffingtonpost.com/2014/01/22/failing-brands-2014_n_4604534.html

Liker, Jeffery. *The Toyota Way: 14 Management Principles from the World's Greatest Manufacturer.* Madison: McGraw-Hill, 2004.

"Fortune 500 Mission Statements." *MissionStatements*.com. http://www.missionstatements.com/fortune_500_mission_statements.html

Oyedele, Akin. "Lumber Liquidators is Tanking." *Business Insider.com.* Mar. 13, 2015. http://www.businessinsider.com/lumber-liquidators-is-tanking-2015-3

Pendrith, Mike. "12 Reasons Why New Businesses Fail." *evancarmichael.com.* May 2014. http://www.evancarmichael.com/Starting-A-Business/866/12-REASONS-WHY-NEW-BUSINESSES-FAIL.html

Tichy, N. M., & Bennis, W. G. *Judgment: How Winning Leaders Make Great Calls.* New York: Penguin Group, 2009.

Yukl, G. *Leadership in Organizations* (7 ed.). Upper Saddle River: Prentice Hall, 2010.

INDEX

A

B

C

– D

– E

H

I

J

K

— L

— M

— N

O

P

Q

R

– Z

ABOUT THE AUTHORS

We are father and son, best friends, coauthors, and military officers who were inspired to write this book after more than forty years (and counting) in leadership positions. We have always taken our leadership roles very seriously and strive to make a difference each day in developing people and processes into "the best they can be," to use an old US Army slogan.

We wanted to offer a little insight and perspective into who we are so that you can better understand the basis for our approach to leadership and the life lessons that have led us to embark on this publication. We truly believe that we can offer unique insight into developing you as a good, complete leader and spare you many of the hard lessons typically taught in the "school of hard knocks." Given that we're both veterans, we intersperse some war stories that support key points in the book that we trust will serve as practical applications that you can relate to and use, in theory, in your day to day role as a complete leader.

Mike, the dad, spent his civilian career in various areas of supply chain and logistics management, and in the telecommunications industry where he was a process improvement consultant. He is also a thirty-five-year military veteran, having achieved the rank of Army Major General with service spanning from post-Vietnam to OPERATION: Iraqi Freedom. He was deployed many times the final eight years of his military career and briefed, negotiated, and consulted with foreign dignitaries and military leaders with his last assignment as Director of Coalition Coordination for US Central Command. He has been a leader of organizations with as few as ten employees and as many as twenty seven thousand military members. He has been blessed to serve with a few great leaders who were instrumental in shaping him into the leader he is today. However more times than not, he was underwhelmed with many wannabe leaders who simply missed the boat and gave leadership a bad name. Mike feels that his experience in various leadership roles, especially as a senior military leader, gives you, the reader, a unique bird's-eye view of leadership from a kaleidoscope of life. He remains very passionate about mentoring, coaching, and serving as an advisor to many who have served with him during his career.

Chris, the son, is a 23-year military veteran. He is currently a Captain in the Air Force and serves as an Acquisition Program Manager. He grew up with a lot of irons in the fire at a young age, having played football from the neighborhood park level through high school. He was active in church and school activities in his youth and spent many years in the Boy Scouts, earning Eagle Scout rank, and he also served several years as a staffer to junior Scouts. Chris exemplified leadership traits early in life with a "take charge" approach to his many activities. He mapped out his career path at a tender age of seventeen when he enrolled in the US Navy's delayed entry program at the start of his junior year of high school.

During his nine-year career as a naval air traffic controller, he identified a few "complete leaders," but saw a lot of room for improvement and development in the leadership ranks. He left active duty Navy and enlisted in the Alabama Air National Guard, where he served in an Intelligence Squadron that supported remotely-piloted aircraft (RPA) missions during OPERATIONS: Iraqi and Enduring Freedom. He later moved back home to Alabama where he graduated ROTC from the University of Alabama—just like dear ole Dad. As a matter of fact, Dad commissioned him, along with his classmates, when he graduated from the Roll Tide roster.

Having taken a leadership role at a very young age, Chris feels he has a lot of insight to offer young leaders in giving them the confidence to step up to the plate and be a good, effective, strong leader very early in life. He continues to develop and hone his skills as a complete leader each day.

We feel that our accomplished backgrounds have equipped us to offer you sound and credible guidance and direction that will further develop your leadership skills. Our approach is unique in that we blend processes and people in developing complete leaders, and we believe wholeheartedly in this tried-and-true approach to great leadership. More than anything, we want you to experience some of the memorable rewards in store for you as a complete leader. And we ask that you pay it forward in making a difference in the lives of those you lead at work, in your churches and communities, and especially the young people who see you as a role model. We know that with your help, we can make a difference in the leaders of today and those of tomorrow, one leader at a time.